Psychoanalysis and Hypnosis

Mental Health Library Series

Monograph 5

edited by
George H. Pollock, M.D., Ph.D.

Psychoanalysis and Hypnosis

Erika Fromm, Ph.D.
University of Chicago

Michael R. Nash, Ph.D.
University of Tennessee

International Universities Press, Inc.
Madison   Connecticut

INTERNATIONAL UNIVERSITIES PRESS and IUP (& design) ® are registered trademarks of International Universities Press, Inc.

Library of Congress Cataloging-in-Publication Data

Fromm, Erika.
    Psychoanalysis and hypnosis / Erika Fromm, Michael R. Nash.
        p.   cm. — (Mental health library series ; 5)
    Includes bibliographical references and index.
    ISBN 0-8236-5181-9
    1. Hypnotism—Therapeutic use.   2. Psychoanalysis.   I. Nash,
Michael R.   II. Title.   III. Series: Mental health library series ;
monograph 5.
    RC495.F74   1996
    616.89′162—DC20   96-43561
                                                            CIP

Manufactured in the United States of America

Contents

Foreword

A visit to Freud's final study near Swiss Cottage in the north of London provides fascinating evidence of how persistent was his interest in hypnosis, despite his early rejection of the use of hypnosis. After, as he noted in his autobiography, a female emerged from her trance and threw her arms around his neck, "I was modest enough not to attribute the event to my own irresistible personal attraction, and I felt that I had now grasped the nature of the mysterious element that was at work behind hypnotism" (1925, p. 27). This element was, of course, transference, and he conceived of psychoanalysis as a means of analyzing and working with rather than simply utilizing irrational feelings about the therapist. However, when one enters Freud's study, which was personally organized by him when he arrived in London after escaping the Nazis in Vienna, one sees something fascinating. In the sacred spot, the wall over the couch, one is confronted with of all things, a famous picture of Charcot inducing hypnotic catalepsy. Thus, at the end of his career Freud revisited his fascination with hypnosis. Indeed he had stated that "the pure gold of analysis might have to be alloyed with the baser metal of suggestion." This was indeed for Freud the return of the repressed. Hypnosis simply would not go away, and for good reason, as readers of this volume will discover.

In this clearly written, thoughtful, and fascinating book, Drs. Fromm and Nash, both leading hypnosis experts, provide a useful historical review of the rather uneasy relationship between hypnosis and psychoanalysis, apply more modern theories from ego psychology and hypnosis research, and provide clear and useful examples of the applications of hypnosis to psychoanalytic psychotherapy.

There are three prominent reasons why this book is especially timely:

1. Renewed interest in the unconscious: Cognitive psychologists have reinvigorated the study of unconscious mental functioning, which began with Janet, Freud, and their contemporaries. While some continue to insist that there is no evidence for phenomena such as repression and dissociation, the extraordinary complexity and wealth of information processed in the brain makes it implausible to believe that anything but a small minority of mental functions can occur in consciousness. Everything from regulation of body functions through major components of perception, to the use of language, storage, encoding, and retrieval of memories, to complex motor activity, must involve information processing rules that are not consciously thought out. Thus there is renewed reason for understanding a phenomenon such as hypnosis in which the boundaries between conscious and unconscious mental processing can be shifted. Furthermore, sophisticated utilization of these phenomena in assessment and psychotherapy is enhanced, as the authors demonstrate, by an understanding and mobilization of hypnotic phenomena.

2. Concern about the effects of abuse and other trauma, dissociative processes, and repressed memories: A formidable debate has emerged in recent years regarding the prevalence and effects of sexual and physical abuse in childhood and the use of techniques such as hypnosis to facilitate the working through of such memories. Some claim that any psychotherapeutic interest in a history of trauma amounts to a coercive suggestion that the trauma must have occurred, leading to the construction of false memories. This position is untenable. While the influence of questions must be acknowledged, the logical outcome of this point of view is that a therapist cannot inquire about any aspects of a patient's history without suggesting the answer. On the other side of this debate are people who see repressed memories of sexual abuse behind all symptoms present or absent, insisting that to treat almost any psychiatric problem the patient must acknowledge and bear memories

of trauma no matter how tenuous the reality of such memories. The authors here provide a reasoned, sensible, and useful approach, acknowledging that sexual trauma in childhood may have lasting effects, and providing a thoughtful means for working through these memories in psychotherapy.

3. The fields of medicine and psychotherapy have been radically transformed in the last decade by the increasing control over health care delivery services by insurance and managed care companies, increasing costs and fierce disagreement about the appropriate role of federal as well as state governments in health care delivery. There was a time when psychotherapy patients fully expected to pay for their treatment out-of-pocket; that time is gone. In many ways, it was preferable. Psychotherapy patients at that time were far more in control of their treatment. Because they paid for this care they could choose any therapist they wanted and negotiate the terms of their treatment. Now treatment decisions are made and restricted by managers, many of whom have little or no training in psychotherapy. These factors have combined to put tremendous pressure on psychotherapists to deliver treatment that is briefer and more efficient. Not all of this is bad. Some forms of psychotherapy, especially many of the psychoanalytic ones, were in fact too long. As the authors of the volume describe well, hypnosis can be a tremendous facilitator of psychotherapy, intensifying the expression of emotion, the exploration of the therapeutic relationship, the examination of memory, and the treatment of a variety of symptoms. Indeed the authors provide a useful section on treatments of smoking, obesity, pain, and other behavioral problems which are facilitated by the application of hypnosis.

Hypnosis is a fascinating state of aroused, attentive focal concentration. As the authors demonstrate in this book, it can substantially facilitate psychotherapeutic treatment. There is nothing one can do with hypnosis that one could not also do without it, but especially in these times of renewed interest in cognitive processes, heightened concern about the effects of trauma, and means of retrieving memories of trauma, and the need to develop treatments that are more effective and efficient, hypnosis deserves the kind of attention it receives in this volume. It can make you a more effective therapist. Enjoy it.

David Spiegel, M.D.
Stanford, California

1

The Evolution of Freud's
Ideas about Hypnosis

Freud was unambiguous about the role hypnosis played in the development of psychoanalytic theory and treatment: "It is not easy to over-estimate the importance of the part played by hypnotism in the history of the origin of psycho-analysis. From a theoretical as well as from a therapeutic point of view, psycho-analysis has at its command a legacy which it has inherited from hypnotism" (Freud, 1924, p. 192). His eventual abandonment of hypnosis as a technique, coupled with his self-acknowledged indebtedness to it, has left many analysts with the impression that hypnosis is an outdated concept of merely historical interest. We, along with others (Gill and Brenman, 1959; Kubie, 1961; Fromm, 1965a, 1977, 1979, 1984; Chertok, 1977; Brown and Fromm, 1986; Nash, 1987) challenge this view. In fact, hypnosis remained an enigma to Freud throughout his life, and, as Kubie (1961) points out, psychoanalytically informed examination of hypnotic phenomena holds immense potential to illuminate contemporary controversies in psychoanalysis: the complex interface between affect and soma, the development and maturation of object relations, the nature of therapeutic and pathological regressions, primitive manifestations of the transference, and the relationship between historical event, mnemonic experience, and self-narrative.

In large part our book is an invitation for psychoanalytically oriented clinicians to reconsider hypnosis both as a topic of psychoanalytic inquiry and as therapeutic technique. As a kind of conceptual staging area we will first focus on how some of Freud's most enduring metapsychological and technical formulations were provoked by the problems and challenges posed by hypnosis. We will identify how Freud's early and ongoing exposure to psychopathology in the context of experimental and clinical hypnosis defined and sharpened his understanding of human experience, therapeutic encounter, and in turn hypnosis itself.

To appreciate what Freud called the "legacy" of hypnosis, one must understand that at the time of his medical training and early professional life (1880s and 1890s) hypnosis, hysteria, and psychopathology were inextricably linked in a heated debate within the scientific and medical communities. The dominant figures in this earliest phase of experimental psychopathology, Jean-Martin Charcot and Hippolyte Bernheim, were based in France, each surrounded by a cadre of devoted colleagues and students. Their clinical observations, laboratory findings, and theoretical formulations had an immense impact on psychiatry, virtually defining a generation's understanding of psychopathology. During the latter part of the nineteenth century and early years of the twentieth, hypnosis was highly touted as a means of studying and treating psychopathology. Naturally enough a young Freud was drawn to the personalities, issues, and arguments surrounding this cutting edge work. Just four years out of medical school, and before opening his private practice, Freud visited and worked with Charcot for four months (1885–1886). Three years later he visited and worked with Bernheim. Over the years Freud shifted loyalties more than once in the complex theoretical debate between Charcot and Bernheim. At issue were the two most puzzling aspects of hypnosis:

1. *Altered state of the organism.*[1] The status of hypnosis as an altered or pathological condition of the organism akin to sleep and

---

[1]Here we are not referring to the later, narrower concept of "altered state of consciousness." We are instead referencing the nineteenth century understanding of hypnosis as involving a broad and dramatic alteration in neurophysiological functioning.

somnambulism, which involves diminished attention to external stimuli, shifts in mentation and memory, and functional aberrations characteristic of hysteria.

2. *Suggestibility.* The hypnotic subject's extraordinary responsiveness to the hypnotist's influence, even when this involves gross distortions of reality.

Charcot invoked an anatomical explanation, with the above aspects of hypnosis resulting from "functional dynamic" lesions in the physiological substratum. Bernheim countered with an explanation of these same phenomena as resulting from the normative process of suggestion alone (although he too construed suggestion itself as a neural mechanism, albeit a "normal" one, confined to the cortex [Chertok, 1977]).

The altered state and suggestibility aspects of hypnotic response (along with the personal relationship Freud established with each of the protagonists)[2] were to prove enormously influential in his later theorizing on the nature of the unconscious and on the primacy of transference. By far the most celebrated connection is between Freud's early observations of posthypnotic suggestion and his theoretical statements concerning unconscious motivation and repression: Freud reported himself to be astonished by the effects of hypnosis on consciousness: "I received the profoundest impression of the possibility that there could be powerful mental processes which nevertheless remained hidden from the consciousness of men" (Freud, 1910, p. 17). In this sense the altered state aspects of hypnosis and Charcot's idea of altered physiological structure convinced Freud that ideas, experiences, and motives could operate without being conscious. A cornerstone of the topographic hypothesis was thus secured. Less recognized by the psychoanalytic community, but of equal moment, is the connection between the hypnotic subject's dramatic responsiveness to the hypnotist's "will" (suggestibility) and the evolution of Freud's concept of transference. It was through his clinical experience with hypnosis that Freud discovered hypnotic suggestion to be a matter of relationship, for him rooted in the

---

[2]Freud named his first son Jean Martin, known as Martin, after Jean Martin Charcot.

biological substrate of sexuality. Freud came to believe that *sugges-tion* is most fundamentally *transference*: an unconscious libidinal condition involving an ontogenic, and later phylogenetic, regres-sion to an archaic and masochistic relationship with the father. In a sense the tension between explanations of hypnosis based on a presumed altered state of the organism and explanations based on a regressed relationship endured throughout Freud's life. Though he somewhat expansively elaborated on the latter in an attempt to explain the former, he was never really satisfied with the result. It was left to others to pick up the thread of how nonrelational shifts in consciousness may operate in concert with relational factors to explain the phenomena of hypnosis.

CHARCOT AND HYPNOSIS AS AN ALTERED STATE OF THE ORGANISM

During the latter quarter of the nineteenth century Jean Mar-tin Charcot, based at the Salpêtrière Clinic in Paris, was the world's most renowned figure in neurology and neuropathology. Members of his hypnosis/hysteria research group included such notables as Pierre Janet, Alfred Binet, Joseph Babinski, and Gilles de la Tourette. At the age of 30 Freud applied for and received a stipend to travel to Paris for a brief period of study with Charcot (October 1885 to February 1886). Charcot was quite self-con-sciously the champion of scientific rigor and physiological deter-minism, which for him dictated that the functional anomalies of hysteria and hypnosis must be grounded in some form of perma-nent neurological lesion or impairment. Importantly though, he was prepared to accept the role of past psychic trauma, in interac-tion with hereditary defect, as a causal antecedent to symptom formation in hysteria. As evidence of this relationship between "idea" and symptom Charcot dramatically demonstrated over and over again in his laboratory that hysterical paralyses and other hysterical symptoms could be produced experimentally merely by hypnotizing hysterical patients and giving suggestions. For Char-cot spontaneous hysterical symptoms were precisely the same in scope, character, and mechanism as those produced experimen-tally using hypnosis with hysterical patients. Both involved an un-derlying hysterical neuropathy diagnosable by the presence of a major hysterical or hypnotic episode. According to Charcot only patients with this pervasive, yet subtle neuropathy of hysteria could be hypnotized.

Elicitation of an hypnotic episode following induction was thus pathognomonic for hysteria. For Charcot an hypnotic episode had three invariant periods: catalepsy, lethargy, and somnambulism. Each period had its own phases such as aura hysterica (a type of prodromal phase), hysteric-epilepsy, and interestingly, hysterogenic zones (peculiar sensations of pain usually in the vaginal region for women and the genital region for men). These periods were accompanied by dramatic changes in consciousness, cognition, sensation, and motoric patterns, ultimately leading to a sleeplike state of somnambulism. In sum, Charcot viewed the seemingly random disorganization observed among hypnotized and hysterical patients as the invariant and lawful unfolding of disrupted biological processes.

The four-month association with Charcot and his colleagues was exhilarating for Freud: "there was something positively seductive in working with hypnotism. For the first time there was a sense of having overcome one's helplessness; and it was highly flattering to enjoy the reputation of being a miracle-worker" (Freud, 1910, p. 17). But Freud's enthusiasm did not detract from his acute sense that much was left unanswered. Clearly Charcot had posed the first challenge of hypnosis with dramatic flair: hypnosis (and by implication hysterical episodes) involved a profound alteration in mental state which rendered the individual particularly vulnerable to nonconscious psychical influence. Freud, like Charcot, remained unwilling to forgo reliance on an organic base to explain such broad and extreme alterations of state. The momentous, and courageous, step Freud was to eventually take was to jettison neurophysiology and embrace sexuality, as the biological substrate operative in both hypnosis and hysteria.[3]

[3]In 1914 Freud noted that Charcot was willing to acknowledge in private the pivotal role of sexuality in the development of hysterical symptomatology: At an evening reception hosted by Charcot, Freud listened to Charcot and a French colleague discuss a case of hysteria in a young Asian woman. Freud reported: "For Charcot suddenly broke out with great animation: '*Mais, dans des cas pareils c'est toujours la chose genitale, toujours . . . toujours*'; and he crossed his arms over his stomach, hugging himself and jumping up and down on his toes several times in his own characteristically lively way. I know that for a moment I was almost paralysed with amazement and said to myself: 'Well, but if he knows that, why does he never say so?' But the impression was soon forgotten; brain

Elaboration of this revolutionary idea would await further work with Breuer, a visit to the clinic of Hippolyte Bernheim, and more extensive clinical experience with the concept and consequences of suggestion.

BERNHEIM AND SUGGESTION

Operating from the medical school at Nancy, and elaborating on the writings and clinical work of A. A. Liébeault, Hippolyte Bernheim utterly rejected Charcot's contention that hypnosis and hysteria were manifestations of neuropathy. Unlike Charcot, Bernheim viewed hypnosis as a perfectly normal physiological condition that could be produced in healthy persons, not just neurotics. Bernheim championed the role of suggestion as the defining agent responsible for all hypnotic phenomena, including age regressions, paralyses, hallucinations, and Charcot's three phases. For Bernheim there was a normal physiologically based predisposition among humans to translate "idea" into action. This process he termed suggestion. The Nancy School position was that the elegant somatic and behavioral syndromes observed at Charcot's Salpêtrière were artifactual, results of direct and indirect suggestion by the experimenters rather than invariant markers of an underlying neuropathy. In a somewhat sardonic moment Bernheim noted that on one occasion he did encounter a subject who actually displayed Charcot's three stages with meticulous accuracy: "Only once have I seen a subject who could demonstrate perfectly the three stages: lethargic, cataleptic, and somnambulism. It was a young woman who had spent three years at the Salpêtrière. . . . She was not a naturally hypnotized subject, any more" (Bernheim [1886a, p. 95], translated and cited by Laurence and Perry [1988, pp. 203–204]).

In the summer of 1889, Freud, accompanied by one of his patients (probably Emma Von N), journeyed to Nancy to visit and study with Bernheim for a few weeks. Though Bernheim made no better progress with Freud's patient, Freud was nevertheless

anatomy and the experimental induction of hysterical paralysis absorbed all my interest" (Freud, 1914, p. 14).

impressed with the profound responsiveness of other patients to the words and actions of Liébeault and Bernheim. While Freud retained his construction of hypnosis as an altered state of the organism, he was moved by the strikingly compliant, submissive posture of hypnotized individuals vis-à-vis the hypnotist. One year after his visit, Freud made an extraordinarily acute observation which was to echo throughout his later work on the nature of transference.

> [C]redulity such as the subject has in relation to his hypnotist is shown only by a child towards his beloved parents, and that an attitude of similar subjection on the part of one person towards another has only one parallel, though a complete one—namely in certain love relationships where there is extreme devotion. A combination of exclusive attachment and credulous obedience is in general among the characteristics of love [Freud, 1890, p. 296].

The door was beginning to open on conceptualizing hypnosis, hypnotherapy, and psychotherapy as relationship based.

Though Charcot and Bernheim sharply clashed on interpretation, they generally agreed that there are two broad classes of hypnotic phenomena to explain, as cited earlier in this chapter: *Altered state of the organism* (there seems to be an aberrant shift in neurological function); and *Suggestibility* (the subject appears unduly influenced by the words and actions of the hypnotist). Charcot understood these characteristics of hypnosis as manifestations of a disrupted neural process, thereby emphasizing a biologically grounded shift in state. Bernheim just as forcefully championed the sovereignty of suggestion as antecedent cause, thus implying that hypnotic phenomena can only be fully understood in terms of the interaction of the subject and the hypnotist. It was Freud's clinical genius and his relentless curiosity which led him to a startlingly creative reformulation of hypnosis, one that at once embraced relationship and organic determinism, one that led him to transference, infantile sexuality, and unconscious processes.

For Freud then, *both* the heightened suggestibility and altered state characteristics of hypnosis came to be viewed as products of a single mental process involving regression: Hypnotic

subjects are hypersuggestible because, under the sway of powerfully regressive sexual factors, they are repeating with the hypnotist early infantile modes of relating to objects, involving passivity,
compliance, submission, and surrender. At the same time, hypnotic subjects undergo a transformation of mental state because they
are experiencing a regressive dreamlike shift in consciousness, a
topographic regression in which primary process thinking pre-
dominates. The type of regression associated with suggestion-
transference and the type associated with shift in consciousness
were distinct for Freud. If we are to trace how Freud's ongoing
encounter with suggestion led him to the discovery of transference, and how his recognition of an altered state in hypnosis
alerted him to the importance of primitive mentation, we must
define what he meant by regression.

TEMPORAL AND TOPOGRAPHIC
REGRESSION

Citing the work of Breuer and J. Hughlings Jackson, Freud
invoked the concept of psychological regression to explain
changes evident during special states (e.g., sleep, dreaming, psychopathological conditions, hypnosis, and some phases of psychoanalytic treatment). Beginning very early in his career Freud
worked with two concepts of regression, temporal regression and
topographic regression, each derived from a distinct biologically
based metaphor, and each serving different functions in his metapsychology and clinical theory (Freud, 1891, 1909, 1917; S. W.
Jackson, 1969; Tuttman, 1982; Marcel, 1983). Though in *The Interpretation of Dreams* (1900) and in later writings Freud was elegantly
concise in drawing the distinction between these two types of
regression (Freud, 1917), the difference became quite muddled
again even during his lifetime (S. W. Jackson, 1969; Tuttman,
1982).

Temporal Regression

Freud patterned his concept of temporal regression on work
in developmental morphology basing it on the assumption that

there is an orderly pattern of human development from simpler, less organized forms to more complex, advanced ones. He also maintained that these earlier stages in human development are imperishable, and that under special circumstances "The primitive stages can always be re-established" (1915, p. 285), and that "the essence of mental disease lies in a return to earlier states of affective life and of functioning" (p. 286). For Freud then, the hysteric's mode of relating represented a return of archaic psychic structures, laid down long ago, but nonetheless defining the patient's response to self and others. This concept was to serve a defining role in Freud's understanding of hypnotic suggestion, transference, and (in even more expanded form) group psychology.

TOPOGRAPHIC REGRESSION

Freud's concept of topographic regression was based on the system of the reflex arc in neurology and physiology (Freud, 1917). Here, the regression had nothing to do with time, but was a spatial retrogression in a hypothetical psychical apparatus: It was a reverse movement along a path "from the region of thought-structures to that of sensory perceptions" (Freud, 1905c, p. 162); "The process begun in the Pcs. and reinforced by the Ucs., pursues a backward course through the Ucs. to perception which is pressing upon consciousness" (Freud, 1917, p. 227); a backward course that results in a transformation of thoughts into visual imagery (Freud, 1933). Freud noted that the regressive shift from thought to imagery carried with it a shift in form (secondary to primary processing [Freud, 1916–1917]). Indeed, there is a rich literature suggesting that imagery and primary process are linked, and that these manifestations of topographic regression can be operationalized in the consulting room and the laboratory (Sperling, 1960; Paivio, 1971; Atwood, 1971; Bogen, 1973; Galin, 1974; Schwartz, Davidson, and Maer, 1975; Fromm, 1978–1979; Dixon, 1981; Marcel, 1983a, b; Erdelyi, 1985; Fromm and Kahn, 1990). Thus, a cornerstone of psychoanalytic thinking became the notion that psychopathology and certain altered states involve a regressive shift away from secondary-process thinking toward primary-process thinking—a form of regression that does not involve an undoing of development.

FROM SUGGESTION TO TRANSFERENCE: FREUD'S ONE-FACTOR EXPLANATION OF HYPNOSIS BASED ON TEMPORAL REGRESSION

Two times[4] Freud mentioned a clinical incident, which he cited as pivotal in his discovery that the mechanism underlying hypnotic suggestion is rooted in sexuality:

> And one day I had an experience which showed me in the crudest light what I had long suspected. It related to one of my most acquiescent patients, with whom hypnotism had enabled me to bring about the most marvellous results, and whom I was engaged in relieving of her suffering by tracing back her attacks of pain to their origins. As she woke up on one occasion, she threw her arms round my neck. The unexpected entrance of a servant relieved us from a painful discussion, but from that time onwards there was a tacit understanding between us that the hypnotic treatment should be discontinued. I was modest enough not to attribute the event to my own irresistible personal attraction, and I felt that I had now grasped the nature of the mysterious element that was at work behind hypnotism [Freud, 1925, p. 27].

Chertok (1977) asserts with some plausibility that this was the beginning of a "long march" which was to bring Freud to the ideas of transference, infantile sexuality, and temporal regression.

Probably somewhere around 1896 Freud began to turn away from hypnosis proper as a technique (Jones, 1955), but without abandoning catharsis. For a period of time he experimented with the "pressure" technique and something he called "concentration hypnosis." But by the time of his "Three Essays on the Theory of Sexuality" (1905c) he could write: "I can not help recalling the credulous submissiveness shown by a hypnotized subject towards his hypnotist. This leads me to suspect that the essence of

---

[4]In "A General Introduction to Psychoanalysis" (1920); and in his autobiography (1925).

hypnosis lies in an unconscious fixation of the subject's libido to the figure of the hypnotist, through the medium of the masochistic components of the sexual instinct" (p. 150). At the same time he was beginning to articulate the technical implications of this theoretical breakthrough (see "Dora"), with increasing emphasis on analysis of the ongoing interaction between patient and therapist.

For the remainder of his life Freud adhered to this one-factor formulation of hypnosis, elaborating on it only once to explain some state characteristics of hypnosis that seemed inconsistent with a purely ontogenic regression. The analogy between the adult hypnotic subject's relationship to the hypnotist and the child's relationship to the parent was a compelling one for Freud. He defined hypnosis as "the influencing of a person by means of the transference phenomena . . ." (1912, p. 106), and he understood this influence to be a thinly disguised and inhibited expression of the sexual drive. This model explained the hypnotic subject's extraordinary compliance and submissiveness quite nicely, but it did not really account for the altered state characteristics of hypnosis (extraordinary immobility, changes in psychophysiological and somatic functioning), and Freud knew it:

> [Hypnosis] exhibits some features which are not met by the rational explanation we have hitherto given of it as a state of being in love with the directly sexual trends excluded. There is still a great deal in it which we must recognize as unexplained and mysterious. It contains an additional element of paralysis derived from the relation between someone with superior power and someone who is without power and helpless. . . . The manner in which it is produced and its relationship to sleep are not clear . . . [Freud, 1921, p. 115].

In "Group Psychology and the Analysis of the Ego" (1921) Freud made his final bid to resolve this problem. He acknowledged that hypnosis entails an alteration in the subject's state of consciousness and proposed that this alteration is due to a temporal regression of dramatic proportions involving not just a retracing of the individual's psychosexual development, but a reanimation of the phylogenetic heritage of the human species.

By the measures that he takes, then, the hypnotist awakens in the subject a portion of his archaic heritage which had also made him compliant towards his parents and which had experienced an individual re-animation in his relation to his father; what is thus awakened is the idea of a paramount and dangerous personality, towards whom only a passive-masochistic attitude is possible, to whom one's will has to be surrendered,—while to be alone with him, "to look him in the face," appears a hazardous enterprise. It is only in some such way as this that we can picture the relation of the individual member of the primal horde to the primal father. As we know from other reactions, individuals have preserved a variable degree of personal aptitude for reviving old situations of this kind. Some knowledge that in spite of everything hypnosis is only a game, a deceptive renewal of these old impressions, may, however, remain behind and take care that there is a resistance against any too serious consequences of the suspension of the will in hypnosis [Freud, 1921, p. 127].

In a footnote Freud recognized that he had now come full circle to embrace Charcot's view that hypnosis is indeed a radically different state of the organism (Freud, 1921, p. 128). From this perspective hypnotic compliance and transference are not merely a repetition of an individual's past experience with significant others, but a reanimation of a primitive biophysiological matrix, with specific behavioral and experiential features (immobility, dreamlike mentation, impaired reality testing) presumably characteristic of early stages in mankind's evolution. In this sweeping appeal to the concept of temporal regression Freud attributed psychopathological conditions and the hypnotic state to a reactivation of earlier stages in the development of the individual, the species, and the culture. As Chertok (1977) points out, the strained, overly abstract, almost "science-fictional" nature of these final formulations concerning hypnosis betray the fact that the statelike shifts in soma and mentation associated with hypnosis posed a problem for psychoanalytic theory that was far from solved. Whereas Freud's earlier clinical formulations linking suggestion to relationship factors were as seminal as they were elegant, his attempts to subsume the cognitive–physiological shifts in hypnosis under the expanded banner of temporal regression were neither. The fact is that in clinging to his one-factor explanation of hypnosis based on temporal regression, he failed to satisfactorily address the sometimes profound changes in mentation and somatic functioning undergone by the hypnotic subject, changes which came to be understood by many of his later adherents as consequences, not of relational forces per se, but of shifts in certain functions of the ego. It is unfortunate that Freud's last word on hypnosis was in "Group Psychology" (1921); he never attempted a reformulation in light of his structural theory as presented in "The Ego and the Id" (1923). Nonetheless, Freud's stress on the ego and ego functioning was formative for later psychoanalytic explanations of hypnosis.

THE LINGERING PROBLEM OF STATE: FROM TOPOGRAPHIC REGRESSION TO SHIFTS IN EGO FUNCTIONING

SOMETHING MORE THAN TRANSFERENCE

As early as *The Project* (1895, p. 337) Freud was beginning to define his concept of topographic regression, connecting it with emergence of primary process thinking in sleep, dreaming, and hypnosis. Here Freud noted the "motor paralysis" in sleep, the "unexcitability of the sense organs" in hypnosis, and the "withdrawal of the cathexis of attention" in both, and concluded that these were the proximal causes of a statelike reorganization of thought processes, characterized by a predominance of primary process mentation in sleep and hypnosis (p. 337). From this point of view, the sleeping subject's and the hypnotic subject's experience is a psychical expression of an underlying neurological reorganization. In both sleep and hypnosis, dramatic shifts in perception, reality testing, and affect tone take place, and are explained by the profound reorganization of psychic structure attendant upon the altered neurological status of the organism. Here prepsychoanalytic/pretransference ideas of a sleeplike state persist in Freud's formulation of hypnosis.

In *The Interpretation of Dreams* (1900) Freud gives a very clear example of how free association, the process of dream interpretation, self-observation, sleep, and hypnosis share a kinship. In outlining the state of mind required for dream interpretation Freud notes:

> This involves some psychological preparation of the patient. We must aim at bringing about two changes in him: an increase in the attention he pays to his own psychical perceptions and the elimination of the criticism by which he normally sifts the thoughts that occur to him. . . . I have noticed in my psycho-analytical work that the whole frame of mind of a man who is reflecting is totally different from that of a man who is observing his own psychical processes. In reflection there is one more psychical activity at work than in the most attentive self-observation. . . . In both cases attention must be concentrated, but the man who is reflecting is also exercising his *critical* faculty. . . . The self-observer on the other hand need only take the trouble to suppress his critical faculty. If he succeeds in doing that, innumerable ideas come into his consciousness of which he could otherwise never have got hold. . . . What is in question, evidently, is the establishment of a psychical state which, in its distribution of psychical energy (that is, of mobile attention), bears some analogy to the state before falling asleep—and no doubt also to hypnosis. . . . As the involuntary ideas emerge, they change into visual and acoustic images . . . [pp. 101–102].

Much later in his *Introductory Lectures on Psychoanalysis* (1916–1917), Freud seems to acknowledge that hypnosis is more than a transference reaction:

> [T]here is an obvious kinship between the hypnotic state and the state of sleep. . . . The psychical situations in the two cases are really analogous. In natural sleep we withdraw our interest from the whole external world; and in hypnotic sleep we also withdraw it from the whole world, but with the single exception of the person who has hypnotized us and with whom we remain in rapport [p. 104].

The period of time during which the *Introductory Lectures* were written is aptly enough referred to as Freud's "topographic period" (Silverstein and Silverstein, 1990). Indeed a common element in this "kinship" between sleep, dreaming, free association, self-observation, hypnagogic state, and hypnosis might be most concisely framed as topographic regression. Both Silverstein and Silverstein (1990) and Chertok (1977) point out that construing hypnosis as something more than transference was almost a logical necessity given the ubiquity of transference reactions in casual and intimate interpersonal relationships. Transference reactions, even the most dramatic ones, do not really "look like" hypnosis. A transference reaction simply does not explain "the transition to an altered state of consciousness which imparts to hypnosis its very special character" (Chertok, 1977, p. 107).

THE FIRST STRUCTURAL MODEL: EGO IDEAL OR EGO

From a contemporary psychoanalytic perspective it seems patently obvious that the alterations which characterize hypnosis (and sleep) reflect, at least in part, alterations in ego functioning. Changes in volition, reality testing, perception, mobility, planfulness, cognition, self awareness, experience of time, and affect availability are all characteristics of hypnosis which puzzled Freud and strained his one-factor explanation. We now know that these are all operations of one particular intrapsychic structure: the ego (Bellak, 1955; Hartmann, 1958; Fromm, 1965a, 1977, 1979, 1984; Rapaport, 1967). Unfortunately Freud's final word on hypnosis came after his first rough attempt at articulating intrapsychic structure ("Group Psychology and the Analysis of the Ego," 1921), but before his more complete and polished formulation in "The Ego and the Id" (1923).

In "Group Psychology and the Analysis of the Ego" (1921) Freud proposed that "*Hypnosis* resembles being in love in being limited to these two persons, but it is based entirely on sexual impulsions that are inhibited in their aims and puts the object in the place of the ego ideal" (p. 143). Thus the hypnotist replaces the subject's ego ideal. Since, at that time, Freud attributed reality to the ego ideal (and not the ego) he eliminated identification as a factor in hypnosis: "The fact that the ego experiences in a dream-like way whatever he (the hypnotist) may request or assert reminds us that we omitted to mention among the functions of the ego ideal the business of testing the reality of things" (p. 114). Of course Freud was to define and expand the role of the ego to incorporate almost all of the person's interactions with the world, including perception and reality testing (Freud, 1923). But he never elaborated on how this model might be applied to hypnosis, or how it might address the dramatic alterations in experience which seem to operate in concert with transferentially based temporal regression during hypnosis.

FREUD'S ABANDONMENT OF HYPNOSIS
AS TECHNIQUE

Several reasons have been offered for why Freud discontinued use of hypnosis in the clinical settings (Jones, 1955; Kline, 1958). But one must first consider how he employed hypnosis in his prepsychoanalytic work with patients. Following the lead of his French and German mentors Freud utilized induction techniques which were exceedingly authoritarian: He would often place his hand on the patient's forehead, or grasp the patient's head between his two hands and command sleep. Or, as in the case of Emmy von N, he sternly positioned his index finger in front of the patient's face and called out "Sleep!" (Breuer and Freud, 1893–1895). While these techniques might seem very strange to contemporary clinicians, they constituted the conventional hypnotic procedures as practiced by physicians throughout Europe during the latter part of the nineteenth century.

The stern, paternalistic tone of nineteenth century hypnotic inductions in the context of the attendant touching that took place (usually with the patient in a reclined position) undoubtedly produced some dramatic examples of passive–dependent and oppositional–defiant reactions on the part of patients, both of which preclude the kind of effortless attention to mental experience which Freud came to champion. It is no wonder then that Freud turned away from a technique that had more to do with coercion than understanding. Freud viewed himself as an intrepid scientist. The idea of coercing data from a patient was at painful odds with the natural science model of patiently attending to and interpreting data, from a position of detached neutrality. As

Freud and others used it, hypnosis was indeed a gross breach of scientific and therapeutic neutrality which distorted and obstructed the processes of discovery. By jettisoning hypnosis about 1896 Freud protected psychoanalysis from some of the obvious sources of methodological contamination (witness Charcot). But in so doing he discouraged examination of how the hypnotic state might be utilized, not in service of obfuscation and repetition, but of uncovering and insight. In a sense the problem with hypnosis may not have been in the state itself, but in the way it was utilized: after all, the solution for "Wild Analysis" is not the abandonment of interpretation as technique. Perhaps the same can be said for "Wild Suggestion." Indeed, following the First World War Freud acknowledged the resurgence of interest in hypnosis as a treatment for "shell shock" by conceding that if psychoanalysis is to be more widely applied to a greater number of patients hypnosis might find a place in it again (Freud, 1918, p. 168).

SUMMARY

Though Freud's view of hypnosis changed dramatically several times over the course of his career, one basic assumption about its nature endured from the earliest days: Whatever else hypnosis may involve, it is most fundamentally an organically based alteration in consciousness. Freud struggled with two competing metaphors to explain this alteration: First, there is the idea of hypnosis as a sleeplike state of the organism. The organic substrate is thus neurological, the mentation akin to that of dreaming, and the regression topographic in nature. The influence of Charcot and the Salpêtrière School is most recognizable when Freud invokes this metaphor. Second, there is the idea of hypnosis as a return to childhood. Here the organic substrate is sexual, the mentation akin to that of earlier ontogenetic or phylogenetic stages of the organism, and the regression temporal in nature. The influence of Bernheim and his concepts of suggestion and compliance are most salient here.

By 1921 Freud had settled on a one-factor explanation, based on hypnosis as a reinstatement of primitive, archaic functioning. The temporal regression metaphor had become transcendent in

Freud's thinking, the hypnotic experience was to be cast both as a retracing of the maturational process, and an undoing of cultural evolution. Put simply, hypnosis *is* transference. But there was always the nagging problem posed by the patient's clinical presentation itself: Hypnotic subjects were almost never entirely compliant; as a group their behavior and affect expression were undeniably more intense, focused, and dreamlike than those of typical analysands, even those in the grips of transference; and hypnotic phenomena such as anesthesia, negative hallucination, and amnesia simply were not consistent with the concept of the hypnotic subject as child or primitive human being. That Freud was quite aware of these problems is evident in his persistent allusions to sleeplike states and his final musings over the enigmatic nature of hypnosis: "There is still a great deal in it which we must recognize as unexplained and mysterious" (Freud, 1921, p. 115). It was the ego psychologists who began to build a more complicated and satisfactory model of hypnosis, weaving aspects of both topographic and temporal regression into an explanation based on structure and adaptation. But it was Freud, challenged and informed by the likes of Charcot and Bernheim, who first defined the landscape of psychoanalytic inquiry into hypnosis. No longer was hypnosis to be viewed in terms of neurological impairment or mechanical compliance, but as a complex product of fundamental human strivings for relationship, identity, and structure.

2

From Views Based on Libido Theory to Ego Psychological Theories of Hypnosis

For most psychoanalysts, particularly those in the United States, hypnosis became a taboo topic after Freud abandoned it in the 1890s (Freud, 1900, 1916–1917). For a hundred years analysts did not know, or did not want to know, that there were always a few well-known members of the profession who continued to use it with their patients and even produced interesting theories of hypnosis.

PREDECESSORS TO THE REAL DEVELOPMENT OF EGO PSYCHOLOGICAL THEORIES OF HYPNOSIS

Sandor Ferenczi

Before he became enchanted with the method of free association around 1907, Ferenczi was an ardent hypnotherapist, and

19

he continued to employ hypnotherapy after that time. In 1909 he developed a theory of hypnosis based on psychoanalytic libido theory. He conceived of hypnosis as a reactivation of the Oedipus complex, with the adult patient occupying in the relationship to the hypnotist the role of the child during the oedipal period; that is, the child who has strong libidinal feelings toward one of the parents, usually the parent of the opposite sex, but in more homosexually inclined children, the parent of the same sex.

To this libidinal root of hypnosis, Ferenczi added a second root: the wish to submit to a beloved authority. The oedipal child, he said, is not only in love with one of the parents, but also admires this parent's strength and authority. Unconsciously the child identifies with that parent, hoping to partake in that parent's magical power by subjugating her- or himself to the parental authority.

In his paper "Introjection and Transference," Ferenczi (1909) also introduced the idea of the hypnotist as a strong transference figure. He stated that the capacity to be hypnotized and influenced by suggestion depends on the possibility of a positive transference taking place. He defined transference as the positive, though unconscious, sexual attitude that the person being hypnotized adopts with regard to the hypnotist. He felt that transference, like every object love, has its deepest roots in repressed sexual childhood feelings toward one's parents. Ferenczi was far ahead of his time, permissive in an era of authoritarian hypnotherapy. For authoritarian hypnosis was popular in the nineteenth and early twentieth century. Permissive hypnosis was hardly known or employed until World War II, except perhaps by the late nineteenth century French hypnotherapist and founder of the Nancy School, Liébeault (1866), and in the United States, starting in the 1930s, by Milton Erickson. However, Erickson actually vacillated quite a bit between authoritarianism and permissiveness.

The idea of hypnosis as a regressive phenomenon is in some way already contained in Ferenczi's 1909 article, when he states that in his opinion in hypnosis and in suggestion the child that is dominant in the unconscious of the adult is somehow reawakened. Ferenczi differentiated between two forms of hypnosis, according to the nature of the transferences involved, that is, whether it was maternal or paternal. Maternal hypnosis, he theorized, was based on love, paternal hypnosis on fear of the authority figure.

PAUL SCHILDER

Schilder, a psychoanalyst from Vienna, came to the United States a few years before the Nazis gained power in Austria. He was a sophisticated clinical theorist, an accomplished researcher, and a prolific writer, as much at home in the fields of physiology, neurology, and the anatomy of the brain as he was in psychiatry and psychoanalysis.

Schilder (1923) elaborated on Ferenczi's theory of the infantile erotic nature of hypnosis (i.e., the ideas Ferenczi had developed on the basis of the libido theory). Schilder added to them a twist that stressed "the creative power of the word" with which outer reality can with apparent magic be changed into a world in which all of one's wishes come true. It is a world of imagery, the magical world in which primary process thinking takes over from secondary process. The regression, he felt, is to preoedipal and oedipal forms of thinking.

Schilder (Schilder and Kauders, 1926, Schilder, 1927) expanded on Ferenczi's work. The oedipal child's relationship to the parents, he said, characteristically shows goal-inhibited libidinal drives combined with unconditional trust in and a wish to subjugate oneself to the parent's demands and attitudes.

With regard to the regressive aspects of hypnosis, Schilder showed that the hypnotized adult ascribes to the hypnotist the magical powers of omniscience and omnipotence. The small child thinks the parents possess these Godlike qualities. However, Schilder also points out that in attributing the same irrealistic qualities to the object of the transference—the hypnotist—the adult patient regresses to the irrealistic, magical thinking of early childhood. This regression is only a partial regression, he says; in special ways the individual, while seemingly unaware of reality, actually is aware of it. His or her behavior in negative hallucination and in certain other experiments shows that clearly. For instance, if it has been suggested to the subject that there is nothing red in the room (while actually there is a red armchair right in front of him), and that he should cross the room, he will furtively look around and away from the red object, hallucinate it away, walk around it and across the room, and avoid running into it. Experiments like this indicated already to Schilder that even in very deep hypnosis and even when a suggestion to the contrary has been given, some part of the ego secretly retains reality awareness.[1] Three years after ego psychology was born (Freud, 1923), Schilder already was dimly aware of the fact that the ego plays a role in hypnosis: The subject, in order to avoid crashing into the chair, somehow must perceive it, but is not aware of perceiving it. Perception, in hypnosis as well as in the waking state, is an ego function. In negative hallucinations a perception is kept out of conscious awareness because the hypnotist suggested that the stimulus would not be perceived.

It is perceived, however. Not consciously, but preconsciously. Fromm (1992) pointed out that all negative hallucinations, including those that demonstrate the existence of the "Hidden Observer," are perceived preconsciously.

Like Ferenczi, Schilder and Kauders (1926) felt that suggestibility and the phenomena of hypnosis and suggestibility have the same libidinal root going back to the dynamics of the Oedipus complex. Schilder, too, viewed hypnosis as a sort of regression in which the child hopes for and fears sexual abuse by the parent. The not uncommon fears of female patients, that the male hypnotist would seduce them during the trance, are often the expression of the underlying (childhood) oedipal wish-and-fear of being seduced by the father.

Schilder did believe that besides the id drives, ego drives exist, too. As ego drives he names hunger, thirst, grasping, holding, fending off, repelling, and intentionality. (Strangely enough, he does not include curiosity in this list.) The higher sensory organs—vision, hearing, etc.—are their physiological appartuses.

Like Schilder, the authors of this book believe that ego drives do exist. They conceive of curiosity as the most important ego drive, a drive that in their view propels forward most intellectual and developmental progress.

---

[1]This finding, as discussed in 1926 by Schilder and Kauders, seems to us to anticipate by 50 years Hilgard's (1977) discovery of the "Hidden Observer" phenomenon.

Schilder (Schilder and Kauders, 1926, 1956) believes that a person hardly ever is *totally* involved in the hypnotic experience; he feels that there is always a certain part, the "more central" part of the ego, that stays awake and in contact with reality. That is the part, it seems to us, which E. R. Hilgard calls "the Hidden Observer."

While some of Schilder's work represents the very beginning of a theory of hypnosis based on an ego psychological point of view, his theory is mainly a drive theory.

LAWRENCE S. KUBIE AND SIDNEY MARGOLIN

Kubie and Margolin (1944) view the hypnotic process as a phenomenon of partial regression to the sensorimotor state of the infant in the first few weeks of life. Their reason for conceiving of it as a partial regression is different from that of Schilder. They stress that it is partial, because the human being in hypnosis can by no means fully divest her- or himself of all the facets of development acquired after infancy. This view foreshadows Nash's ideas of hypnosis as a topographical regression.

For the hypnotized person there is a restriction in the motor and perceptual spheres. The hypnotized subject usually hardly moves while in trance, and reality for him or her fades into the background of awareness.[2] The major ego psychological concept with which Kubie and Margolin work is the concept of ego boundaries between the inner and the outer world. Strong ego boundaries depend on variegated perceptual–sensory contrasts. As the hypnotized person usually restricts sensory input and motor output, Kubie and Margolin hypothesized that in hypnosis ego boundaries become blurred.

Kubie and Margolin differentiate between induction of hypnosis and the state of being hypnotized. In the induction, they say, ego boundaries are narrowed; in the hypnotic state itself they

---

[2]While Schilder and Kauders published together, only Schilder was psychoanalytically oriented and looked at hypnosis from a psychoanalytic point of view (see his Foreword in Schilder and Kauders [1926]). However, together, Schilder and Kauders also developed interesting neurophysiological ideas about hypnosis. We cannot concern ourselves with these here, because it would lead us away from our central topic of hypnosis and psychoanalysis.

can be reexpanded. This idea is somewhat similar to what Fromm and her student collaborators (Fromm, 1979; Fromm, Brown, Hurt, Oberlander, Boxer, and Pfeifer, 1981; Fromm and Kahn, 1990) have described as the swinging back and forth from concentration to expansion of attention, with more concentration in the beginning phase of trance, where instructions are given, and more freedom and more expansive attention when the state of trance has been achieved.

Ferenczi, Schilder, and Kubie and Margolin are not really ego psychological theory makers. Rather, they represent the transition from libido theory to ego psychology with regard to hypnosis.

EGO PSYCHOLOGICAL THEORISTS OF HYPNOSIS

Lewis R. Wolberg

Wolberg, a New York psychoanalyst, was perhaps the first fully ego psychologically oriented analyst who wrote extensively on hypnoanalysis. He advised his colleagues to use hypnoanalysis, feeling that it could accomplish the same results as psychoanalysis in a much shorter time, both in the uncovering as well as in the reeducative periods. He pointed out that in hypnosis, from the very beginning, transference resistances are much diminished as compared to psychoanalysis, and that hypnosis has a remarkable influence on resistances related to the repression of traumatic memories. In hypnosis, one can circumvent and more easily resolve ego defenses that keep unconscious material from gaining access to awareness. In addition, Wolberg felt that hypnosis can shorten the time needed for therapy because "the hypnotic relationship permits easier incorporation and absorption of wholesome interpersonal attitudes" (p. 163), a phenomenon that today we would call healthy internalization.

Wolberg advised using hypnosis as an adjunct to psychoanalysis, as a method that would speed it up. In his three books (1945,

1948a,b), he describes the phenomena of hypnosis and hypnotic techniques, and carefully shows how the psychoanalyst can use hypnosis in various neuroses, psychosomatic conditions, character disorders, alcoholism, and psychoses. Nearly 50 years later, his books, which have been ignored by the psychoanalytic community, remain sound dynamic works that can profitably be used by the beginning psychoanalyst as well as the beginning hypnoanalyst to understand the principles of dynamic psychology and hypnosis. Wolberg was a psychoanalyst who innovatively and daringly advocated the use of hypnoanalysis at a time when psychoanalysts were very antagonistic toward it.

FREDERICKA FREYTAG

Freytag, another psychoanalyst, wrote a book in 1959 that does not contribute new elements to the theory of hypnoanalysis, but describes carefully and extensively the process in a case of hypnoanalysis and therefore deserves to be mentioned here.

JOHN G. WATKINS

Watkins, a psychologist-psychoanalyst, has used hypnosis since World War II (Watkins, 1949). His early practice was influenced mainly by libido theory. He used abreaction as one of his main techniques. Later (Watkins, 1978, 1992; Watkins and Watkins, 1981) he developed an ego psychological theory of hypnosis based on the ego psychological theory of personality structure originated by the Hungarian psychoanalyst Paul Federn (1952), a close associate of Freud. In contrast to Freud, who postulated that all energy comes from the id, Federn stated that the ego itself has two kinds of energy: ego cathexis and object cathexis. Mental and physiological processes invested with ego cathexis are experienced as belonging to "me" and as having "selfness" because, according to Federn, this ego energy *is* "the self." "Object" cathexis is a sort of not-self energy which also can activate physiological and psychological processes.

Watkins has applied these concepts of Federn's to hypnosis and uses them to explain the phenomena of dissociation. If I lift "my" arm, he says, the arm is experienced as part of me because it has ego cathexis. If the hypnotist suggests that "the" arm will levitate by itself, or will become the arm of a marble statue, and I cannot bend it, then the arm has become dissociated, has become a "thing," and has been invested with object cathexis.

At different times and under different circumstances, frequently on the same day, people take on different roles and behaviors (e.g., the role of the mother, the professional woman, etc.). Federn spoke of these as being different "ego states." Each ego state "represents a body of behaviors and experiences bound together by a common principle and separated by a boundary from other states which have been integrated about other factors" (Watkins, 1987a, p. 49). Watkins (1978) extended Federn's ego states theory and made it the basis for his own ego state therapy, particularly with regard to hypnosis, and even more so with regard to the treatment of multiple personalities. At any given time, a particular ego state is felt as being the executor, the self, and as being in charge of experiences and behaviors currently activated or acted upon. That ego state is at this particular time the one most highly energized with ego cathexis. Other ego states are, in a way, dissociated from it and from each other, though at times they can overlap (as, for instance, when the professional woman at work worries about her sick child at home).

Because hypnosis is a state in which dissociation occurs easily, it can be used to withdraw ego cathexis and substitute object cathexis, or vice versa. For instance, one might help a patient with severe burns who feels *he* hurts very badly (or the pain hurts *him*) by substituting for this ego cathected state a state of object cathexis, one in which the patient in fantasy in hypnosis removes himself from his body, goes over to sit in a corner, and watches "that man" who is lying on his bed, and whose bandages have to be changed, go through these painful procedures. "That man," the body on the bed, has then become an "object," and been object cathected; while the ego cathexis remains with the observing part of the person, who in the hypnotic fantasy removes himself from the suffering body, goes over to the corner, and just watches.

Watkins and his wife, Helen (Watkins and Watkins, 1979–1980, 1980, 1990), have also worked a good deal with multiple personalities. They conceive of multiple personalities as a large family, the members of which are fighting each other covertly or are unaware of each other. Watkins and Watkins try to help them therapeutically by attempting to integrate the various personalities into one person, more unifiedly cathected with ego cathexis.

EDITH KLEMPERER

The psychoanalyst Edith Klemperer (1965) combined hypnosis with psychoanalysis, in similar fashion to Watkins' adoption of Federn's theory of ego states, and described past ego states emerging in hypnoanalysis. She described the types of visualization shown in hypnoanalytic age regression and revivifications, and compared patients with anxiety, conversion, and phobic reactions, on the one hand, to obsessive-compulsives. She did not produce a new theory, but nonetheless her work should be noted. Her stance, too, is ego psychological.

MERTON M. GILL AND MARGARET BRENMAN

In 1959 Gill and Brenman published a book on hypnoanalysis that became a classic, *Hypnosis and Related States: Psychoanalytic Studies in Regression*,[3] one of the most important books in the field. In it Gill and Brenman differentiate explicitly between: (1) hypnosis as a transference phenomenon, and (2) hypnosis as an altered state (ASC).

The major theses Gill and Brenman propose and investigate in this book are:

1. Hypnosis expresses both oedipal and preoedipal, libidinal and aggressive wishes.
2. Hypnosis is an altered state of consciousness (ASC). It has some analogy to stage 1 sleep and is also characterized by a suspension of criticality.

---

[3]The title of Gill and Brenman's (1959) book *Hypnosis and Related States*, echoes the beginning of the title of Liébeault's famous (1866) book *Du sommeil et des états analogues considérés surtout au point de vue de l'action moral sur le physique. (Of sleep and related states, considered mainly from the viewpoint of the action of the psyche upon the soma).*

3. The distribution of psychic energy and tension in a trance is different from that in the waking state. In the hypnotic state, involuntary ideas slip from the unconscious into consciousness more easily and more frequently than in the normal waking state.
4. The transference relationship to the hypnotist is the essence of hypnosis.
5. Hypnosis is an induced regression in the service of the ego.

Gill and Brenman's mentor and colleague, David Rapaport (1950), had proposed a few years earlier that there are various states of consciousness, such as the waking state, reverie, dreams, the hypnotic state, and sleep. Gill and Brenman felt that certain ego states are coordinated with certain states of consciousness; that is, with conscious, with preconscious, or with unconscious awareness. They call them "States of Altered Ego Functioning"; altered because they are different from the ordinary waking state. An example would be a hypnotically produced hallucination (the hypnotist says to the patient, "Look over there. Your brother is sitting there," when in reality he is a thousand miles away. The patient "*sees*" the brother sitting on the empty chair. He does not pretend. He hallucinates him sitting there).[4]

The metapsychology of hypnosis as a regression in the service of the ego is Gill and Brenman's (1959) most important theoretical contribution.

The concept of regression in the service of the ego was originated by Kris (1936); Hartmann (1939) called it "adaptive regression." It means to relax and, for a limited time, go back on the developmental ladder one step in order to be able subsequently to make greater progress and to go forward two steps. Typical examples are the fact that we go to bed and sleep at night in order to be fresh and active again in the morning; or that when sick we allow ourselves to be nursed and taken care of, which makes it possible to get well faster.

Bellak (1955) independently conceived of the idea that hypnosis is a regression in the service of the ego. But he called hypnosis "a special case of the self-excluding function of the ego,"

---

[4] Good hypnotic subjects experience imagery, their own or that which has been suggested, as if it were real. This phenomenon is called "hypnotic hallucination." It is a *normal* phenomenon, not pathological.

because he was more impressed by the ego's decision to relinquish certain important ego functions during trance, such as reality orientation and criticality. While in trance, people trustingly turn over these functions of their own to the hypnotist. It is therefore of utter importance that the hypnotist be a highly ethical human being and under no circumstances take advantage of patients or subjects who, in the hypnotic state, cannot protect themselves as they can when awake.

Gill and Brenman (1959) also have shown that what the hypnotist does during induction can be understood as an attempt to disrupt the (conscious) ego's control over its own apparatuses. The hypnotist encourages the patient to "let things occur" rather than to *make* them occur. This can be seen clearly with regard to the perceptual and motor apparatuses, but it holds also for those relating to attention and cognitive processes—and we would like to add that it also holds with regard to memory.

Another one of Gill and Brenman's central proposals for a theory of hypnosis is that in hypnosis a subsystem is set up within the ego. This subsystem is a regressive one which, however, is in the service of the overall ego (as well as under partial control of the hypnotist). Separately the overall ego maintains a nonhypnotic, reality-oriented relationship with the hypnotist. We think there is some similarity between this part of Gill and Brenman's (1959) theory and E. R. Hilgard's (1977) theory of the "Hidden Observer," in which part of the subject stays out of trance and in contact with reality.

ERIKA FROMM

We shall now discuss the ego psychological concepts and principles Fromm has investigated during the last twenty-five years. We feel they explain important aspects of hypnosis. Put together as a whole, they form Fromm's theory of hypnosis. Taking off mainly from Gill and Brenman's work, Erika Fromm developed a complex ego psychological theory of hypnosis. By means of laboratory experiments, she checked out every step she took in theory formation as well as ego psychological hypotheses that other psychoanalysts who preceded her had made.

Hypnosis as a Regression in the Service of the Ego
Regressions in the service of the ego are nonpathological, healthy,
short-term regressions. Like Gill and Brenman (1959), Fromm
(1977, 1978–1979, 1979) and her collaborators (Fromm and
Gardner, 1979; Fromm and Hurt, 1980) have theorized that hypnosis is an adaptive regression or a regression in the service of the
ego. Hypnotic relaxation Fromm feels causes an ego-modulated
relaxation of defensive barriers with a return to earlier, less realistic, primary process thinking. The cognitive changes are temporary, limited to the time of the trance state. In successful
relaxation the productive changes carry over into the waking
state.

The creative act also is a regression in the service of the ego.
According to the psychological researcher Wallas (1926, p. 80),
creativity comprises four phases: 1) preparation, 2) incubation,
3) illumination, and 4) verification, or evaluation. The second
phase, "incubation," we consider to be the relaxation phase; and
the phase of "illumination," we feel, is the equivalent of regression in the service of the ego with a breakthrough of unconscious
material into consciousness. The artist or creative scientist must
follow it up by evaluating whether this combined product of conscious and unconsious material is really creative and viable.

Ego Activity and Ego Passivity
In the late 1940s, Rapaport initiated a psychoanalytic theory of
the modes of the ego, the theory of ego activity and ego passivity
(Gill, 1967). He never was fully satisfied with this theory, but
could not improve it nor did he apply it to hypnosis. He was very
ambivalent about publishing it. Eventually, in 1961, he published
it (in English) in an Ecuadorian psychological journal, one that
few of his American colleagues read. By chance the Ecuadorian
government sent this particular issue of its journal to the senior
author who became very excited about the paper and thought it
was the best one that David Rapaport, whom she admired, had
ever written. She and her students later applied Rapaport's psychoanalytic ideas on ego modes to the fields of heterohypnosis
(Fromm, 1972, 1977, 1979; Fromm, Lombard, Skinner, and Kahn,
1987–1988) and self-hypnosis (Fromm, Brown, Hurt, Oberlander,

Boxer, and Pfeifer, 1981; Fromm and Kahn, 1990), and enlarged on them (Stolar and Fromm, 1974).

The issue of ego activity, the senior author feels, is tied to the concepts of choice, free will (Fromm, 1992), defense, and mastery; that of ego passivity is tied to a feeling of being over-whelmed and unable to cope.

Fromm defines ego activity with regard to the hypnotic state as a volitional mental activity during trance (Fromm, 1992). It can be a decision by the patient to go along with what the hypnotist is suggesting because the person *wants* to do it; or *not* to go along with it (Fromm, 1972). In self-hypnosis it can be the act of giving oneself a self-suggestion or of deciding to break off the trance (Fromm et al., 1981; Fromm and Kahn, 1990).

Ego passivity is a state in which the patient feels overwhelmed or helpless and is unable to handle the situation. Except perhaps in highly masochistic people, this is always accompanied by un-pleasant affect. The ego dystonic, the unacceptable demand may come from the instincts, from the external world, or from the superego (Stolar and Fromm, 1974). The person goes along with the demand, as, for example, the drug addict or the person who runs amok does, even though unwillingly, or because of feeling overwhelmed and experiencing that he or she *has* to submit (e.g., in the case of rape). With hypnosis, ego passivity could occur when an authoritarian hypnotist forces a patient into doing, feel-ing, experiencing, or bringing up into the conscious waking state something that individual definitely does not want to do or is not ready to experience (Fromm, 1972).

Ego Receptivity
In 1971 Deikman, a San Francisco psychoanalyst interested in meditation, added to Rapaport's scheme the exciting concept of ego receptivity. Fromm has applied this concept to the field of hypnosis and found that in hypnosis ego receptivity occurs when the generalized reality orientation (GRO) has faded into the background of awareness, sinking into the preconscious (Fromm, 1992). Then there exists a greater openness to experience stimuli that arise from within or stem from just *one* outside source, the hypnotist, on whom the patient's attention is concentrated and

to whom he has a special transference relationship. Active, goal-directed, logical thinking, and voluntarism are temporarily suspended in the ego receptive hypnotic phases, and the patient "just lets go." The patient is more open to the hypnotist's suggestions and some of the patient's own unconscious and preconscious materials float effortlessly into awareness (Fromm, 1977, 1979; Brown and Fromm, 1986; Fromm and Kahn, 1990; Fromm and Nash, 1992).

The reader can get a feeling for what this state is like, if he or she tonight in the hypnagogic state (i.e., the state just before falling asleep) listens to the stream of consciousness in his or her head, but without trying to direct it. This talk in our heads goes on more or less all the time; rarely is it noticed in the waking state. The state of relaxation in which ego receptivity occurs, probably is—or in any case is close to—the relaxation state that accesses free association on the one hand, and on the other hand it is similar to the hypnagogic state.

When the ego is receptive, defenses are more relaxed, allowing into consciousness the emergence of fluid thought and images which in the waking state are below the level of conscious awareness. In heterohypnosis ego receptivity is encountered primarily as suggestibility, that is, increased openness to stimuli coming from the hypnotist (Fromm, 1979). Trust in the hypnotist is a prerequisite. Ego receptivity to stimuli arising from within appears in heterohypnosis as well as in self-hypnosis, and has highly beneficial consequences for hypnotherapy and hypnoanalysis. It helps to speed up the processes of uncovering and reintegrating. Ego receptivity also is an important aspect of creativity (Fromm, 1988).

Ego receptivity in hypnosis is basically the same as what Patricia Bowers (1978, 1982–1983) has called "effortless experiencing." She found this to be an important aspect of heterohypnosis and creativity.

Changes in Thought Processes in Hypnosis: From Prevalence of Secondary Process to Increase in Primary Process
The production of imagery is a pictorial form of thinking. It has been well researched with regard to hypnosis by J. R. Hilgard (1965, 1970, 1979), by Gill and Brenman (1959), and by Fromm

and her students (Fromm, Oberlander, and Gruenewald, 1970; Gruenewald, Fromm, and Oberlander, 1972; Lombard, Kahn, and Fromm, 1990). Primary process (Freud, 1900) is the mental functioning typical of early childhood; that is, before reality orientation has developed. In primary process the form of thinking is that of preverbal imagery. Primary process thinking is nonsequential and does not follow the rules of logic.

Secondary process thinking occurs in language rather than in imagery, pictures, and symbols. It results from the impact of reality, and is reality oriented. It is goal directed, verbal thinking and operates by logically ordered, practical, or abstract concepts. It is the dominant, everyday, cognitive mode of the adult in the waking state. When primary process occurs spontaneously in the healthy adult, it represents an input from the drives or from the unconscious ego, both of which can creatively enrich waking, logical modes of thought.

Primary process thinking is not given up when secondary process thinking has developed. Even in the adult waking state, our thoughts are hardly ever devoid of some form of imagery; and even in the deepest stages of trance or in the state of nocturnal dreaming, some elements of realism and logic can be found.

Primary process and secondary process are ranged along a continuum (Fromm, 1978–1979), and no sharp line of distinction separates one from the other. The primary process end is drive dominated, characterized by vivid, healthy imagery (for instance in the artist), by psychotic hallucinations in the emotionally severely disturbed patient. Secondary process characteristically shows step-by-step logic and reasoning and good reality orientation. Healthy primary process is particularly characteristic of the inspirational phase of the creative act and of intuitive thought. In the psychotic, primary process overwhelms and drowns out secondary process logic and reality orientation.

In various of our researches examining changes in thought processes in hypnosis (Fromm et al., 1970; Gruenewald, Fromm, and Oberlander, 1972; Fromm and Kahn, 1990), we found that hypnosis does involve a shift in mental functioning from secondary process to more imagistic, nonlogical primary process thinking. There are two types of imagery: primary process imagery and the reality-oriented, secondary process imagery, that can be

TABLE 2.1

Primary/Secondary Process in Waking & Hypnotic States

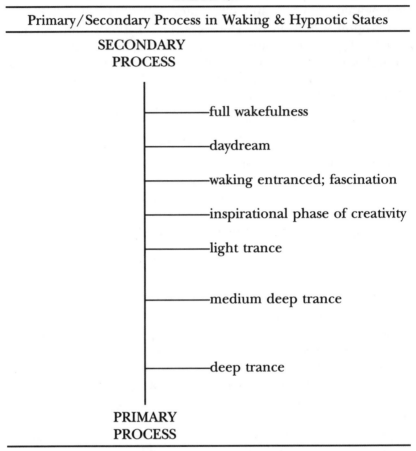

SECONDARY
PROCESS

——full wakefulness

——daydream

——waking entranced; fascination

——inspirational phase of creativity

——light trance

——medium deep trance

——deep trance

PRIMARY
PROCESS

produced voluntarily (but not equally vividly by all people). Primary process imagery usually arises spontaneously and involuntarily from within. It has fantastic, irreal qualities. Both primary and secondary process imagery and thinking are products of the ego. Only the ego can perceive, think, and produce imagery. Voluntarily produced fantasy represents an ego active process. Imagery that arises spontaneously from within, as in dreams, is an ego receptive process.

Imagery is the preferred way in which the hypnotized individual expresses himself. It can arise spontaneously, or it can be stimulated by suggestions from the hypnotist. These suggestions should be given in an open-ended way: "An image or a scene will now appear in front of your eyes that will give us some insight into aspects of the conflict you are working on. Notice what you see and tell me."

Attention, Absorption, and the General Reality Orientation (GRO)

Three other concepts that play a role in Fromm's theory of hypnosis are attention, absorption, and the GRO (Shor, 1959). Attention and absorption are concepts that stem from cognitive psychology. Absorption and the GRO have long been recognized as important characteristics of hypnosis. The former has been researched by Tellegen and Atkinson (1974), the latter by Shor (1959).

With regard to attention, Fromm differentiates between concentrative or focused attention on the one hand, and expansive, that is, free-floating attention on the other (Fromm, 1977, 1979). In expansive attention the patient "lets go," and a wide variety of thoughts, feelings, and memories enter into attentional awareness.

In their researches on self-hypnosis, Fromm and her collaborators found that concentrated attention always goes along with ego activity, and expansion of attention coincides with letting go and giving oneself over to ego receptivity (Fromm and Kahn, 1990). Ego receptivity and expanded attention are inextricably interwoven.

While attention and absorption are not concepts originally described in the psychoanalytic literature, Fromm conceives of both of them as ego functions—in the same way in which perception and cognition are ego functions. In the current psychological literature, attention is called a cognitive function; and in psychoanalysis we think of cognition as a function of the ego. Absorption is a result of both concentrated attention and ego receptivity. It denotes the extent to which a patient's attention has been gripped at a given moment by an outside event or by an ongoing inner experience that fascinates him.[5]

---

[5]While mainstream psychology has always been at odds with psychoanalysis and denied the existence of the unconscious, recently there has been a rapprochement between cognitive psychology and psychoanalysis (Epstein, 1994). Cognitive theorists have become

Structural and Content Categories
In the studies done in Fromm's laboratory we have come to recognize that there are two types of variables, structural and content, that differentiate hypnosis from the waking state (Fromm et al., 1981; Fromm and Kahn, 1990). Structural factors are those that essentially characterize the nature of the state. They are absorption-fascination, letting the GRO fade into the background of awareness, increased ego receptivity, more frequent expansive attention, and the experience of deep trance. Content categories comprise the phenomena of increased imagery production, hypermnesia, stronger affect, more enjoyable as well as more conflictful thoughts, hypnotic dreams, working on personal problems, and self-suggested sensory and motor phenomena.

SHAPING THE FROMM THEORY OF HYPNOSIS

Fromm has developed her theory of hypnosis by applying to the understanding of the phenomena of hypnosis the concepts described above and some other psychoanalytic concepts, as well as the three other concepts stemming from cognitive psychology. At times she made theoretical formulations first and followed them up with experimentation which would prove or disprove the theory she had made. At other times experimental findings came first and led her to add to, modify, or discard parts of the theory she was building (Fromm and Nash, 1992, pp. 131–148).

MICHAEL R. NASH

While the regression that is "in the service of the ego" is usually conceptualized as both temporal and topographic in char-

---

aware of the fact that most human information processing occurs outside of conscious awareness. They now postulate a "cognitive unconscious," by which they mean an automatic intuitive mode of information processing which operates in a different mode from the rational one. It is a nonverbal, experiential mode of thinking and functioning in which imagery and emotions play a much greater role than they do in the rational mode. Thus cognitive psychologists have come quite close to what we psychoanalysts call primary and secondary process thinking, and now recognize that an unconscious exists. Kihlstrom (1990), a cognitive psychologist and hypnosis researcher, has described the cognitive unconscious as a "kinder, gentler" unconscious than the Freudian one.

acter, Nash contends that the regression in hypnosis is solely topo-graphic. Citing the work of cognitive and psychoanalytic theorists (Spitz, 1965; Piaget, 1973; Peterfreund, 1978; Gill [cited in Tutt-man, 1982 as personal communication]; Rubinfine, 1981), Nash posits that in the course of development the psychic structure of the child is permanently changed, and that it is therefore impossi-ble to retrieve in pristine form early stages of development or early memories in statu. He agrees that there is a regression dur-ing hypnosis; and that the regression might be fairly described as a regression in the service of the ego; but in his view the regression is topographic and not temporal in character. This helps explain the fact that over one hundred years of research on hypnotic age regression has failed to uncover any credible evidence that hypnosis "brings back" genuinely childlike cognitive, perceptual, physiological, or psychological functioning (Nash, 1987). Fur-ther, this position is consistent with current theories of memory which reject the "immaculate perception" model of memory ac-quisition and storage in favor of an ongoing interaction between memory traces and contemporary factors such as expectation, cultural press, suggestion, and transference. On the other hand, there is good reason to believe that hypnosis alters the balance between primary and secondary process mentation in a way that is consonant with Freud's (1905b) original construct of *topographic* regression: more primary process, greater availability of affect, prevalence of condensation-displacement, body distortion, and changes in the experience of volition. If the regression in hypno-sis is indeed topographic, involving a state of consciousness akin to fantasy, reverie, and dreaming, we have an explanation which accounts for both its effectiveness as a therapeutic tool and its limitations as a forensic technique.

It should be clear by now that the respective positions taken by the authors of this book diverge on the nature of hypnotic regression. While we agree hypnosis can best be characterized as a "regression in the service of the ego," Fromm maintains that hypnotic regression is both temporal and topographic, and that these types of regression are in fact quite inseparable. Nash posits that hypnotic regression is solely topographic, and that likening the hypnotic state to earlier stages of psychic functioning is mis-leading. For example, in the case of Don, described in chapter

7, Fromm cites the affect-laden return of a long unused language as evidence for a transient reinstatement of an archaic psychic structure (temporal regression). Nash contends that use of language in this way is not mediated by the return of archaic structures in pristine form, but instead represents an eruption of dynamically loaded primary process material in an essentially contemporary psychic structure. Of course the only real remedy for this disagreement is rigorous psychoanalytically informed study of the changes in mentation undergone by hypnotic subjects. We hope that such a study will be undertaken soon. But one can anticipate that this divergence underlies the degree to which each author is willing to attribute historical authenticity to material emerging in the course of hypnotherapy.

3

Object Relations Theory,

Self Psychology, and

Hypnosis

According to two contemporary psychoanalytic theories, the theory of object relationships (Mahler, Pine, and Bergman, 1975; Kernberg, 1975, 1976; Masterson, 1981; and Adler, 1985), and the self theory[1] (Kohut, 1971, 1977) normal preoedipal child development proceeds along the following lines:

NORMAL AND DEFICIENT PREOEDIPAL
DEVELOPMENT

In the first three months after birth, the child has little knowledge of the outside world and is only aware of whether his or her needs are being gratified or frustrated. When fed, the child relaxes, smiles, or goes back to restful sleep; when left hungry, the child frets and cries. The baby is not able yet to differentiate between himself and the outside world,[2] or leave psychological space between himself and a nurturing or frustrating mother.

---

[1] The authors think that these two theories really are one, namely that self theory is a variant of object relationship theory.

[2] Daniel N. Stern's (1985) empirical observations on infants have cast some doubt on this notion.

There is no clear-cut demarcation yet between the "me" and the "not-me."

TABLE 3.1
Preoedipal Child Development

Age	Preoedipal Developmental Progression and/or Fixations	Pathological Regression
1–3 years	Need to see "gleam in mother's eye" to develop self-confidence Attaining object- and self-constancy	Narcissism
4 months to 1 year	Splitting of people into "all good" and "all bad" Desire to merge with "good" mother versus fear of being engulfed and annihilated by "bad" mother	Borderline
0–3 months	Lack of demarcation between "me" and "not me" Awareness of need gratification	Psychosis

In the second period, ages 4 months to 1 year, the child begins to conceive of the caretaking, nurturing parent who fulfills his or her needs as an "all-good" person; and of the same parent who is sometimes frustrating as an "all-bad" person. The child does not yet have the capacity to see that the mother (or father) cannot always be at his or her disposal at once, nor that both the giving and the frustrating caretaking parent are one and the same person. But the child does see them both as people outside of him- or herself. The child wishes to merge with the "good" mother (or father), but at the same time greatly fears being engulfed and swallowed up by the "bad" mother (or father). The technical term for this in the psychoanalytic literature is *splitting*,[3] splitting of people into all-good and all-bad ones.

---

[3]We think that with regard to child development *splitting* is a poor term: You can only split something that is a unit. In the *development* of the child, however, the good and the bad mother at this point have not yet reached object constancy (i.e., unity).

When it comes to describing the phenomena that occur in pathological regression, however, that is *after* self and object constancies developmentally have been established but start to fail, "splitting" is an apt expression to describe what happens in the regressive breakdown.

Borderline patients are constantly in danger that affect storms may fragment their very weak personality structure. They are suffering from a deficit in structure and integration. They see others, and themselves, as either all-good or all-bad; most of the time as all-bad. They are highly unstable and vulnerable to fragmentation of the personality resulting in psychotic breaks. They also are prone to suffer panic states, and to lose self-confidence as well as realistic knowledge of and trust in other people.

In the third period of normal development, ages 1 to 3 years, the child gains what has been called object- and self-constancy. The normally developing child during that time gains the ability to conceive of the mother as *one* person who is neither all-good nor all-bad; a person who satisfies the child's wishes many a time but at other times may not be able to do so and thus frustrates him. The child also begins to think of himself as *one* person. That is, he develops object- and self-constancy, and with it a feeling of identity. The age period of 1 to 3 years is the time in which object- and self-constancy are being established.

According to Kernberg (1975), the borderline syndrome is characterized by three facets: (1) splitting as a primary defense mechanism; (2) lack of selfobject differentiation in close relationships, resulting in a delusional transference psychosis with regard to people who are in a close family or friendship relationship and who are seen alternately as "all-good" or "all-bad" objects; and, on the other hand, (3) the ability to maintain selfobject differentiation and thus to behave in a reality-oriented manner in relationships that are *not* close (for instance, with colleagues in work situations). It is the splitting and the selfobject merger as manifested in the delusional (unconscious) transference to closely related others that distinguish the borderline personality organization from character disorders (Kernberg, 1975). And the tendency to fuse self and object images distinguishes the borderline from pathological narcissism, a condition in which such a merger does not exist. In narcissistic patients, even when the object is idealized, it is not confused with the grandiose self. The borderline is interested in others only with regard to whether they will gratify or frustrate his needs, allow or reject merger. The narcissistic patient uses others either as confirming or in some ways frustrating his defense of grandiosity which conceals vulnerable self-esteem and protects him against rage, envy, and psychic helplessness. For Kernberg (1975), pathological narcissism is a variant of the borderline personality organization. For Kohut (1971) pathological narcissism is a specific, unique form of developmental deficit disease based on the 1- to 3-year-old child's not having received enough admiration and proud "mirroring" in the mother's eye to develop solid pride in his own achievements; that is, healthy self-confidence and healthy narcissism.

What has been described so far is the preoedipal development of the child according to object relationship theory. Self theory adds to this that in order to develop self-confidence, the child needs the mother's admiration; to see "the gleam in the mother's eye" (Kohut, 1971) and the pride the mothering and/ or fathering person takes in all of the child's newly developing skills, such as walking, talking, and climbing.

The person who gets fixated on the 0 to 3 months level of development is a psychotic; the one who splits people into the all-good and the all-bad, and also has a fear of being engulfed or annihilated by others, is a borderline. The person who needs constant reassurance about their self-worth or who at other times has an exaggerated opinion of himself, suffers from narcissism. Frequently, people develop relatively normally, but when under too much stress they go into a pathological regression, moving backwards from normality or neurosis to narcissism; or even deeper to the borderline state, or to psychosis.

The upward-directed arrow on the left side of Table 3.1 indicates normal developmental progression. The downward-directed arrow on the right side indicates pathological regression.

TRANSFERENCES OF PATIENTS WITH
DEVELOPMENTAL DEFICIT

Until the 1960s psychoanalysts felt that only neurotic patients, character disorders, and patients with psychosomatic illnesses could be analyzed. Narcissistic, borderline, and psychotic patients were considered unanalyzable. Supposedly, these patients could not develop a transference. With the advent of object relations theory and self theory, psychoanalysts became aware of the fact that the latter group of patients, suffering from developmental deficit, also develop transference (Kernberg, 1975; Masterson, 1976; Kohut, 1971): preoedipal transferences. These transferences differ from those of patients suffering from neuroses and psychosomatic illnesses. Nonetheless they are transferences and such patients therefore are now recognized as being analyzable.

Narcissistic patients form what Kohut (1971) has called the selfobject transference by means of which they attempt to obtain from the therapist something they have not yet internalized, namely, feelings of self-worth and healthy pride in their own accomplishments. The therapist must provide "mirroring" (Kohut, 1971) and admiration to make up for the deficit caused by the parents not having provided for these needs at the critical ages of 1 to 3 years.

The borderline transference is characterized by boundary diffusion, splitting (Kernberg, 1975), panic states (Buie and Adler, 1982), and transient loss or fragmentation of selfobject representations. The hypnoanalyst must provide a safe and facilitating environment in which the patient can recapitulate the development of the early subphases of the separation–individuation period (Mahler, Pine, and Bergman, 1975) with a better parent figure, in a safe climate. The hypnoanalyst must help the patient to develop object constancy and overcome "splitting," and freely and unstintingly give a great deal to the patient for a long time.

In the transference of the psychotic the basic problem is the need–fear dilemma (Adler, 1985). The psychotic needs "the other" to define himself as a person. He has a strong need to merge with the love object and at the same time fears to be swallowed up by that person, or to lose his identity in the merger. He behaves in the same way in his relationship with the therapist.

HYPNOANALYSIS OF PATIENTS WITH DEVELOPMENTAL DEFICIT OR REGRESSION ALONG THE DEVELOPMENTAL LINE

Until the 1980s, hypnotherapists did not dare to use hypnosis with psychotic patients or with borderlines, mainly on account of

Harold Rosen's (1953) widely publicized notion that hypnosis is dangerous for such patients, that it could lead to suicide, and that it could throw people, particularly borderline cases, into a psychosis. Rosen feared that the natural tendency to produce dissociation in hypnosis might increase the decompensation potential. This, however, is a danger only if deep uncovering techniques such as age regression, free-floating imagery, and the interpretation of hypnotically produced dreams are employed in the beginning treatment of psychotics and prepsychotics. Prepsychotic patients must first be helped to learn more about reality rather than about their unconscious motivations. Because psychotic and prepsychotic patients have weak egos, one must also first help them in hypnosis to gain ego strength and coping mechanisms, so that eventually they will be able to face reality rather than deny it and erect as defenses their own hallucinatory fantasies or splitting.

In the past 20 years a few hypnotherapists have courageously gone ahead and worked hypnotically with psychotic and borderline patients (Lavoie, Sabourin, and Langlois, 1973; Lavoie, Sabourin, Ally, and Langlois, 1976; Scagnelli, 1976; Zeig, 1974).

Psychoanalysts (Fromm-Reichmann, 1948, 1954; Karon, 1963; Searles, 1965) had found that in working with psychotic and borderline patients they must assume a more active role than when working with neurotic patients. Similarly, the hypnotherapist must be more active and directive in building up the therapeutic scenario for borderline patients. He or she must actively try to become for the patient a focal point for selfobject interactions by providing an environment that is constant, stable, protective, and nurturing. The hypnotherapist must be a very real person for the patient, not just a transference object but a person who can "hold" the boundaries of reality much as a good mother does when holding the infant (Winnicott, 1965). The establishing of such a boundary then begins to provide a sense of demarcation between the "me" and "not-me," the self and the other. It also (Baker, 1981) "provides a bridge for restoring appropriate investment with external objects and the internalization of their appropriate representations" (p. 40).

The most outstanding hypnoanalytic work with psychotics has been done by Elgan Baker (1981), who is well grounded in psychoanalytic theory. He has combined the techniques of psychoanalytic object relations theory and self theory with guided imagery in hypnosis, so that now it is possible to treat psychotic and borderline patients with hypnoanalysis. He was the first hypnoanalyst to translate the theoretical insights of object relations theory and self theory into a protocol of primary process language to be used with psychotic patients, so they can progress upward and forward again along the developmental line (see Table 3.1). It is a seven-step program anchored clearly, step by step, upon the insights of object relationship theory, the successive steps the normal child has to take in the developmental progression in his relationship with other people. He specifically bases his technique upon Mahler's description of preoedipal child development. The primary focus of this protocol of hypnoanalysis is helping the patient relate to the therapist as someone who can nurture and protect him in a dependable, consistent manner, and in a way that does not arouse anxiety in the patient.

In hypnosis, and in most other altered states of consciousness, thinking occurs to a great extent along the lines of primary process (Fromm, 1978–1979, 1979). Visualizations, imagery, and symbolizations play a much greater role in hypnosis than they do in the waking state. From the beginning of treatment, the primary focus of therapy is to help the borderline relate to the therapist as someone who can nurture and protect the patient in a consistent and dependable fashion. The hypnoanalyst actively attempts to help these patients to live through a normal developmental process of differentiating self and object, gaining object constancy and identity, and to follow this up by introjection of the good object and integration. In order to achieve this goal, the therapist follows a progressive sequence of techniques in hypnosis which develop in the patient feelings of relaxation coupled with phase-appropriate imagery and fantasies. Elgan Baker (1981) devised this ingenious seven-step sequence for hypnoanalytic work with psychotic patients. It is one of the most important innovations in the whole field of hypnotherapy.

BAKER'S PROTOCOL FOR
HYPNOANALYTIC WORK WITH
PSYCHOTICS[4]

The patient is first helped into a light to medium state of
trance by means of permissive induction methods. Feelings of
comfort, calm, and well-being are suggested in a soothing voice.

Step 1: Evocation of Images of Primary Narcissism. When the patient
shows through body posture or through verbalization that
he or she feels relaxed, the patient is helped to imagine
being *alone* and involved in some pleasant activity. From
time to time the therapist continues to suggest feelings
of comfort and well-being. This usually needs to be done
for a number of weeks.

Step 2: Beginning Separation. The patient is again instructed to
visualize the self-image that feels comfortable, then to
open her eyes and look at the therapist; then to close her
eyes and see the self-image. Suggestions for relaxation are
interspersed. The process is repeated several times. The
purpose is to reassure the patient that the therapist exists
even when not seen and to lay the groundwork for the
concept of separateness of object and self.

Step 3: Working toward Object Constancy. The patient is asked to
develop visual images of the therapist while being given
continuing suggestions of feelings of relaxation and well-
being. It is frequently difficult for psychotic and borderline patients to visualize the therapist. If such is the case,
the hypnoanalyst changes the tactic somewhat and asks
the patient to produce "deanimated"[5]—and thus less
dangerous—images that can serve as symbols for the therapist or as imaginary transitional phenomena (Winnicott,

---

[4]An earlier version of this description of Elgan Baker's work was published by the
senior author in *Psychoanalytic Psychology* (1984), 1:61–76, as part of a paper entitled "Hypnoanalysis—With Particular Emphasis on the Borderline Patient."

[5]This is parallel to deanimation in dreams which, as French and Fromm (1964, pp.
64–70) have shown, is a defensive maneuver patients execute when they strongly need to
protect themselves against becoming aware of the nature and depth of the conflict they
are struggling with.

1965). For instance, the hypnoanalyst may suggest that the patient imagine the therapist's name written on a blackboard or that the patient imagine holding in his hand an object selected from the therapist's desk. If the patient becomes anxious or upset, the imaging is discontinued and the therapist reinstates feelings of calm relaxation in the patient. But the purpose is eventually to help the patient develop visual images of the therapist as an alive, whole, and separate person.

The borderline patient is further along on the road to object constancy than the schizophrenic. Thus hypnoanalytic work with borderlines can be started with step 3 or 4. But in all hypnotic sessions with borderlines (as well as with psychotics), it is imperative to start the session with induction of relaxation and comfort.

Step 4: Separate but Together. The patient is instructed to alternate between developing images of the therapist and images of the self; then in imagery to picture himself or herself and the therapist together. The measure of their proximity is left to the patient. One of our patients at first developed the image of himself sitting on top of a peak in the Rockies and seeing the therapist wave to him from the top of the Empire State Building in New York. In the next session he saw us both swimming in Lake Michigan, but he was swimming at a Chicago beach on the west side of the lake and the therapist was swimming on the east side of the lake, 40 miles away. It took several weeks before he could visualize himself and the hypnoanalyst in the same room. The hypnoanalyst attempts, gradually, to help the patient decrease the distance in the images while maintaining comfort and relaxation.

Step 5: Working toward Introjection of the "Good" Object. The next step in the sequence consists of helping the patient to develop fantasies involving the patient and the therapist in *parallel activity,* and then in *interaction.* The suggested interactional fantasies should emphasize the nurturing, protecting, and supportive role of the hypnotherapist.

These positive visual images of the therapist and the patient in interaction provide a cognitive–affective *pairing* that makes it possible *to introject the therapist as a gratifying ("good") object* and *to see the self as a positive, "good me."* The images can then be used to reduce anxiety and to induce positive feelings of self-worth.

Step 6: Controlled Externalization of Distorted Self and Object Representations.[6] Step 6 is the counterpart of step 5. The patient is asked in the hypnotic state to visualize the distorted bad object and self representations that have been internalized; then to externalize them and get rid of them.

For instance, the patient may be told that now he can look deep inside himself, and that when doing this he will see, as if in an X ray, inside of his body, the old image of the "bad" parent. Furthermore, the patient may be told that he can now take this image out from within and attach the bad part of the parent to a balloon that lies "over there" on the ground. The balloon can then be blown up with helium and released. It will float far away, up into the sky—so far away that as the patient watches it float away, it becomes smaller and smaller, a tiny point in the sky that eventually vanishes, and no longer exists. This is not resorting to magic, but it is making use of symbolism, of communicating with the patient in primary process language.

The hypnoanalyst also suggests to the patient that he can keep the good, loving part of the parent within the self (or it can be taken back into the self). Sometimes taking the incorporated bad, and often distorted, parent out of the self can be quite a dramatic performance with abreaction of strong affect.

In addition, the patient can also be asked during this period of hypnotherapy to visualize himself in the mask of the "bad" child who sometimes may have provoked the parent's anger and thus became deprived. Now the patient can tear off the constraining mask of the "bad" small child, and really grow and

---

[6]In Baker's work, which deals with psychotics, step 6 employs visualizations of voices and threatening delusional figures and their management. We have used the principle of this step but modified the content of the imagery to fit the phenomena of the borderline patients' experiences and the dynamics of the borderline and narcissistic personalities.

unfold all the good potential the patient has within (Fromm and Eisen, 1982). Or the patient can be asked to visualize the new self, putting the bad incorporated object and self representations into a paper garbage bag (not a plastic one because that might imply nonbiodegradability and thus continued existence), and dumping them somewhere, so that the patient will be rid of them for good.

In general, it is preferable as much as possible to let the patient's own imagery and visualizations come up and then to guide them in the therapeutic direction (Fromm and Eisen, 1982).

Step 7: Integrating Love and Hate Objects Solidly: Achieving Solid, Separate Self and Object Constancy. As stability of ego functioning increases, other significant love-and-hate objects appear in the patient's hypnotic imagery. Emphasis in the hypnoanalysis continues to be placed upon the integration of both positive and negative interpersonal experiences. Dynamic issues now emerging can be examined and worked through in the hypnotic state and in the waking state, alternatively.

The authors have found steps 3 to 7 to be extremely useful in hypnoanalytic work with borderline patients. With patients at the upper end of the borderline syndrome, and with narcissistic patients, we only use Baker's (1981) step 5 (emphasis on the nurturing and protectiveness of the therapist), step 6, and step 7.

We have added an eighth step of our own:

Step 8: Gaining Control Over Splitting as a Defense. Once the good object introject is well established, it can be used to gain control over "splitting." The hypnoanalyst can now begin to explain to the patient that a mother cannot always gratify a child's needs; that some frustration of dependent wishes leads to the child's moving toward autonomy and growth; furthermore, that the world is not black and white; that all people have good characteristics and bad ones, and that people can even be giving when they withhold. The hypnoanalyst can now point out how the patient has transferred his or her early defense of splitting the good and the bad object and the feelings connected with it to current adult family members; and how unrealistic it is to see these same people at times as all-good and at other times as all-bad. Feelings and fantasies that need to be made increasingly ego dystonic can now be talked about in terms of their destructive effect on the patient and on his or her environment. Or the patient may be asked to look at these irrealistic feelings carefully in the imagery and see that perhaps he or she can let them go or float away. Here guided imagery would be used in hypnosis.

Elements that represent aspects of defensive object splitting also may be moved toward integration through emphasis on merging in imagery the good and the bad parts into a single, whole object. This goal can be achieved through various fantasies and guided images in hypnosis that emphasize temporal and spatial pairing of the bad image of the mother with the now safely internalized good image of the therapist. In this phase the patient must constantly be shown that the good relationship with the therapist is not destroyed by this merger, and that the therapist continues to stand by the patient. The following case may serve as an example:

One of our patients was suffering from a narcissistic character disorder with borderline features. She conceived of her mother as having rejected her since birth and of having abused her emotionally as well as physically (through what in the first two years of therapy she described as "daily" beatings with a strap and "nearly daily"[7] enemas being forced upon her). At one point, when the patient was in hypnosis, her hand was lying in her lap in a rather unnatural position, fingers outstretched, with the index finger separated from the other three fingers by a wide *V* of open space. To me, the senior author, this seemed to symbolize splitting. We had been talking about her tendency to see authority figures only in black and white, and to feel that some, including the hypnoanalyst, were all-good but most others, like her mother,

---

[7]Toward the end of the hypnoanalysis the patient told the hypnoanalyst that she had been given an enema only *once* in childhood, but that the beatings had occurred about once a week.

all-bad. In order to undercut the splitting, I suggested to the patient at this point that the four fingers of her hand would now move together and would want to stay together; that is, I suggested that if the patient now unconsciously was ready for merging the good and the bad objects, a symbolic and involuntary ideomotor activity would occur. Some involuntary movement of the fingers toward each other did occur, haltingly. But the patient then tore the index finger away from greater closeness to the other three fingers and exclaimed with great affect, "I can't do that. I can't do that." I asked why. Again with great affect she remonstrated: "You're good, you're good to me and I cannot allow you to become poisoned with my mother's terrible poison."[8] I calmly assured her that I would refuse to let this happen and asked her to allow the fingers of the hand to do whatever her unconscious was ready for them to do. Hesitantly, and in little lapses, the fingers moved toward the index finger (which we later found out represented the bad mother, while the other three fingers represented me). Shortly after the index finger and the middle finger had touched, a beatific expression came over the patient's face, and she said, "I suddenly saw a beautiful image in front of my eyes: a young woman holding a baby in her arms and looking at the baby lovingly." I asked her whether she recognized the young woman. At first the face of the woman was vague, but slowly it became clearer and clearer. Eventually the patient said, "Oh it's my mother, and I seem to be the baby in her arms! My mother can't always have been bad. She must have loved me, too, at least when I was a baby. And perhaps later, too, even though she was too harsh and strict and gave me enemas."

This event occurred during the therapy hour which just preceded my going overseas for a month. The patient, who had always felt abandoned by me when I had to go out of town even for a few days, now withstood the separation without any difficulty. (I sent her two postcards from Europe as "transitional objects.") Her progress after this symbolization of the good and the bad object and moving toward object constancy was indeed remarkable.

---

[8] Several months later the patient told me that during that moment she had felt "in danger of disintegration or fragmentation, or death, or loss of you and the love I feel for you or you feel for me."

Spontaneous imagery plays an extremely important role in hypnoanalysis. However, one should remember that changes in fantasy and visual imagery do not automatically alter psychic structure or the organization of self and object representations. Rather, they are a symbolic primary process expression of the patient's dawning insight that psychic structure and the organization of self and object representations have changed. The cause of the change is the relationship between the hypnoanalyst and the patient both in its real, contemporary aspects and in the transference manifestations with their historical meanings. In this relationship, through symbolically interplaying in hypnoanalysis the rational and irrational aspects of the patient's inner early experiences, the patient is led to restructuralization and to healthier introjects, a process which makes further growth and maturation possible.

The importance of imagery and primary process language in the hypnoanalyst's communication with severely disturbed patients cannot be overstressed. Hypnosis lends itself much better than the waking state to the use of imagery—guided imagery produced in interplay between patient and therapist as well as imagery produced spontaneously by the patient alone. In psychoanalysis, where the patient is in the waking state, the therapist employs mostly secondary process language. But when the patient is in hypnosis the therapist must use—with any patient, not only with the severely disturbed ones—*much more* primary process language and *much more* imagery. The insights gained in hypnosis are therefore much deeper; they go to the gut. In waking-state psychoanalysis, insights often remain purely intellectual, but in hypnosis they become deep emotional insights. This is one of the reasons why we prefer hypnoanalysis over psychoanalysis.

In summary, in the hypnoanalysis of the psychotic and the borderline patient we try to achieve basic structure building by means of developing within the patient solid object constancy and internal representation—first of the good, nourishing mother figure, and then of the realistic object with its good and its bad qualities, which we hope the patient no longer needs to split.

With psychotic and borderline patients the hypnoanalyst needs to assume a somewhat more active and more structuring role than with neurotic patients. The patient needs to be guided toward the development of a stable, gratifying, and positive inner representation of the object, the therapist—a representation which he or she can assimilate as a new and mending introject. When the process of assimilation has occurred, the new introject enriches the integrative and organizing functions of the patient's ego. The introject then can provide a stable "magnetic" core around which split and fragmented images can begin to coalesce. The identification with the therapist provides a "re-educative experience" (Alexander and French, 1946). By means of internalization, the patient can then develop better and more realistic self representations. This will lead to appropriate differentiation and integration of the self system in an enduring fashion.

The hypnoanalysis of borderline and narcissistic cases takes more time than the hypnoanalysis of neurotics or character neuroses. But it does *not* take the amount of time that psychoanalysis takes because in hypnoanalysis, as opposed to the waking state, the therapist talks much more directly to the patient's unconscious, and the patient's unconscious communicates much more directly with the therapist. The dream is not the only royal road to the unconscious. There are at least two others: altered states of consciousness (one of which is hypnosis) and imagery. In hypnoanalysis all three roads are available.

DIAMOND'S DUAL INTERACTION THEORY

The psychoanalyst and hypnoanalyst Michael Jay Diamond (1984, 1987) thinks of hypnosis as being an object relationship in which two people are intensely involved, the patient and the therapist; more intensely than in any other kind of therapy. He states that he has come to regard hypnoanalysis and hypnotherapy as a "dual" interaction phenomenon of great intensity. He feels that it has four dimensions which constantly interact: (1) the transference; (2) the therapeutic or working alliance; (3) a symbiotic or fusional alliance; (4) the realistic, here-and-now relationship between the patient and the therapist. These four dimensions overlap, and at any point in hypnosis, one or another of these four dimensions may predominate. However, the essential thread of the other three exists also at all times. Each person in the hypnotic relationship experiences these four dimensions and contributes to their existence in a truly interactive manner. From moment to moment within the hour (and even outside of it) these object relations interactions between the hypnoanalyst and the patient are interwoven and intertwined, sometimes changing in constellation and emphasis very quickly between the two partners in the dyad.

The symbiotic or fusional alliance component plays a much greater role in the hypnoanalysis of patients suffering from deficit in or regression to a point along the preoedipal developmental line than in those with oedipal conflicts and relatively mature psychic structuralization. Many a time the patient experiences the therapist symbiotically (i.e., as an actual part of the self), "incorporated as 'inside' one's own psychic system. . . . The degree of symbiosis can range from partial (i.e., a self/object attachment) to complete (i.e., union or merger)" in the psychotic (Diamond, 1987, p. 100).

In the vibrant world of the hypnotic relationship, the hypnotherapist is not an external, detached, objective observer. He is more active, more involved in the relationship than the kind of psychoanalyst who sees his task to be only a blank screen on which the patient projects his feelings. Diamond conceives of the hypnotist as part of a system to which both the hypnotherapist and the patient belong. "What occurs transpires between the 'us' that comprises the dyad" (Diamond, 1987, p. 101).

What Diamond has called the *real relationship* between the interacting parties is what has been described by Brown and Fromm as the "realistic Perception of the Therapist as a Person" (Brown and Fromm, 1987, pp. 20–21). It implies that while all the complicated interpersonal transference reactions between hypnotherapist and patient are there, the patient also, to some degree, has a realistic, here-and-now appreciation of what the hypnotherapist really is like.

4

Fundamentals of Hypnotic

Technique

This chapter is a distillation of current research findings and general clinical protocols on the therapeutic applications of hypnosis: What is hypnosis, how is it done, and why does it work. We begin with an operational definition of hypnosis; we then identify six key research findings bearing most directly on clinical practice; and finally we outline in detail specific aims and methods of clinical intervention with hypnosis.

Though for the most part conducted by investigators who are relatively uninformed about psychoanalysis, the robust tradition of basic research in hypnosis is vitally relevant to any clinician wishing to incorporate hypnosis into his or her psychoanalytic practice. We invite the reader to endure the rather generic, sometimes reductionistic language of basic research in service of developing sharper clinical formulations and treatment plans. In *Science*, the centerpiece journal of the American Association for the Advancement of Science, Kihlstom (1987) offered a sensible and relatively theory-neutral definition of hypnosis: "Hypnosis is a social interaction in which one person, the subject, responds to suggestions offered by another person, the hypnotist, for experiences involving alterations in perception, memory, and action" (p. 1449). Even the most hidebound adherent of one hypnosis theory or another would probably agree that this statement is satisfactory as a working definition. In fact, this type of operational definition has proved immensely heuristic—hundreds of hypnosis research articles are published each year in scientific and medical journals.

SIX RESEARCH DISCOVERIES THAT ARE CORE TO CLINICAL PRACTICE

We will eschew the inter- and intranicene turmoil between competing theoretical models about the "essence" of hypnosis, and concentrate rather on the six broadly replicated research discoveries which most inform responsible clinical application. Though these six findings are generally accepted, we caution that in all but two cases there are dissenting minority opinions championed by perfectly respectable theorists and clinicians.[1]

HYPNOTIC RESPONSIVENESS CAN BE RELIABLY MEASURED AND IT IS A RELATIVELY STABLE PERSONALITY TRAIT

Observations that people differ in their general level of responsiveness to hypnotic procedures date back to the eighteenth century. Attempts to measure hypnotic susceptibility began in the nineteenth century with Braid (1843) and Bernheim (1886b) leading the way. But it was not until the late 1950s that a rigorously normed and standardized procedure for measuring hypnotizability emerged from the programmatic research of Ernest Hilgard at Stanford University: The Stanford Hypnotic Susceptibility Scales, forms A, B, a little later C (Weitzenhoffer and Hilgard, 1959, 1962). While the Stanford Scales (especially form C) remain somewhat of a "gold standard" in hypnosis research, many other standardized protocols have been developed in the ensuing years

---

[1]Below we supply dissenting opinions on four of the six positions based on credible research:

    Point 1: Spanos (1986)
    Point 2: Lynn, Rhue, and Weekes (1990)
    Point 3: No credible contrary evidence
    Point 4: Spanos, Perlini, and Robertson (1989)
    Point 5: No credible contrary evidence
    Point 6: Smith, Womack, and Chen (1989)

(see Table 4.1). But all operate from the basic premise that hypnotic responsiveness is best measured by hypnotizing a subject, administering a series of suggestions which are either passed or failed, and adding the number of "passed" items to obtain a score. For example the Stanford scales involve administration of an induction along with 12 suggestions including ideomotor suggestions (e.g., an extended arm that becomes unbearably heavy and moves down; hands that become so tightly interlocked that they cannot be separated), cognitive suggestions (e.g., amnesia), and perceptual suggestions (e.g., positive visual or auditory hallucination). Specific behavioral criteria are established for obtaining a "pass" score on each of the 12 items. The total number of suggestions *is* the subject's score. The range of possible scores is thus 0 to 12, with individuals scoring on the lower end of the spectrum being less hypnotizable, and those at the upper end being more hypnotizable.

This methodological breakthrough enabled researchers and clinicians to more confidently examine the nature of hypnotizability, especially its stability. Four important discoveries emerged from this work. First, hypnotic susceptibility is for the most part normally distributed across the population, with almost everyone able to experience hypnosis to some extent. Second, a person's responsiveness to hypnosis is relatively unaffected by the technique used, environmental surroundings, and person of the hypnotist. In other words, the person's ability to be hypnotized accounts for his or her responsiveness, not the specific technique used, not the expertise of the hypnotist, not the situational variables surrounding the test administration. Third, hypnotic susceptibility is a personality trait that changes little, if any, across time. Test–retest reliabilities for hypnotizability scales compare favorably with those of IQ tests. In fact, Piccione, Hilgard, and Zimbardo (1989) reported an extended follow-up study which revealed an impressive correlation of .71 between the scores subjects obtained initially, and those obtained 10 to 25 years later. Fourth, children as young as 4 years of age can be hypnotized. Hypnotizability appears to increase with age into early adolescence, when it plateaus, perhaps decreasing slightly among the elderly. Later in this chapter we will discuss how each of these

TABLE 4.1
Commonly Used Hypnotic Susceptibility Procedures

Scale Name	Modality	No. of Items	Duration	Typical Uses
The Stanford Hypnotic Susceptibility Scale (Forms A and B) Weitzenhoffer & Hilgard (1959). *Stanford Hypnotic Susceptibility Scale, Forms A and B.* Palo Alto, CA: Consulting Psychologists Press.	Adult Individual	12	1 hr 15 min	Used primarily in research as a preliminary screening device to serve as a nonthreatening initial estimate of hypnotic responsivity. Sometimes used clinically for assessment.
The Stanford Hypnotic Susceptibility Scale (Form C) Weitzenhoffer & Hilgard (1962). *Stanford Hypnotic Susceptibility Scale, Form C.* Palo Alto, CA: Consulting Psychologists Press.	Adult Individual	12	1 hr 15 min	Generally used in research, and considered the touchstone against which all other measures of susceptibility are gauged. Some demanding items which give it more "top." More regressive items.
Stanford Profile Scales of Hypnotic Susceptibility (Forms I and II) Weitzenhoffer & Hilgard (1967). *Revised Stanford Profile Scales of Hypnotic Susceptibility, Forms I and II.* Palo Alto, CA: Consulting Psychologists Press.	Adult Individual	12	1 hr 30 min	The most thorough hypnotizability test yielding a profile of abilities for each subject. Some exceedingly difficult items. Rarely used in either research or clinical settings.
Stanford Clinical Hypnosis Scale (Adult and Child Forms) Morgan & Hilgard (1978–1979). The Stanford Hypnotic Clinical Scale for adults and children. *American Journal of Clinical Hypnosis,* 21:134–169.	Child and Adult Individual	5	20 min	Brief 5-item versions of the Stanford Scales designed for clinical use. There is a form for children (ages 3–16) and adults.

TABLE 4.1
Commonly Used Hypnotic Susceptibility Procedures

Harvard Group Scale of Hypnotic Susceptibility (Forms A and B) Shor & Orne (1962). *Harvard Group Scale of Hypnotic Susceptibility, Form A.* Palo Alto, CA: Consulting Psychologists Press.	Adult Group	12	1 hr 15 min	Used in research as a preliminary screening device designed to serve as a nonthreatening initial estimate of hypnotic responsivity. A relatively "easy" scales.
The Waterloo-Stanford Group C Scale of Hypnotic Susceptibility Bowers (1993). The Waterloo-Stanford Group C Scale of Hypnotic Susceptibility: Normative and comparative data. *International Journal of Clinical and Experimental Hypnosis*, 41:35–46.	Adult Individual	12	1 hr 15 min	Developed as a substitute for the Stanford C. Contains more difficult items than other group scales. Used exclusively for research.
The Computer Assisted Hypnosis Scale Grant & Nash (1995). The Computer Assisted Hypnosis Scale: Standardization and norming of a computer-administered measure of hypnotic ability. *Psychological Assessment.*	Adult Individual	12	1 hr 15 min	Interactive computer software (for both MAC and DOS for Windows) which utilizes graphics and digital voice technology to administer and score a hypnotizability test. The items are similar to the Standard C scale in content and difficulty. Research and clinical screening uses.

TABLE 4.1 (continued)
Commonly Used Hypnotic Susceptibility Procedures

Scale Name	Modality	No. of Items	Duration	Typical Uses
The Children's Hypnotic Susceptibility Scale London (1963). *The Children's Hypnotic Susceptibility Scale.* Palo Alto, CA: Consulting Psychologists Press.	Child Individual	12	1 hr 15 min	A modification of the Stanford A scale but modified for the understanding and behavior of children.
Hypnotic Induction Profile Spiegel & Bridger (1970). *Manual for the Hypnotic Induction Profile.* New York: Soni Medica.	Adult Individual	5	10 min	A scale using extent of eye roll, arm levitation, involuntariness, dissociation, and ability to terminate hypnosis. A relatively easy scale employed clinically and in some research settings.
The Carleton University Responsiveness to Suggestion Scale Spanos, Radtke, Hodgins, Stam, & Bertrand (1983). The Carleton University Responsiveness to Suggestion Scale: Normative data and psychometric properties. *Psychological Reports,* 53:523–535.	Adult Group or Individual	7	30 min	A scale that yields four responsiveness subscores: behavioral, subjective, involuntariness, and compliance. Used almost exclusively in research settings.

four points has important implications for the clinician who is contemplating a hypnotic intervention.

HYPNOTIC SUBJECTS REPORT EFFORTLESS
UNBIDDEN EXPERIENCES BUT IN FACT REMAIN
ACTIVE PARTICIPANTS

Good hypnotic subjects invariably report that their hypnotic responses were nonvolitional, that their experience happened *to* them (e.g., "my hand became heavy and moved down by itself"; "suddenly I found myself feeling 3 years old again"). In fact hypnotic subjects are not passive automatons, mechanically responding to the immutable imperatives of an altered state of consciousness or the explicit demands embodied in the hypnotist's suggestions. Instead, there is ample evidence from laboratories operating from a variety of theoretical perspectives that hypnotic subjects are cognitively active problem solvers who are, albeit unconsciously, incorporating cultural ideas about hypnosis into their response, and responding to implicit expectations inherent in the immediate interpersonal matrix (E. R. Hilgard, 1977; Sheehan and McConkey, 1982; P. G. Bowers, 1986; Spanos and Chaves, 1989; Coe and Sarbin, 1991). As psychoanalytic clinicians we immediately recognize this pattern of nonconscious participation as something similar to how our patients report and experience many of their symptoms—they are ego alien, but nevertheless profoundly affected by intra- and interpersonal factors. Thus, while the peculiar features of the hypnotic state may in part determine the hypnotic subject's response, there is the added feature of the subject's nonconscious involvement in the role of "a hypnotized person." It is sometimes important to understand when a therapeutic outcome is attributable to a technique-specific effect, and when it is a consequence of nonspecific factors inherent in any helping relationship (e.g., expectations, demand characteristics, placebo).

HYPNOSIS INVOLVES A SHIFT IN COGNITIVE
PROCESSES SUCH THAT DISTINCTION BETWEEN
HISTORICALLY REAL AND IMAGINED EVENTS
BECOMES MUDDLED

Hypnosis is sometimes mistakenly employed to "find out the real truth" about the past. Like traditional psychoanalytic psycho- therapy, hypnosis can aid in establishing narrative coherence and contextualization to mental representations, but it in no way en- sures their correspondence with previous life events. Citing the basic memory research of Johnson and her colleagues (Johnson, Hashtroudi, and Lindsay, in press) K. Bowers (1992) cautions that "any factor or combination of factors that renders an imagined event vivid, effortless, and well-contextualized will increase the likelihood that it will mistakenly be accepted [by the patient] as memory" (p. 8). Given the effortless character of hypnotic responding and the sometimes compelling vividness of hypnotic imagery, hypnosis can actually obscure rather than clarify what really happened in the past. There is now a rich forensic literature documenting just this point (Pettinati, 1988; Wagstaff, 1989; McConkey, 1992). A psychoanalytic therapist is already mindful that any intervention (hypnotic or otherwise) that invites topo- graphic regression invites the emergence of compelling affect, vivid imagery, and believed-in fantasy. While all of these elements have immense therapeutic potential, their relationship to histori- cal event is of course complex and nonlinear.

HYPNOTIC RESPONSE IS NOT PLACEBO RESPONSE

It is tempting for clinicians unfamiliar with hypnosis to equate responsiveness to placebo with responsiveness to hypnosis. In fact there appears to be little or no relationship between the two. There are two lines of research addressing this question. First, it has been empirically demonstrated that forms of social suggestibility variously described as "conformity," "gullibility," "low autonomy," or "external locus of control" are not corre- lated with responsiveness to hypnosis (Moore, 1964; Burns and

Hammer, 1970; Kihlstrom, Diaz, McClellan, Ruskin, Pistole, and Shor, 1980).

Second, the research literature, most notably McGlashan, Evans, and Orne (1969) and Spanos, Perlini, and Robertson (1989), has demonstrated that for individuals who have little or no hypnotic ability, and *only* for them, an hypnotic intervention actually does act like a placebo. Thus among insusceptible individuals, hypnosis engenders a modest therapeutic effect, the extent of which is comparable to how these subjects respond to placebo. In addition, for these insusceptible subjects the extent of the hypnotic effect is highly correlated with their responsiveness to placebo alone. But the picture changes dramatically when we consider highly hypnotizable individuals. For these people not only is the therapeutic effect of hypnosis far greater than that of placebo, the extent of the hypnotic effect bears no relationship with their response to placebo alone. In fact, highly hypnotizable individuals as a group demonstrate little placebo response, and sometimes their placebo response is actually negative. While there is much disagreement as to what is the "active therapeutic element" in hypnosis, there is general consensus on the point that it is not a placebo mechanism.

THE HYPNOTIC SUBJECT QUICKLY DEVELOPS A SPECIAL EMOTIONAL BOND TO THE HYPNOTIST

Certainly no psychoanalytically trained therapist is surprised by the above research finding. But this interpersonal aspect of hypnosis gains all the more credibility precisely because it emerged from laboratory research conducted by investigators who were neutral or even antagonistic toward psychoanalytic formulations of hypnosis. Two cognitive theorists were led by the data to posit a special quality to the hypnotic subject's experience of the hypnotist. Shor (1979) defined "archaic involvement" with the hypnotist as "the extent to which there occurred a temporary displacement or 'transference' onto the . . . hypnotist of core personality emotive attitudes . . . most typically in regard to parents" (p. 133). Indeed, later empirical work confirmed that hypnotic subjects evidenced three enduring themes in their relationship with the hypnotist involving (1) perceived power of the hypnotist; (2) positive emotional bond; and (3) fear of negative appraisal (Nash and Spinler, 1989). Sheehan (Sheehan and Dolby, 1979), in a brilliant and impeccably controlled analysis of hypnotic dreams and subsequent laboratory behaviors, concluded that "the subject (responds) beyond the role demands of the hypnotic test situation as they are normally defined and (interacts) with the hypnotist in an especially motivated and personally meaningful way" (p. 573). Bear in mind that these rapid and intense transference reactions emerged even though the individuals in these studies were research subjects, not patients. The message to clinicians is quite clear: The flesh and blood of any therapeutic effect of hypnosis is likely to be inextricably linked to the management of the relationship in general, and the transference in particular.

WHEN USED PROPERLY, HYPNOSIS IS AN
EFFECTIVE INTERVENTION

In evaluating the research literature on the effectiveness of hypnotic interventions one immediately encounters a problem. Rarely, if ever is hypnosis the sole form of treatment with a patient. Unlike psychoanalytic, cognitive–behavioral, and client-centered therapies, hypnosis is not a therapy unto itself, it is a technique. Indeed, it can be, and at times is, incorporated into all of the above models of psychotherapy. In this sense then, asking whether hypnosis is effective is like asking whether some specific component of psychoanalysis is, by itself, effective (e.g., dream interpretation, free association, the couch, confrontation). As we see it, hypnosis cannot, and should not, stand alone as the sole intervention in any comprehensive form of uncovering, expressive psychotherapy. Of course, this renders evaluation of its effectiveness in this context quite complex, though not impossible.

Fortunately there is a research literature which examines the impact of relatively brief and pristine hypnotic interventions in the treatment of circumscribed disorders including pain disorders, asthma, gastrointestinal disorders, skin disorders, insomnia, posttraumatic stress disorder, and addictive disorders. In 1982 Wadden and Anderton comprehensively reviewed the empirical literature on the effectiveness of hypnotic interventions with these types of disorders. There was sufficient evidence for them to conclude that hypnosis is effective in the treatment of pain disorders, asthma, and skin disorders. Further, they noted that when measured at the onset of treatment, hypnotizability scores (on standard measures such as the Stanford scales) positively correlated with treatment outcome, with highly hypnotizable patients obtaining more symptom relief than low susceptibles. The latter point is immensely important in helping us be certain that the therapeutic effect in hypnotic treatment of these disorders is due to hypnosis per se rather than to various nonspecific effects of treatment in general. When patients had little or no hypnotic ability then hypnosis was not "present" in the therapy, and outcome seemed to suffer accordingly. Since the Wadden and Anderton (1982) view, a number of controlled studies have been reported which support the contention that hypnosis is effective with a host of other behavioral, psychophysiological, and immune related disorders (Ewer and Stewart, 1986; Cochrane and Friesen, 1986; Spanos, Stenstrom, and Johnston, 1988; A. F. Barabasz and M. Barabasz, 1989; Tosi, Judah, and Murphy, 1989; Brom, Kleber, and Defares, 1989). One of the most heralded studies was conducted at Stanford Medical School by David Spiegel and documented that metastatic breast cancer patients who participated in group therapy (with a substantial hypnosis component) survived longer than control subjects matched on a host of diagnostic prognostic and demographic variables (Spiegel, Bloom, Kraemer, and Gottheil, 1989). Another major contribution to our confidence in the efficacy of hypnosis is a recent meta-analytic study of research comparing cognitive interventions with, and without, hypnosis. Across such studies there is a significant therapeutic effect beyond that which can be attributed to cognitive therapy alone (Kirsch, Montgomery, and Sapirstein, 1995). While these studies are impressive, the field must generate more fine-grained analyses of the effects of hypnosis within and outside the behavioral medicine tradition.

HYPNOTIC INDUCTION AND DEEPENING

In introducing the psychoanalytic therapist to the techniques of hypnotic induction and clinical hypnosis in general, it must be emphasized that the single, most preeminent factor determining how deeply a patient experiences hypnosis has almost nothing to do with therapist technique per se or any other therapist-related factor for that matter. Instead, the patient's ability to enter hypnosis is primarily determined by his or her preexisting traitlike capacity to suspend certain cognitive functions and participate in the experience of trance—simply put, his or her hypnotic susceptibility. As stated earlier, this ability is fairly immutable over time, and seems unrelated to any personality characteristics, at least in any simple linear fashion. A hypnotizable subject will become hypnotized under a host of therapist conditions and therapeutic settings; in fact, formal induction is often not necessary. For all patients then, the extent to which patients become hypnotized has more to do with what they bring to the session in terms of ability, than with what the therapist does or says.

Learning to hypnotize someone per se is fairly easy. It is an elementary skill which involves extending an invitation to regress: some patients respond dramatically to this invitation, some patients do not. However, learning to do hypnosis *therapeutically*, is another matter entirely. Here the therapist must marshall all of his or her clinical abilities; empathy, disciplined compassion, conceptual rigor, theoretical sophistication, and technical savvy, to make the most use of the regressive aspects of hypnosis in service of the therapeutic goal, whether it be symptom removal or insight. Use of hypnosis does not, and cannot, make a poor therapist better. Its use in no way compensates for limitations that the therapist brings to the consulting room. If anything, therapist limitations may be writ larger in sessions when hypnosis is used precisely because the pace and emotional intensity of the interaction can be so accelerated. The analogy to surgery seems apt: Anyone can wield a scalpel so as to cut, but cutting *therapeutically* involves years of training and experience.

Thus, the two necessary preconditions to therapeutic use of hypnosis are: (1) a patient who is at least minimally hypnotically susceptible, and this includes about 80 to 90 percent of the population; and (2) a therapist who has solid diagnostic and clinical skills. One does not really become a better clinical hypnotist by learning new things to say during hypnosis, or new ways to say them, but rather by sharpening and refining ones clinical skills in general, and applying those general clinical skills to the environment of hypnosis. Nothing happens *with* hypnosis that does not also happen *without* hypnosis. Thus, if a clinician is ill-prepared to manage resistance, transference, regression, and primitive mentation in nonhypnotic therapies, the same will hold for hypnotic interventions. Nevertheless, there are certain parameters and techniques specific to hypnosis and suggestion which constitute a helpful body of knowledge for clinicians wishing to employ hypnosis. While we will fully present these technical principles in this chapter, they represent nothing more, or less, than the systematic application of techniques derived from a psychoanalytic understanding of cognition, regression, and object relatedness operative in the therapeutic enterprise. We believe that a mechanistic application of these guidelines, divorced from a more fundamental appreciation of the lawfulness of the therapeutic interaction, represents a serious countertransferentially based attempt to avoid the rigors of engagement with the patient, and invites treatment failure.

THE SETTING FOR A HYPNOTIC SESSION

Hypnosis is possible across a host of environmental settings. There is stage hypnosis, hypnosis in emergency and operating rooms, hypnosis in the research laboratory, and even hypnosis during quite substantial aerobic exercise (Bányai and Hilgard, 1976). For the therapist working in the outpatient environment, the principles of the therapeutic setting that apply to conventional psychoanalytic psychotherapy, apply as well for clinical hypnosis, with only a few modifications. First, there is relatively more silence during hypnosis than is the case with most forms of nonhypnotic psychotherapy. Thus, there is a premium on establishing an environment that is fairly free of auditory distractions. But even with careful soundproofing or placement of a white noise generator there is a certain inevitability to the occasional intrusion of outside noises (e.g., telephones, ambulance sirens, backfires, emergency interruptions). Our experience is that these sounds are far more distracting to the therapist using hypnosis than to the patient in hypnosis. When we supervise therapists beginning to use hypnosis in their clinical work we almost always encounter the therapist's distress and annoyance about outside noises "interfering" with their hypnotic procedure. Our advice is twofold: We instruct the therapist to simply ask the patient if he or she heard any distracting sounds during the procedure. On almost every occasion patients report either not hearing the offending sound, or they report having heard it, but without distraction. In fact, given the usual environment of a consulting room, when a patient fails to experience hypnosis it is rarely due to something as prosaic as a distracting noise, though the beginning therapist may fervently believe this to be the case. Our second bit of advice is to encourage the therapist to use or comment upon a potentially distracting sound. An example of use of a noise might be: "As you hear the sound of the siren you can listen to it fill up the space surrounding you, you can listen to every nuance of its tones and pitch. And as it fades, you can drift deeper and deeper into hypnosis yourself." An example of commenting on a noise might be: "Continue to listen comfortably to my voice, effortlessly letting any other outside sound fade into the background. . . . unimportant, as you go deeper and deeper." In sum, the therapist using hypnosis is mindful of the robust nature of the hypnotic experience: It is not a fragile transient state surviving only in the rarefied atmosphere of the consulting room. It is in almost all cases stable and quite durable. If the therapist remains poised and relaxed in the face of intrusion, the patient will do likewise.

A second principle in regard to the setting of hypnosis sessions is the relative position of the therapist and the patient. Most psychoanalytic psychotherapists work with the therapist in a chair situated at an oblique (180 degrees) angle to the patient who is likewise sitting in a chair. This is a sensible arrangement which facilitates eye contact, without engendering an intrusive, and almost compulsory face-to-face encounter. The arrangement for hypnosis is slightly different. First, since most hypnotic procedures take place with the patient's eyes closed, there is no real need for eye contact. On the other hand, there is still a need for the therapist to observe the patient's nonverbal responses, and hear the sometimes muted verbal production. Therefore we advise that the therapist using hypnosis sit a bit closer to the patient than is usual in nonhypnotic therapies, at an angle of about 90 to 100 degrees. Touching, an old and sometimes helpful hypnotic procedure, is facilitated by this arrangement. Because some hypnotic inductions involve eye fixation, the therapist does not obstruct the patient's view.

THE SET

As in many forms of psychotherapeutic intervention, it is helpful to provide the patient with some expectations about what the hypnotic procedure will be like. There is a modest but informative nonhypnosis literature on the efficacy of preparing patients for the therapy process by describing for them the nature of the intervention and the part they are expected to play in therapy. This formal attention to establishing patient set at intake is referred to in this literature as "role induction" and has been shown to be of benefit for some patients about to enter drug or alcohol abuse programs (Ravndal and Vaglum, 1992), group therapy (Strupp and Bloxom, 1973), behavioral therapy (Marquardt, Sicheneder, and Seidenstucker, 1975), and psychoanalytic psychotherapy (Heitler, 1976).

Formal attention to set is especially important in the preparation of therapy patients about to participate for the first time in hypnosis. We call this preparation the "prehypnotic interview." There are several reasons for doing such an interview: First of all, the therapist will want to be very clear on the patient's expectations and motivations regarding hypnosis so as to sharpen the plan for intervention. Second, the lay literature and the mass media abound with misinformation about hypnosis, so there is often a need to disabuse patients of some of these misconceptions. Third, as a means of further refining potential treatment plans, the therapist will want to explore the patient's construction of what trance is, and whether the patient might already utilize trancelike experiences in their day-to-day activities. Fourth, the therapist will want to clearly articulate the reasons for doing a hypnotic procedure, underscoring that it is not necessary for the patient to "do well" during hypnosis, but merely to experience whatever happens. This prehypnotic "role induction" is typically of 10 to 20 minutes in duration, and is really an interactive process in which the therapist carefully listens to the patient's construction of hypnosis (the inquiry phase), but then more actively shapes the therapeutic frame in light of the aim of therapy, the patient's characterological maturity, and the reality of what hypnosis is and is not (the intervention phase).

Usually during the first part of the inquiry phase the therapist simply asks the patient open-ended questions pertaining to their attitude about hypnosis. If fears are verbalized, then the therapist will want to inquire into these fears. Are there unrealistic expectations about treatment results? Is the patient inclined to an excessively passive stance in regards to hypnosis? Are issues of control figural for this patient? Does the patient anticipate a wildly abreactive experience involving emergence of "long-buried" traumatic memories (suggesting structural problems with affect regulation)? Are there religious values that come into play? Does the patient seem motivated? If the patient has been in therapy for some time the therapist may be able to anticipate conscious and unconscious attitudes and motivations based on the patient's enduring patterns of interactions with the therapist and with others. The point here is to listen for stylistic and interpersonal themes which can later be interpreted, "corrected" with information, or utilized during the hypnotic intervention itself.

The second portion of the inquiry phase involves gently probing for grossly unhelpful misconceptions about the nature of hypnosis. The media, especially soap operas and gothic novels, are saturated with misinformation about hypnosis. In addition, some patients may have had previous experiences with hypnosis in a nontherapeutic setting: friends who have hypnotized them, stage hypnosis, audiotapes, or participation in legitimate research. All of these experiences are important to explore.

The third portion of the inquiry requires the therapist to explore the patient's construction of what the hypnotic experience will be like. Here the therapist asks such questions as: "What do you imagine being in trance will be like?" Sometimes patients meet this request with the very sensible response that they do not know what it will be like because they have never experienced it. Silently noting the resistant quality of such a response, the therapist can acknowledge that the patient does not really know precisely what hypnosis will be like "from the inside out," but may ask, "What do you imagine it will be like?" This often elicits some associations to other types of altered states which the patient has indeed experienced. They might include hypnagogic phenomena, drug states, conditions of extreme relaxation, dissociative states, religious states of ecstasy, meditative states, or dream states. This material can be immensely instructive to patient and therapist alike. With therapist guidance the patient can anchor their expectations to a naturally occurring state which is familiar to them. The therapist can also "mine" this material for preexisting imagery and internal cues which might further facilitate the patient's hypnotic experience. For instance, a patient entered short-term therapy for a life-long problem with trichotillomania. The prehypnotic interview revealed her to be a devoutly religious person with initial reluctance to enter hypnosis because it seemed to conflict with her religious teachings. Upon closer inquiry this woman revealed that when speaking on two or three occasions she had spoken "in tongues" during a church service. She described these experiences as profoundly spiritual and positive. She described her state of mind as involving a quiet sense of patient receptivity followed by a pleasant unbidden involvement in speaking. During the prehypnotic interview the therapist likened these experiences to that of hypnosis, and proceeded to explain hypnosis in spiritual rather than secular terms (e.g., "a quiet meditation," "patiently waiting," "being receptive to the light within"). Further, the therapist fashioned an hypnotic intervention which capitalized on the patient's construction of the hypnotic experience as a kind of Christian meditation and openness.

During the intervention portion of the prehypnotic interview the therapist seeks to shape the patient's expectations and attitudes in terms of what we know about hypnosis and what will be effective during the ensuing treatment. Depending on the patient's attitudes and expectations about hypnosis, typical points we might make concerning hypnosis are:

1. *Addressing performance anxiety.* Next time we will be doing a hypnotic procedure which will take about 30 minutes. It will have nothing to do with your problem. I simply want you to become familiar with hypnosis and I want to understand more

about how you experience it. You do not need to be an extraordinary hypnotic subject to gain benefit from hypnosis. In fact, even people who at first do not experience hypnosis much at all can be helped with hypnosis nonetheless. Almost everyone can experience hypnosis to some extent, and I just want to know what hypnosis is like for you, and I want you to become more familiar with it as well.

2. *Hypnosis is not a matter of losing consciousness.* You will know what is going on around you, you will be attentive, and you will remember what we did during hypnosis just as you would if you were not hypnotized. In fact, this is especially important in our work because I want you to tell me what you are experiencing so that I know what works best for you. Remember, your responses are fully under your control (the latter point might be stressed when working with patients who for structural reasons find it difficult to tolerate their own passive-dependent strivings; for example, some eating disordered patients).

3. *Hypnosis is different from sleeping.* You may find it to be a somewhat dreamy state in which your attention can be fixed on some particular thing, while other things fade into the background. You will probably find that you can become absorbed and focused on interesting events with greater ease.

4. *It would be most helpful not to try to make experiences happen, but instead just let things happen by themselves.* If you find yourself wondering whether or not you are hypnotized, remember that what we are most interested in is *how* you experience what we do, not *if* you experience one thing or another.

5. *Hypnosis is not something that I do to you,* nor is it something that you do by yourself (although that may come later in our work); for now hypnosis is something that we do together. We can be curious about how you will experience hypnosis.

6. *People differ in the way they respond to hypnosis.* It is not necessary that you experience everything I suggest for us to work productively together. No one experiences everything in hypnosis.

7. *Responding to hypnosis is a perfectly natural ability.* It is just that in working together in this way we can use your ability in a more systematic and productive way to help you with your problem.

Of course the difference between imparting accurate information about hypnosis and manipulating patient expectations about it is quite indistinct, and for therapeutic purposes may not be all that important. If the therapist operates from an informed knowledge base, and communicates confidence in the usefulness of the technique, this form of role induction will be useful.

While disabusing patients of gross misconceptions about hypnosis can be helpful, to impart information is in itself to deliver a suggestion, so one must be careful not to "overdo" the disabusing process. For instance, if the patient never voices a fear that "I will be stuck in trance," the therapist would be ill-advised to introduce this topic. With this qualifier, what follows is a list of typical misconceptions about hypnosis.

1. The hypnotist can make me do things that I will not remember later.
2. In hypnosis people can be made to do immoral things that they would not otherwise do.
3. Hypnosis means losing control of my behavior.
4. Hypnosis is a form of brainwashing or an X ray of the mind.
5. I will tell the hypnotist secrets about myself without wanting to.
6. I will be passive and under the complete control of the hypnotist.
7. The therapist will hypnotize me, and when the hypnosis is over, my problem will be solved.

Of course, while any of these misconceptions could be attributed to the abundance and variety of media/news/talkshow hype in regards to hypnosis, it is still true that some may in fact represent the patient's most cherished unconscious wishes, not to mention those of our culture. Still, the prehypnotic interview is not the time to interpret these longings, any more than it would be appropriate to do so during an initial consultation for psychoanalysis, where setting realistic expectations and securing the working relationship is of utmost importance. We impart accurate information about our therapies because it is the honest and responsible thing to do, knowing full well that our reassurances address neurotic as well as realistic needs. Thus, to reassure a patient that hypnosis does not entail surrender to the hypnotist, is not to forget that the patient harbors this concern (or wish) in the first place.

THE STRUCTURE OF THE HYPNOTIC SUGGESTION

There are three structural features of an hypnotic suggestion: There is the role-defining tone of the communication; the extent to which the suggestion invites topographic regression and ego receptivity; and the interactive relational component of the exchange. Below we discuss these three structural features in detail.

The Role-Defining Tone of the Suggestion

Though the patient's inherent ability to experience hypnosis for the most part determines the extent to which he or she will respond to hypnosis, *when and how* this ability is expressed is a function of the patient's understanding of what hypnosis is. These role expectations are influenced by the culture and by the therapist before hypnosis ever takes place. But they are also shaped during the initial phases of the first hypnotic induction, and therapists using hypnosis are advised to be mindful of two basic principles which serve to define and sharpen our communication of the hypnotic role. First, the therapist must communicate an expectant but permissive attitude. This really involves a balance between confidently directing the patient's attention and behavior, and quietly inviting the emergence of material from the patient's own internal experience. Therapists who are new to hypnosis are sometimes quite timid and unsure of their ability to hypnotize patients. They may also be troubled (albeit unconsciously) by unneutralized narcissistic yearnings which render them hesitant to robustly define for the patient what is being suggested. Either way these therapists tend to phrase their suggestions in such vague and irresolute language that the patient becomes confused and anxious about responding. In general, it is a good idea for hypnotherapists to refrain from overusing conditional words like *maybe, perhaps, can,* or *might.* As Brown and Fromm (1986) point out: "To produce arm levitation . . . do not say 'your arm *might* be getting lighter.' " Be definitive and certain in the wording of

TABLE 4.2
The Structure of Hypnotic Suggestion

Structural Element	Technical Implication
I. The Role-Defining Tone	Expectant but permissive attitude Discouragement of passivity Paced/graded quality of suggestions
II. Facilitation of Ego Receptivity and Suspension of Executive Ego Functions	Absorption and focusing of attention Repetitions which lead the patient Monitoring and adjusting patient response Labeling patient responses and making causal attributions
III. Encouragement of Topographic Regression	Facilitation of nonconscious involvement Dedifferentiation of thought and action Language of discovery Imagery and language of sensation Condensation, displacement, and affect
IV. Elicitation and Utilization of Interactive/Relational Features	Active solicitation of patient's private experience Utilization of positive transference Suggestions rooted in the same developmental tasks as the symptom Attention to, and utilization of, resistance embedded in the transference Utilization of patient's defensive structure

the suggestion; use words like 'is' or 'will.' Say for example: 'the arm *is* getting lighter' or 'the arm *will* get lighter.' It is likewise important to avoid questions that convey doubt such as 'Is your arm light?' As a rule of thumb make questions into gentle requests: '*allow* the arm to become light, and as it becomes light, it *will* move in a way we both can see' '' (pp. 62–63).

While this authoritative and direct stance communicates to the patient a certain nonanxious attitude concerning a joint patient–therapist encounter, it can also transmit an expectation that the good hypnotic subject is to be passive, externally focused, and obedient at all times. This eventuality is to be devoutly avoided,

as it is *receptivity* we are after, not passivity. Accordingly the therapist must combine authoritative clarity and definition with a permissive–evocative style, thereby communicating and modeling
curiosity and openness to spontaneously occurring promptings
from the patient's own internal experience. In this regard, what
is to be avoided is language that communicates command and
authority: For instance: "*I want* your right leg to become numb."
Instead, a therapist might be better advised to say: "Now I would
like you to pay close attention to your right leg . . . . . all the feelings you may be having in it. . . . . As you do so, you will discover
that a feeling of numbness is beginning to form. . . . you find your
leg is becoming numb. . . ." Further, the therapist can best model
observing ego functions by leaving suggestions open. Instead of
directly suggesting: "At the end of the spiral staircase you will
find a door. . . . . open it up and step into a beautiful ocean beach
setting. . . . I want you to feel more and more relaxed in this
setting," the permissive therapist might say: "As you approach
the bottom of the spiral staircase, look around you and you will
find a door which you will soon open when I ask you to. . . . Do
you see the door? (yes). . . . . Now, in just a moment I will ask you
to open this door, and when you do you will walk into a place
that *means* relaxation. A place where you are safe and at peace
with yourself. . . . . We can be curious about what this wonderful
place behind the door is like. . . . . go ahead now and open the
door and tell me all about it." In sum, even when working exclusively in a supportive (as opposed to expressive) therapy mode,
the therapist is not creating imagery as much as amplifying it.
Once a patient describes his or her imagery the therapist might
say: "Now that you have gone through the door and are in this
beautiful mountain setting, I would like you to pay especially close
attention to the stream you noted. . . . . approach it and listen to
the rich sounds it makes as it passes over the stream bed. . . . Look
carefully, and you can see through this clear water right down to
the rocks and pebbles below. . . . what do you see?. . . ."

A second aspect of role definition is the paced quality of
the hypnotic procedure. As in any form of effective expressive
psychotherapy it is important for the patient to experience the
therapist as being accommodating toward the timing and pacing
of the patient's unfolding experience; to experience a mutuality

in the dyad's management of the ebb and flow of clinical material. By ignoring patient reactions, or suggesting immediate and complete production, the therapist invites multiple empathic breaks and therefore considerable resistance. Instead, we advise that therapists utilize graded suggestions which gradually move toward some desired experience. Instead of saying: "Now that you are holding your left arm straight out in front of you, when I touch your left shoulder your hand and arm will be so heavy that they will immediately fall down by your side . . ," the more empathic therapist says: "As you hold your left hand and arm out in this way you find that they are becoming quite heavy . . . . . much more heavy than they ordinarily would be if you held them out like this for a little while. . . . In a moment I am going to count from 1 to 10, and as I do your hand and arm will become quite heavy, more and more heavy. . . . As they become heavy you will find they begin to move down, more and more down. 1, heavier and heavier, like lead . . . 2, heavier and heavier, beginning to move down . . . 3, heavier and heavier, down more and more. . . . . ." Astute use of the future tense can be of help here as well: "Soon you will begin to experience the spreading lightness," or "As we continue you will become more and more drowsy and sleepy," or "The tingling sensation is gradually replacing your discomfort until soon there will be no room at all for the pain."

Encouragement of Ego Receptivity
As discussed in chapters 1 to 3 the shifts in state associated with hypnosis can best be described as a movement from secondary to primary process mentation, and an attendant transient restructuring in a subsystem of the ego such that executive ego functions are suspended and receptive functions become figural. Not surprisingly then, the linguistic structure of effective hypnotic suggestion compliments and supports this shift by providing narrative forms and contents compatible with such a topographic regression. Essentially the structure of hypnotic suggestion is the language of psychological regression—a language with which psychoanalytically trained clinicians are intimately familiar. Thus the linguistic modifications a psychoanalyst not using hypnosis might employ with a patient in the throws of the transference

neurosis or with a patient under the "spell" of a half-remembered dream, are precisely the same modifications used in structuring a hypnotic suggestion. Here we arbitrarily divide these modifications of syntax into two categories: those which support the suspension of executive ego functions, and those which facilitate a relative shift from secondary to primary process mentation. For illustrative purposes we report a series of suggestions (occurring over several sessions) that were given to a patient who presented with trichotillomania.

The initial phases of hypnotic induction and suggestion must facilitate emergence of receptive ego functions in part by inviting an alteration in the patient's general reality orientation and by supporting a suspension of executive ego functions. Four structural components of the suggestion are relevant to this aim.

1. *Absorption and focusing of attention.* The patient is instructed to focus attention on some particular aspect of his or her experience: This could be somatosensory (e.g., internally generated imagery, or somatic experience such as breathing), or external (e.g., some stimuli originating outside the body such as the hypnotists voice, a dot on the wall, a sound). It is probably helpful to be quite explicit with the patient about the importance of focusing attention. The benefits of doing so are twofold: It extends an invitation to the patient to conditionally suspend autonomous ego functions involving attention, and it begins the process of deautomatizing response to internally and externally generated experiences. In the case of the trichotillomania patient the therapist might say: "I know that you do not just pull a hair out and then throw it away, but that you pull it out and then, with your right hand, you roll the hair and feel it in a very special way. Today we can begin to understand what that means. Now, I would like you to focus your attention on your right hand, every sensation that the right hand is experiencing at this moment. . . . . ."

2. *Repetition which leads the patient.* Here the suggestion can be given again and again, with some variation and flexibility. This serves to support the continuity of focus and sets the stage for the patient to respond in her own fashion. The therapist might say:

> You find yourself paying close attention to everything the hand is feeling right now. You are becoming keenly aware of every nuance

of sensation that is happening in the right hand . . . . . how the air feels against the skin of the hand. . . . Tell me, what sensations are you having in your hand right now. . . . . That's right, rub your fingers together and feel the surface of your skin . . . . the sensation of how one surface feels as it moves across another. . . . As you become even more clearly aware of the surfaces, you also become mindful of how the hand feels itself . . . . . the width and length of its fingers . . . . . the way part of the hand is just slightly at a different temperature than another part. . . . .''

3. *Monitoring and adjustment of the response.* By asking questions such as: "Tell me what you are noticing right now" the therapist can monitor the patient's rate of response and its quality. If the pace is too slow, the therapist might note whatever positive response has been obtained and encourage further response by saying: "You mentioned the interesting tingling in your hand, and soon you will experience an even fuller range of sensations that the hand is having." If the pace is too fast the therapist might encourage the patient to selectively focus on one feeling at a time. In some sense this technique enables the therapist to titrate the ensuing regression. If the patient fails entirely to experience the suggested event it is important that the therapist make some attempt to understand what the patient *is* experiencing and why. For example, attention to bodily sensation is difficult for some patients for structural reasons (e.g., anorectic patients); there may be some impinging physical sensation (e.g., pain) that mitigates against attention to some part of the body; or there may be dynamically determined reasons for a patient to resist a suggestion (in for example the patient's right hand may be associated with some early trauma). As we will discuss later, the therapist follows and sensitively utilizes resistances to gain a better understanding of the patient's hypnotic experience. In any event, the therapist clearly communicates the acceptibility of not experiencing a suggestion: "Not everyone experiences their hand in just this way during hypnosis . . . let's move to something else."

4. *Therapist labels response and makes attributions.* The therapist can further facilitate suspension of executive ego functions by serving as a gentle organizer of the patient's ongoing experience. This is particularly helpful when the patient is being asked to

respond behaviorally: ".... Your arm is getting heavier and heavier as you hold it out in front of you .... and it begins to move down .... [as the arm moves] *there, that's right, the arm is moving down because it is becoming heavy ..... yes, the arm is moving down quite nicely now because you are so deeply and comfortably hypnotized ...*" But this strategy can also be employed when suggesting changes in tactile experiences as in our trichotillomania example: ".... [the patient reports some sensations in her hand] *yes that is right, you are doing quite well, you're experiencing these sensations so much more fully now because you are hypnotized.*"

Encouragement of Topographic Regression
Throughout the hypnotic procedure the therapist strives to encourage a topographic regression such that there is a gentle press for emergence of primary process mentation. There are five principles of technique which can further this effect.

1. *Facilitation of nonconscious involvement.* The therapist structures suggestions in such a manner as to enable the patient to experience a response as "happening by itself" rather than being experienced as consciously volitional. There is of course nothing the least bit interesting about someone holding their arm in the air and slowly moving it down by conscious will. But when this person performs the same behavior while experiencing the arm as moving down by itself, the patient has undergone a striking change in the experience of agency and self, one that is akin to the changes seen in dream states or dissociative states. Suggestions can be linguistically structured to encourage such involuntariness by manipulation of grammar (use of passive voice) and content (avoiding words connoting volition or agency). In the simple case of suggesting that an extended arm will become heavy, the therapist says: "the arm is becoming heavy" or "you find the arm is moving down by itself." Not only do the words *becoming, find,* and *by itself* connote involuntariness, the form of the suggestions is grammatically passive rather than active. Further, it is "*the* arm" not "your arm," thereby encouraging dissociation. Certainly the patient's experience of nonvolition, and thereby his or her topographic regression, is likely to be attenuated by suggestions phrased in an active voice with attendant linguistic acoutrements of agency. An absurd example would be: "You will

make your arm heavy and move it down." In our trichotillomania example the therapist might say: "As you pay attention to the right hand you become aware of the changes that are coming over it . . . . . . you observe these changes in an effortless manner, as they change and shift by themselves . . . . as these sensations occur, you find your attention focusing on one sensation, and then another . . . . ."

2. *Dedifferentiation of thought and action.* Another figural aspect of topographic regression is the relative equivalence of thought, perception, and action. In the language of Freud's topographic model, secondary process mentation involves fairly sharp distinctions between perception, thought, and action. Freud noted, however, that in hypnosis and some pathological conditions this distinction is muddled: Thoughts are sometimes experienced as action, and action as thoughts. The therapist inducing hypnosis can facilitate this process of regression by employing ideomotor suggestions which conflate action and thought. For instance, using the example above:

> You are now very aware of all the sensations in your right hand and arm as you hold them out in this way. Now I would like you to *think* about your arm and hand getting heavy . . . . quite heavy. And as you think about this heaviness in your arm and hand something very interesting begins to happen . . . . . they are *becoming* heavy . . . . . heavier and heavier . . . . and as they become increasingly heavy, you can think about how they would begin to move down under such a weight . . . . . and now we find that they are moving down. . . . ."

3. *The language of discovery.* Closely related to the concept of nonvolition, is the language of discovery. Because night dreams represent a topographic regression they are discovered not created, at least from the point of view of the dreamer. The same holds true for the hypnotized subject, and it is important for the therapist to support this trend under most conditions. Language that supports this attitude of discovery will support the therapeutic regression. Thus, we expect to find suggestions peppered with words and phrases like: *search, observe, perceive, discover, find, find out, see, hear, surprised by, curious about, learn more about, experience.*

4. *Imagery and the language of the senses.* The extent to which the therapist creatively employs imagery is often the extent to which the patient undergoes a topographic regression. We seek to facilitate the process that Freud defined as a backward course that results in a transformation of thoughts into visual imagery (Freud, 1933), and a process in which "thoughts are transformed into images" (Freud, 1917, p. 227). Accordingly suggestions utilize imagery, most preferably the imagery that emerges from the patient's associations. An extended arm becomes heavy because it feels "like lead" or because the patient can visualize "a heavy bucket of water in your hand." In our trichotillomania case it might be time to make a definitive suggestion concerning tactile imagery:

> As your right hand now is so exquisitely sensitive to all the rich nuances of sensation, you begin to feel a hair that you have plucked between your thumb and forefinger. And as I speak, you begin to feel this hair in greater and greater detail . . . tell me how it feels right now, go ahead and roll it the way you so much like to do . . . . what does it feel like? . . . [answer]. . . . that's right, you can feel every edge of the hair, whether it's knotted here or there, whether it's thick or very thin, how the thickness and thinness change across its course. . . . it is as though you *feel* the color of the hair and *sense* its sound as it responds to your rolling it like this . . . you are discovering everything there is to know about this hair. . . ."

The rationale for this suggested imagery will become clear below, but its emphasis on experience-near sensation is illustrative of the way in which the therapist can invoke a dreamlike regressive experience by employing rich, personal imagery.

5. *Condensation, displacement, and affect.* If, as Freud suggested, dreaming, hypnosis, poetry, art, ritual, myth, and psychopathology share a common strand it is perhaps most essentially the expression of symbol, simile, and metaphor in immediate experience. Add to these enhanced access to emotion, and we come very close to defining the intrapsychic architecture of a topographic regression. Once a hypnotic session has proceeded this far, the difference between *utilizing* trance and *facilitating* trance becomes quite indistinct. Whether or not hypnosis is used,

the competent therapist is mindful that employing the language of condensation and displacement invites further regression, with increased availability of affect, and enhanced access to unconscious material. This can be quite mutative, *if* the patient can tolerate the regression, maintaining it in a subsystem of the ego. Assuming this is the case, speaking "poetically," using the language of the patient's unconscious, and embedding condensation and displacement into suggestions, can serve to strengthen the therapeutic effect of hypnosis. What we do *not* endorse is the sometimes "cosmic" and rather self-indulgent imposition of the therapist's own metaphors into the therapeutic mix. The primary process material must emerge naturally from the patient: The therapist sharpens, extends, and articulates through interpretation, but does not *originate* the metaphors. If the patient does not "get it," it is a pretty reliable sign that the therapist has just indulged in a hypnotic counterpart to Freud's "wild analysis" which we call "wild suggestion." What follows is an example of responsibly and gently utilizing primary process mentation for the purpose of abreactive displacement with our trichotillo-mania patient:

> As you continue to roll the hair over and over again between your fingers, you are becoming more fully aware of your feelings, your emotions. . . . how do you feel right now? [patient answers that she feels wonderfully secure] Fine, now allow this wonderful feeling of safety to be center stage right now . . . . how good it feels . . . . there is something so familiar, so safe, so good about the feel of the hair. [As the patient reports feeling more and more fully secure and safe]: Now, as this wonderful feeling continues in its warmth and safety, allow yourself to drift back to a time, any time, when you felt this way before . . . . touching, and feeling so safe and good [here we are inviting a displacement].

Under these circumstances it is not surprising that the patient reports soothingly embracing her transitional object after an oft-repeated episode of leave-taking by her father during childhood. The texture and the tactile richness of the embrace are figural. What was once experienced as an exclusively ego-alien visitation of self-mutilative behavior, becomes understood as an attempt to cope (albeit desperately) with loss. This then informs subsequent therapeutic work.

Interactive and Relational Features of the Hypnotic Suggestion
The third structural facet of hypnotic suggestion is the relational component, which include real and transferentially based aspects of the dyadic exchange. Even cognitive theorists (Sheehan and Dolby, 1979; Shor, 1979) observe, in concert with Freud, that the real flesh and blood of the hypnotic experience is revealed in the quality of the patient's experience of the therapist. Because the hypnotic state itself is so saturated with primary process mentation, the condensation and displacement in regards to the person of the therapist are characteristically rapid and intense. Patients are quick to transfer onto the person of the hypnotist core attitudes, wishes, and emotions which can disrupt or can facilitate movement toward the therapeutic goal, depending primarily on whether the therapist recognizes that they are in operation. One of the oldest and most effective means of deepening a patient's hypnotic experience is the careful, neutralized application of touch. Of course any touching is preceded by suggestions that the touch will increase the comfort and depth of hypnosis. Gently pressing down on the patient's shoulder for one or two seconds can invoke pleasant and useful archaic experiences of being protected and nurtured. It must be recognized, however, that with some patients this type of powerfully regressive pull cannot be tolerated without the emergence of disturbingly dark shadows from the past. As touching is in no way necessary for hypnosis, we advise that it only be employed when the therapist is quite certain that disavowed malevolent selfobjects will not emerge.

Recognition of transferential distortion and resistance is predicated upon communication. The hypnotic experience is a very private one, and patients are sometimes reluctant to talk or even more unless encouraged to do so. Interestingly, therapists who are inexperienced with hypnosis often unwittingly foster this incommunicado condition by becoming engrossed in long, intricately detailed, sometimes rather self-absorbed hypnotic monologues, without ever really noticing the patient, let alone inviting the patient to speak. Of course structuring an intervention in this way can engender a host of real and transferentially based reactions on the patient's part. In the realm of the real relationship, the patient, not unreasonably, infers that hypnosis must be something that "the therapist does to me," and accordingly lapses into inert passivity. Potential transferential reactions are legion, including reexperience of early neglect by caretakers, oppositional withdrawal, and emergence of primitive anaclitic material around abandonment. Thus, as noted in our earlier discussion of structural aspects of suggestion, the therapist must query patients early and often about their ongoing experience, listening carefully for the transferential implications of patient responses. Further, the therapist must observe the nonverbal cues of the patient, especially those involving facial expression. It is not all that uncommon, even in the midst of what would seem to be a patently innocuous hypnotic procedure (e.g., an arm levitation suggestion), for a patient to silently cry. If the therapist's attention is elsewhere, an important therapeutic opportunity is missed, and empathy is disrupted.

One of the authors (M.N.) supervised a relatively inexperienced doctoral graduate student in the use of hypnosis during the very early phase of treatment with a young female patient who had a history of repeated loss. The student therapist proceeded somewhat mechanistically through an initial hypnotic procedure which was designed to test the patient's general hypnotizability. Mindful of our admonition to invite feedback from hypnotic subjects, the therapist earnestly incorporated a procedure to probe for how deep the patient felt herself to be at different points in the hypnotic session. The therapist said something like this: "Now that you are deeply hypnotized I will give you a series of suggestions, but every once in a while I will say the word *depth*. Whenever I say the word *depth* you will say the first number between 1 and 10 that indicates to you how deeply hypnotized you are at that moment; 1 being wide awake, and 10 being very very deeply hypnotized, although some people go beyond 10." She then repeated these instructions. The therapist proceeded with the hypnotic procedure, but was clearly ignoring some early signs of patient discomfort. At about six or seven points during the session, the therapist said the word *depth*. The patient replied accordingly. These were the only times the therapist really queried the patient.

But as the end of the session neared, the patient suddenly began to sob, and came out of hypnosis spontaneously. When asked about this, the patient angrily replied: "Why did you keep saying the word *death* all the time. I felt so good at first, but when you said *death* I just could not do it anymore. And you kept doing it!"

Assuming suggestions provide sufficient space for examination of the interaction, the task of the therapist is to utilize manifestations of the transference to structure suggestions that are rooted in similar developmental tasks as the target symptom, and to employ symbolic language related to the patient's defensive structure and dominant primary process themes. For some patients merely being with the therapist for 50 minutes is associated with fears of being overwhelmed or destroyed. For these patients the theme of initial suggestions must be containment: reinforcement of ego boundaries, support of body integrity, reassurance of capacity to tolerate affect, and focus on positive transference, all converging to create and secure a safe "holding environment." For instance, the therapist can employ suggestions that will enable such patients to open their eyes occasionally to reestablish concrete connection with the therapist, and to modulate the regression. Suggested images of mutuality, autonomy, and joint effort support the working alliance, reinforce ego-syntonic adaptive defenses, and assuage fears of incorporation. With all patients, transferentially based resistances, when recognized, can be employed to fashion an hypnotic approach which is compatible with the patient's defensive structure. Here the hypnotic approach to a brief supportive intervention for smoking cessation with an obsessive–compulsive patient, will differ from that with an hysterical patient. An obsessive–compulsive patient whose experience of the hypnotist is saturated with issues of competition, power, and disavowed anger, and whose defenses of choice are undoing and affect isolation, will respond more effortlessly to hypnotic suggestions framed in the language of self-control, autonomy, and tidiness. On the other hand, a patient presenting as hysterical, whose experience of the hypnotist is replete with themes of affiliation, nurturance, and disavowed erotic yearnings, and whose defenses of choice are denial and projection, will find hypnotic suggestions framed in the language of protection, supply, and compelling affect to be more easily digestible. Of course, resistance and defenses are interpreted in therapies which have a more ambitious, expressive goal, and even in the later phases of supportive work.

THE INITIAL HYPNOTIC PROCEDURE

For pedagogical reasons we move through this section on specific technique with two guiding assumptions: (1) that the clinician and the patient are relatively inexperienced with hypnosis. This allows us to illustrate for the clinician how a novice patient can be guided through all phases of his or her initial encounter with hypnosis. (2) That the nature of hypnosis has been explained as per our discussion above on the prehypnotic interview. Typically there are six phases of the initial hypnotic session: induction, deepening, exploration of hypnotic experience, preparation for subsequent hypnosis, termination, and posthypnotic interview. Of course, in later therapeutic work a utilization phase (employing hypnosis in the service of therapeutic movement) figures prominently, and the need for exhaustive exploration and preparation recedes. Before we launch into annotated protocols for hypnotic induction and deepening we reiterate our caution about mechanistic application of any element in this book. With regards to induction specifically, a trenchant (if somewhat rumpled) comment attributed to Hippolyte Bernheim at the turn of the century seems apt: "any induction of more than 30 seconds duration is a waste of time." Though we regard this as an overstatement, at least during initial phases of therapeutic work, it does communicate quite nicely the relative unimportance of technique in the induction of the hypnotic state. While some clinicians might like to attribute the patient's hypnotic responsiveness to their own particularly masterful grasp of technical esoterica, the fact remains that for the most part patients will, or will not, respond to hypnosis according to their ability, regardless of who is doing the hypnosis and how it is induced. *"Good" hypnotic technique is indexed, not by the patient's responsiveness per se, but by the extent to which the clinician establishes the necessary conditions for subsequent hypnotherapeutic work.* What follow are examples of procedure that both invite patients to experience hypnosis as best they can, and set the stage for later utilization of hypnosis in the therapeutic enterprise. Table 4.3 summarizes the six phases of the initial hypnotic session.

TABLE 4.3
Phases and Technique for Initial Hypnotic Procedure

	Phases of Initial Hypnotic Procedure	Annotated Examples in This Book
I.	Induction Phase	Eye Fixation/Relaxation
		Arm Drop
		Arm Levitation
		Coin Drop
II.	Deepening Phase	Staircase
	Fantasy Techniques	The Beach
		Underwater
	Somatic Techniques	Breathing
		Heaviness
	Fractionalization	Watkin's Fractionalization
III.	Introductory Suggestions	Arm Levitation/Lowering
		Hands Together
		Dream
IV.	Instructions for Rapid Induction	Counting Technique
V.	Termination	Counting Technique
		Breath Technique
VI.	Post-Hypnotic Interview	Semi-Structured Interview

PHASE 1: INDUCTIONS

Perhaps the most common type of hypnotic induction is one that incorporates suggestions for eye fixation, eye closure, and relaxation. However, there is nothing sacrosanct about these responses: historically, hypnosis was not always associated with sleeplike behaviors, and inductions emphasizing physical tension and alertness are equally effective in suggestibility. The eye fixation/relaxation is probably popular clinically because it soothingly invites regression in a manner consistent with the tenor and aims of psychotherapy. What follows is a procedure that owes much to the family of Stanford Hypnotic Susceptibility scales.

The Eye Fixation/Relation Induction

Permissive attitude.	Now I would like you to find a spot or an object on the wall or the ceiling, any spot will do. Perhaps it will be a spot on one of the paintings or perhaps a spot on the wall or an area where the sun strikes the wall or the ceiling in some particularly interesting manner.
Facilitating ego receptivity via focusing of attention and absorption.	I would like you to find a spot and focus your eyes on that spot. I am going to call that spot the target. I would like you to focus your eyes on the target and listen to my words.
Expectant attitude, language of discovery.	By doing so you will find out what it is like to experience hypnosis.
Discouragement of passivity. Emphasis on interactive/ relational.	I assure you that no matter how deeply hypnotized you become you will remain in complete control. Hypnosis is really something that you and I do together.
Repetition.	Eyes comfortable and heavy, focus on the target, continue focusing your eyes on the target and listening to my words.
Absorption. Facilitation of nonconscious involvement.	There is nothing particularly mysterious or other worldly about hypnosis. It really is a quite natural ability that almost everyone has to some extent. In a way hypnosis is like being absorbed in a movie that you are watching and forgetting that you are part of the audience but instead you become part of the story. Or perhaps you are one of those people who enjoys listening to music and can be transported by that music so that everything else fades into the background and the music becomes figural, center stage.

Attention to resistance.
Imagery and language of
sensation. Expectant attitude.

Continue to focus on the target, if your
eyes should wander away from the
target, that's fine but just bring them
back to the target. You may notice that
the target moves about or again changes
color, and if that should happen you can
let it take place.

Paced/graded suggestions.
Repetition. Nonconscious
involvement. Language of
discovery.

Just concentrate on the target and listen
to my words, allowing yourself to relax
more and more. As you relax more and
more you become aware of a certain
kind of drowsiness, a relaxation coming
across your entire body. Pretty soon you
will notice that the object that you are
staring at is changing a bit, perhaps it is
becoming nebulous or perhaps
changing colors. You find that your
eyelids are beginning to get heavier and
heavier and you are looking forward to
finding out what it is like for your eyelids
to grow heavy and close in this way; what
it is like to go into hypnosis. What do
you notice?

Repetition. Nonconscious
involvement. Language of
sensation. Making causal
attributions. Paced/graded
suggestions.

It is a strain to look at a single object
for so long and it would be so
nice to relax completely. *Allow*
yourself to relax completely. As
your eyelids become heavier and
heavier you may notice that your eyes
become wet from straining—so tired
and wet from straining. Your eyes may
soon close by themselves and
when they do you can let that happen,
and then drift into a comfortable
state of relaxation because you will
gradually, and at your own pace,
be drifting into hypnosis.

Labeling patient responses and making causal attributions. Repetition.

Soon your eyes will close themselves and when they do, you can really allow yourself to relax completely. As your *eyes* become heavier your *body* becomes more and more limp and relaxed. Your eyes and your body drift together into hypnosis. Your eyelids become heavier, [patient's eyes begin to blink] blinking, blinking [patient closes eyes]. Notice what you are experiencing and tell me.

Permissive attitude. Attention to resistance. Nonconscious involvement. Monitoring and adjusting patient response.

That's right, your eyes are closed now and they will remain closed for the duration of our work together, but if you would wish to open your eyes while remaining deeply hypnotized, you could do so, but you would do so only for a moment and then close them again. But most likely your eyes will remain comfortably closed as you continue to listen effortlessly to my voice.

Utilization of positive transference via touching. Language of sensation. Repetition.

Now that your eyes are closed you can really settle into a deep state of relaxation and hypnosis. In a moment I'm going to touch the very top of your head with my hand and when I do, I would like you to notice these warm waves of relaxation that begin to emanate from the very top of your head and pass through your entire body. In a little while I will touch the top of your head and when I do you will notice these wonderfully warm waves of relaxation that pass from the top of your head through your entire body. And you will become even more comfortably hypnotized. I am touching your head now. [therapist touches head for 2 seconds].

Language of sensation. Repetition. Nonconscious involvement. Expectant attitude. Imagery.	Allow those warm waves of relaxation to radiate down, down through your entire body. Where do you feel these waves of relaxation right now? [patient responds "at the top of my head"]. Good, I am going to count from 1 to 20 and as I do you will become more and more relaxed and continue to enter a comfortable state of hypnosis in which you can experience many different things.
Language of sensation. Repetition. Nonconscious involvement. Expectant attitude.	1, Allowing those warm comfortably warm waves of relaxation to pass down through the top of your head, across your facial muscles so that the muscles of your forehead, your eyes, your face become limp and relaxed, limp and relaxed. 2, Allowing these warm waves of relaxation to pass down through the back of your head and into your neck, you know how tense your neck can become during the day but as these warm waves of relaxation pass through it, your neck becomes limp and relaxed, limp and relaxed.
Nonconscious involvement.	3, 4, Allowing these warm waves of relaxation now to pass down through your shoulders, your shoulders now dropping limp and relaxed, limp and relaxed as you effortlessly listen to my voice and allow yourself to drift into a comfortable state of relaxation and hypnosis. 5–6, Allowing these warm waves of relaxation to pass down through your shoulders and into your arms, down toward your elbows and down toward your wrists, your arms are now limp and relaxed as these warm

waves of relaxation pass down through your hands pushing any excess energy in your arms and hands out through the ends of your fingertips.

Nonconscious involvement. Language of sensation. Suggesting positive transference. Making causal attributions.

7–8, Now letting these warm waves of relaxation pass down through your chest and your upper back you can be aware, perhaps not for the first time that your breathing is becoming more and more slow and regular, slow and regular as these warm waves of relaxation pass down through your chest, down your back, limp and relaxed, beginning to become more and more sleepy and drowsy as your breathing becomes more and more slow and regular. 9–10, Letting these warm waves of relaxation pass through your stomach muscles and your lower back. How good it feels to be so completely relaxed, how good it feels to feel the support of the couch and these wonderful waves of relaxation that transform the relationship between your body and your mind because you are comfortably drifting into hypnosis at your own pace.

Imagery. Language of sensation. Facilitation of nonconscious involvement.

11–12, And you can be aware of how these warm waves of relaxation passed down through and beyond your waist, down your legs toward your knees and your thighs; relaxed, legs comfortably relaxed, allowing these warm waves of relaxation to continue to pass through your legs, over and through your legs, 13–14. Down beyond your knees, 15, Down toward your ankles and pushing any excess energy out through your toes.

Discouraging passivity. Elicitation of interactive features.	16, More and more sleepy and drowsy, drifting along, sleepy and drowsier, and as you listen to my voice, you can be aware that no matter how deeply hypnotized you become, you will always be able to hear my voice, you will always be able to hear my voice no matter how deeply hypnotized you become.
Language of discovery. Expectant attitude. Language of sensation.	17, And you are now becoming more and more aware of how really relaxed and sleepy and dreamy you have become. More and more relaxed. As you are aware of how these warm waves of relaxation continue to permeate through your entire body, you can continue to listen effortlessly to my voice going deeper and deeper into hypnosis.
Repetition. Language of discovery. Discouragement of passivity. Elicitation of interactive and relational features.	18, More and more deeply relaxed, more and more sleepy, more and more drowsy. You are curious about how your mind and body work together in this hypnotic state. It is so comfortable, so pleasurable to be so deeply hypnotized and relaxed as you are now, with each breath it seems that you go deeper, more and more sleepy, more and more drowsy, yet listening effortlessly to my voice. We are working together to find out more about what hypnosis is like for you.
Labeling patient's response. Language of discovery. Elicitation of interactive and relational features.	19, It feels good to be drowsy, to be hypnotized, as we find out what hypnosis is like for you.
	20, Deeply relaxed and deeply hypnotized.

The Arm Drop and Levitation Induction

There is some merit in using a suggestion for an ideomotor response as an induction: It affords the therapist the opportunity to observe the patient's responsiveness throughout the procedure; it enables the therapist to gauge and encourage dedifferentiation of thought and action; and it provides for the patient a tangible index of his or her own responsiveness to which attributions about state can be made.

The Arm Drop Induction

Absorption and focusing of attention. Language of sensation.	I would like for you to sit comfortably in your chair and close your eyes, that's right, and I would like for you to hold your right hand and arm straight out in front of you, palm facing down, that's right, hold your right arm straight out in front of you, palm facing down. I would like you to concentrate on this right hand and arm and be aware of every feeling that you are having in your right hand and arm right now at this very moment.
Expectant attitude. Language of discovery. Facilitation of nonconscious involvement.	As you know, a person is not usually aware of all the sensations he [use "she" if the patient is female] is having in his body because he is not paying attention to the particular parts of the body where these sensations are taking place. But if you pay attention to a particular part of your body as you are now paying attention to your right arm and hand, then you become aware of many different things.
Expectant but permissive attitude. Discouragement of passivity. Language of sensation. Solicitation of private experience. Nonconscious involvement.	As I have been talking, perhaps you have noticed a feeling of tension in your hand or in your arm or maybe you have noticed a tingling sensation, or a tendency for your fingers to twitch ever so slightly, or you have noticed

something I have not mentioned. There
may be a feeling of warmth or coolness
in your hand or your arm or in both.
Pay very close attention to your hand
and arm and tell me now, what are you
experiencing? {Patient responds}

Condensation and
displacement as patient is
encouraged to dedifferentiate
thought and action. Imagery
and language of sensation.

That's good. Now, I would like you to
continue to pay very close attention to
your arm because something interesting
is about to happen to it. It is beginning
to get heavy, heavier, and heavier, and
as I continue to talk you can be aware
that thinking about this heaviness
creates a tendency for your arm to
become heavy, very heavy and you will
find that in a moment your right hand
and arm will become so heavy like lead,
so heavy that your hand and arm will
gradually very slowly begin to move
down, more and more down. Notice
what it feels like.

Condensation (repetition of
arm lowering as metaphor for
hypnosis). Causal attributions.

The heaviness in your right hand and
arm grows. And as it does you can be
curious about this heaviness because as
the heaviness in your arm grows more
and more it is a sign that you are
becoming more and more deeply
relaxed and more and more hypnotized.

Nonconscious involvement.
Language of discovery.
Labeling responses. Paced
and graded suggestions.

Allow the heaviness in your arm to grow
more and more and as the heaviness
grows you become more and more
relaxed and sleepy, sleepy and dreamy.
Notice how as your arm moves—just as
it is now, gradually moving down, that's
right, your arm gradually moving
down—you can learn what it is like to

be profoundly relaxed and comfortably
hypnotized.

More explicit repetition of metaphor—condensation of arm movement and subjective state.	Deeply relaxed, deeply hypnotized as your arm moves down, you go deeper into this comfortable state of relaxation. That's right, your arm is moving down and you are becoming more and more deeply relaxed, hypnotized, drifting down, more and more deeply, more and more comfortably, relaxed.
Nonconscious involvement. Elicitation of interactive features. Labeling patient responses and making causal attributions.	Notice how your breathing is changing and how as your arm moves down more and more, you can continue to listen to my voice effortlessly letting everything else fade into the background. It is as though your arm as it moves down toward your lap signals to you and to me how deeply relaxed and hypnotized you are.
Imagery and language of sensation. Elicitation of interactive/relational features.	[if patient's arm has not moved much the following component might be added] Your arm is more and more heavy and you are becoming more and more relaxed and hypnotized. Now as I continue to talk, you can imagine holding a bucket in your right hand. It is empty right now, holding a bucket in your right hand, holding a bucket out in front of you in your right hand. You can sense its color and its weight right now. What color is it? [patient answers]. I am going to count from 1 to 10 and with each count I will pour a quart of water in the bucket and your hand and arm will grow heavier and heavier, moving down more and more.

Paced/graded quality of suggestions. Relational features. Repetition.

1, I am adding a quart of water, can you picture the water right now? That's right, you can picture the water right now. I have added a quart and your hand and arm are feeling much heavier.

Further elaboration of condensation. Repetition. Utilization of positive transference.

2, I am pouring another quart of water in, you can hear the water pouring in the bucket and your arm is getting heavier and heavier, moving down more and more. 3, The third quart. 4, Another quart as we continue to work together to help you go deeper and deeper. 5, More water. Moving down more and more, and as your arm moves down you become more sleepy, more drowsy, more and more deeply relaxed, breathing slowly and regularly, letting everything else fade into the background as your *arm* continues to become heavier and heavier and *you* continue to go more and more deeply and completely into hypnosis.

Labeling patient responses and making causal attributions. Nonconscious involvement.

6–7, More water. More and more down, more and more deeply relaxed, more and more hypnotized. 8–9, Almost there. Your hand is almost in your lap and when it reaches your lap you will be completely relaxed, deeply hypnotized, listening without effort to my voice. 10, [hand reaches lap] That's right, your hand has reached your lap now. You are relaxed, dreamily hypnotized, your right hand is in your lap, and while you drift along comfortably and deeply hypnotized, your hand returns to normal. No longer heavy. Now let's move on to something else.

Absorption and focusing of attention. Language of sensation.

Please put your right hand on the table, I want you to concentrate all your attention on that hand. As you look at it, be aware of all the sensations and feelings in the hand. For example, you are aware that it is sitting on the table. There is a weight there. You are aware of the texture of the table. You can keenly sense the position every finger has in relation to every other finger. And there is the temperature of the fingers, which ones are a little warmer and which ones are a little cooler than the others.

Absorption and focusing of attention. Language of sensation. Language of discovery.

As you look at that hand with great concentration, you are going to notice that one of the fingers of that hand will feel especially different from the others. Now, it might be the thumb or the little finger or perhaps the index finger or the big finger or the ring finger, but one of them will feel distinctly different from the other, and that feeling may be that it is a little more warm or that it is a little cold. It could be that it kind of tingles a little bit or that it is numb, it could feel lighter, but if you concentrate well you will be able to find out which finger it is that has the different sensation from the others.

Facilitation of nonconscious involvement. Labeling patient responses and making causal attributions. Dedifferentiating thought and action.

As you pay close attention to that particular finger, that finger will lift itself a little bit from the table over the others. Now concentrate on that, and you will notice that one of the fingers will tend to lift itself up from the table a little. [patient's index finger lifts slightly] Oh yes, it's your index finger.

We can be curious about how light the finger must be to rise in this way. And as you think about this lightness, the lightness in your fingers grows even more.

Repetition, paced/graded quality of suggestions. Monitoring patient response.

Moving up more and more and as you concentrate on this lightness this pleasant lightness in your finger, you will notice that lightness spreads to your other fingers. One by one your fingers and your thumb will rise to the level of your index finger.

Imagery and language of sensory experience. Condensation and displacement.

One by one, that's right, one by one your fingers, the feeling of lightness spreading from one finger to another. That's right, there is a light feeling as though your fingers were corks, just very light and buoyant, floating and buoyant.

Language of discovery. Eye closure prepares patient for imagery.

Now go ahead and close your eyes as you drift along in this relaxed and comfortable state, curious about how becoming more relaxed will enable your hand and arm to experience even more.

Touching and utilization of positive transference. Imagery.

Now what I would like to do is, I'm going to touch your wrist, imagine that I am tying a string loosely to your wrist, here, I am doing it now [therapist touches wrist as though tying a string loosely around wrist], and on the other end of that string is a balloon, a balloon of a particular color, it is not filled yet with helium but it soon will be.

Imagery and language of sensory experience. Repetitions. Condensation and displacement.

And that string is loosely tied to your wrist, and when the balloon is filled with helium, your hand, not just your fingers, your entire hand and arm will begin to feel lighter and lighter. The balloon is not yet filled with helium, but soon it will be. What color is the balloon? [patient responds that the balloon is blue] That's right it is just lying there on the ground now, it's a dark blue color. Now imagine the balloon is being filled with helium, the balloon is getting bigger and you can hear the balloon filling, filling up with helium and you know the way balloons become brighter and lighter when they are filled with helium until the rubber is taut and you can almost see through this beautiful blue balloon filled with helium and rising off the ground, and this string around your wrist becomes taut.

Language of discovery. Dedifferentiation of thought and action. Labeling patient responses and making causal attributions.

You can be curious about what is beginning to happen to your right hand and arm as the balloon begins to tug, tug and pull at your wrist, that's right, your hand and arm are beginning to lift higher and higher and as your hand and arm raise higher, higher and higher, becoming lighter and lighter as the helium balloon tugs on your wrist, your hand and arm began to move up and toward your nose and when your hand touches your nose, you will know you are deeply relaxed and hypnotized.

Facilitation of nonconscious involvement. Imagery and language of sensation. Condensation and displacement.

[patient's hand and arm begin to slowly move upward] That's right, higher and higher and as your hand moves higher and closer to your nose, a gentle breeze can blow the balloon in such a way that your hand and arm move toward your face, closer and closer to your nose, gently pulling, tugging, moving, lighter

and lighter and as your hand is moved
and pulled and made lighter and lighter
by this balloon, *you* drift more and more
comfortable into hypnosis.

Language of discovery
Labeling pt. responses.

More knowledgeable, finding out more
about how your mind affects your body
in this very relaxed, deeply hypnotized
state.

Elicitation and utilization of
positive transference via
interaction and touching.
Repetition. Imagery.

That's fine, the hand has now touched
your nose, and settles there, now I am
going to touch your wrist as I untie the
balloon. . . . [therapist gently takes wrist
between thumb and forefinger and
holds it for a moment] As I touch your
wrist, I will hold your wrist while I
release the string, and as I do you can
watch the balloon go high in the sky and
I will place your wrist back in its resting
position as you remain deeply relaxed
and hypnotized.

Deeply relaxed, deeper and deeper,
deeper into hypnosis. Your hand and
arm are comfortable again, relaxed in
their resting position, normal and
comfortable as you continue,
deeply relaxed and deeply
hypnotized.

The Coin Drop Induction. The coin drop technique can be used in
a number of ways. If the patient is situated over a noncarpeted
floor the sound of the coin dropping can be incorporated in the
procedure in the form of a suggestion that "when you hear the
coin drop to the floor you will know that you are deeply relaxed
and hypnotized."

Elicitation and utilization of interactive features. Condensation and displacement (warmth and coin and therapist).	Now I would like for you to seat yourself comfortably and close your eyes. I am going to put a coin into your right hand like this [puts coin in patient's right hand], and perhaps you would like to hold your arm straight out and make a fist around this coin, I would like you to make a fist around this coin. Be aware now of the warmth in your right hand and the warmth that surrounds this coin.
Absorption and focusing of attention. Expectant but permissive attitude. Condensation (balloon/coin).	As you concentrate on the warmth in your hand at this very moment, you can be aware of how the coin is warming up as well. I would like you to imagine now that this is a very special coin because it has the characteristics of a coin *and* it has the characteristics of a balloon. Imagine this coin as a balloon, your hand is surrounding a balloon, this coin balloon, and the warmth of your hand surrounds the balloon, warming it, warmer.
Language of sensation. Repetition. Continued condensation. Nonconscious involvement.	And as you know, the warmth of a balloon determines how large it is. The air in a balloon expands when it is warmed and as the balloon-coin becomes warmer and warmer it begins to expand, it expands inside your hand. Warmer and beginning to expand.
Imagery and language of sensation. Repetition.	Eventually as the balloon gets warmer and warmer, it will press against the inside of your hand until your hand gradually opens as it presses against your fingers and your hand. Imagine the balloon filling with air in your hand, pushing against the inside of your hand, trying to force the fist open.

Dedifferentiation of thought and action. Paced/graded suggestions. Labeling patient responses. Monitoring and adjusting to patient response.

Warmer and warmer now, gradually, very gradually forcing your fingers open, warmer and warmer, soon your fingers will begin to open of themselves, you can feel the fingers beginning to move by themselves [patient's fingers move, but only very slightly]. That is right, your fingers are just now beginning to move. Your fingers are responding, and moving, the pressure from the balloon-coin is having an effect.

Utilization of positive transference. Condensation.

Now I am going to gently touch the top of your right hand and as I do so, you will notice that the warmth grows even more on the inside of your hand and the balloon-coin expands even more.

Dedifferentiation of thought and action. Paced/graded suggestions. Labeling patient responses and making causal attributions.

I am going to count to 10. Each time that I touch your hand, I will count, and as I do your hand will become warmer and warmer and the balloon will swell more and more. This is a very special balloon-coin so that by the time I reach the count of 10 your fingers will be opened and the balloon-coin will fall upon the floor and you will hear it, and when it does fall on the floor you will know that you are deeply and comfortably hypnotized.

Utilization of positive transference. Paced/graded quality of suggestions. Nonconscious involvement. Labeling patient responses and making causal attributions.

[therapist gently strokes back of hand at each count] Now I will begin to count 1, beginning to press more and more against the inside of your hand. 2, Warmer and warmer, let the warmth flow through your hand. 3, Warmer and warmer, the comfortable warmth increases in the inside of your hand. 4–5, Warmer and warmer, your fingers beginning to move more and more, that's right, moving of themselves, you can find your fingers moving of themselves. 6–7, That's right, fingers beginning to open. 8–9, Soon you will hear the coin drop and when you do you will be deeply relaxed and deeply hypnotized listening effortlessly to my voice. 10, There, that's right, the coin is dropped and you are deeply relaxed and deeply hypnotized.

Language of discovery.

You can be curious about what the hypnotic state is like as you become more and more deeply relaxed and hypnotized with each breath, with each passing moment.

PHASE 2: DEEPENING PROCEDURES

Here we offer two types of techniques which can be employed to further "deepen" the patient's experience of hypnosis. The same structural principles apply for these techniques as apply for the inductions. In fact, any induction technique can also be used as a deepening technique. Essentially the aim of deepening techniques is to broaden the topographic regression in the context of heightened ego receptivity, and to allow the patient further experience in suspension of executive ego functions in service of the therapeutic aim. The "Diving under water" technique is more regressive than others, and should probably be used in later phases of treatment, rather than during an initial hypnotic session (e.g., the two general categories of deepening techniques are: fantasy–imagery techniques and somato/attentional techniques.

Fantasy–Imagery Deepening Technique 1: The Spiral Staircase

Imagery and language of sensation.

In a little while I am going to stop talking for a bit and when I do, I would like you to imagine yourself walking down a very beautiful and quiet spiral staircase. The kind that winds down and around, down and around, down and around.

Imagery and language of sensation. Absorption and focusing of attention. Condensation and displacement (metaphor of depth). Paced/graded suggestions.

Imagine, if you will, a spiral staircase now as I am talking. It is a very beautiful and quiet spiral staircase with an interesting carpet, plush and soft, your favorite color, and as you look further down the stairs seem to fade out into a soft, warm darkness. As you walk down this beautiful staircase you slide your hand along the smooth hardwood banister. In a little while I will ask you to walk down this beautiful spiral staircase at your own pace, and you will note that with each step you take, with each slow step you take down this beautiful spiral staircase, you will go deeper and deeper into hypnosis. [with some more fragile patients the therapist might suggest that they both walk down the stairs together]

Repetition. Paced/graded suggestions. Further elaboration of metaphor of depth.

In a little while I will stop talking for a bit and when I do I would like you to imagine yourself walking down this beautiful spiral staircase. The kind that goes down and around, down and around, down and around, and you will note that with each step you take, with each slow step you take down this beautiful spiral staircase you will go deeper and deeper into hypnosis. You can go at your own pace, going deeper and deeper as you like until when I speak again you will be much more deeply relaxed and deeply hypnotized. Go ahead and imagine yourself walking down this beautiful spiral staircase with each step going deeper and deeper into hypnosis. [Therapist is silent for one minute]. That's right. No longer walking down the spiral staircase now, deeply relaxed and deeply hypnotized.

Fantasy/Imagery Deepening Technique 2: The Beach

Repetition. Expectant but permissive attitude. Facilitation of nonconscious involvement.	Now as you drift along comfortably, deeply relaxed and deeply hypnotized listen carefully to what I have to say. In a little while I am going to count from 1 to 5, and when I reach the count of 5 you will find yourself at that special ocean beach about which you told me today. I am going to count from 1 to 5 and when I reach the count of 5 you will be there, relaxed and comfortable, with each passing moment going deeper and deeper into hypnosis. Now I will begin to count and when I reach the count of 5 you will be there and you will be able to tell me the things that you see and the things that you hear and smell and feel.
Paced/graded quality of suggestions.	1, 2, You are going to the beach, soon you will be there. 3, And you will be able to tell me all about it. 4, Once there at the beach you will find yourself going more completely and deeply into hypnosis. At the next count, you will *be* there, at the beach. 5.
Active elicitation of patient's private experience.	Where are you? [patient responds]. What are you doing? [patient responds], What do you see, hear, feel [the patient responds]. That's good, this is a very special place which *means* relaxation.

Condensation and displacement (use of word *embraces* and *supported*). Imagery and language of sensation. Facilitation of nonconscious involvement. Attentional shifts.	As you lie back on the sand and feel the comfortable warmth of the sun, the comfortable warmth of the sun surrounds you. As you have already noted, you can hear the waves and the sea gulls, feel the support of the sand, how good it is to be supported in this way. I would like you to pay even closer attention now to the sounds of the surf. As you know if you listen to the surf you can hear every individual gentle wave breaking on the shore and if you listen another way, the waves all seem to blend together into a kind of rolling, gentle cascade.
Displacement and condensation. Paced/graded quality of suggestions. Utilization of positive transference.	Listen to the surf so that you can hear different waves breaking at different times, rhythmic waves, one wave after another. How do you hear them? [patient indicates that waves can be heard separately]. And you discover that as you listen, it is almost as though the waves seem to break every time you exhale. There is a certain rhythm, a timing and pacing to our work together.
Repetition and extension of condensation and displacement.	And as you listen to the waves breaking on the shore, you can note that with each wave, with each breath, you go deeper and deeper into hypnosis. A very special rhythm of your breathing and of the waves begins to move together, as you go deeper and deeper. I am going to stop talking now for a bit and you can continue to listen to the waves breaking on the shore gently. With each wave that breaks gently on the shore you go deeper and deeper asleep. [Therapist is silent for one minute]. Good, deeply relaxed and deeply hypnotized.

Fantasy/Imagery Deepening Technique 3: Diving Under the Water. A particularly useful technique to prepare patients for expressive, insight-oriented applications of hypnosis employs a metaphor of going beneath the surface for the sake of discovery. This example is adapted from Brown and Fromm (1986).

Introduction of metaphor involving condensation, displacement, and language of discovery.	Imagine that we are going on a deep-sea exploring trip down in the warm waters off the Caribbean. We have come to a beautiful reef where a group of young deep-sea explorers is preparing a trip in an enclosed capsule into the depth of the ocean.
Utilization of positive transference in references to safety, supply, and communication. Further elaboration of metaphors involving: depth/hypnosis and "going under the surface"/the unconscious.	The capsule can be lowered from a ship on a steel cable. You can safely make a descent of hundreds of feet down into the ocean. Imagine a spacious metal sphere with four portholes, thick plate glass, two or three people can go inside the capsule and sit in it and observe. They are supplied with oxygen lines and a telephone line to the boat on the surface. Imagine yourself for several days watching the young ocean divers on the beach carefully preparing the capsule for their next trip. They have fitted it out with food and with a number of scientific instruments. You have made friends with them and several of them have invited you to join them on their trip to see the wondrous sites of the deep sea.
Language of discovery. Further elaboration of positive transference (themes of protection, expertise, and careful preparation). Imagery and language of sensation.	You have accepted the invitation and you are intrigued, delighted, and curious. Now imagine yourself and the deep-sea explorers standing on the deck of the ship that will take you out to the sea. You are going out to sea now, you see the long, low swell of the sea and

hear the waves rolling in on this calm sunny comfortably warm spring day. You can feel a light breeze on your face. Imagine yourself with two of the explorers who have descended deep into the ocean many times before, we are going into one of the capsules lying on the deck.

Repetitions of themes of safety. Elaboration of discovery. Discouragement of passivity. Imagery and language of sensation.

The portals are being screwed tight so that no water can penetrate, strong cranes swing out your capsule over the side of the ship and you can hear it splash and descend beneath the surface of the water. Notice the sudden shift from the gold and yellow light above the sea to a turquoise green all around you. You see the foam and bubbles from the splash. Look upwards, you see the strong steel cable from which your capsule is being lowered down close to the ship's side, now we are being lowered. Peer up, you can see the watery ceiling crinkling and slowly lifting and settling while here and there pinned to the ceiling are tufts of seaweed. Notice small dots moving just below the weed. You try successfully to focus a pair of binoculars that one of the explorers has handed to you on these moving dots. You have no trouble recognizing a flying fish trailing its half-spread wings as it swims. You can feel the capsule revolving slightly and the bottom of the ship's hull comes into view. It is encrusted with corals and shells. Great streamers of plant and animal life float from it.

Condensation and displacement. Paced/graded suggestions.

There is something unreal and at the same time rather amusing about a port view of a slowly rolling bottom of an unanchored boat. The people on the deck of the boat phone down to tell you that the sun keeps blazing over the ocean, the surface is unusually quiet, and conditions are ideal for going down further. You are being lowered further, the green of the water fades as you go further down and at 200 ft it is impossible to say whether the water is greenish blue or bluish green.

Imagery and language of sensation. Language of discovery.

You make your eyes focus in midwater and see a lovely colony of jellyfish drift past. Gracefully floating in the deep water, they are beautiful. They sweep slowly along, alive and in constant motion. A bit lower a beautifully colored fish looks in on you, two deep sea turtles go by, several silvery squid balance for a moment in front of your porthole then shoot past.

Encouraging ego receptivity. Facilitation of receptivity. Language of discovery.

Now you can take control of how deep you go, which way your capsule turns, and what you see. There are the rich colors of a reef. Observe with interest the texture and colors as the fish gently swim between and around the reef.

Condensation and displacement with extension of metaphor of discovering things under the surface. Imagery and language of sensation.

Slowly, steadily, you guide your vessel—then there are lobsters and some crabs. You are less and less concerned with the upper world, you feel restful, quiet, and happy, removed from it while you plunge into new, interesting, and predictably beautiful sites. Your attention is relaxed, very relaxed, and you keep on going down as far as you like.

Somatoattentional Techniques. Some patients do not possess vivid imaginations. For these patients suggestions to imagine can prove quite frustrating, potentially leading to problems with compliance and discouragement. In these cases other deepening techniques can be employed which do not emphasize imaging ability, but instead invite absorption in internally generated sensation. Two of these are breathing and the kinesthetic sense of heaviness.

Somatoattentional Deepening Technique 1: Breathing

Expectant but permissive attitude. Absorption and focusing of attention.	Now that you are relaxed and deeply hypnotized, I would like you to be aware of your breathing for a moment. One way to go more deeply into hypnosis is to pay attention to your breathing for awhile.
Repetition. Monitoring and adjusting to patient response. Labeling patient responses and making causal attributions.	Notice, as you breathe slowly and normally, how good it feels to exhale, inhale, and exhale [the therapist may time the words *inhale* and *exhale* to the patient's actual breathing pattern] and as you continue to feel all these sensations the way your muscles move quite naturally and effortlessly to facilitate your slow and normal breathing, you become more and more relaxed with each passing breath. More and more hypnotized.
Facilitation of nonconscious involvement. Paced and graded suggestions.	It's as though every time you exhale, you purge your body of the stress and tension of the day. Every time you exhale, while you are hypnotized, every time you exhale, without even thinking about it, you become more and more deeply and comfortably hypnotized as you wish.

Language of sensation. Facilitation of nonconscious involvement. Language of discovery. Discouragement of passivity. Encouragement of activity.

Now I am going to count from 1 to 25, and as I do, you will go more deeply and comfortably into hypnosis because every time you exhale, your body will become more and more limp and relaxed, your mind will become more and more clear, and you will find yourself curious about how your mind and your body work together in this relaxed and interesting state [the therapist might choose to time the counts with patient's breathing]. 1, More and more relaxed, 2, 3, etc.

Somatoattentional Deepening Technique 2: Progressive Heaviness

---

Language of sensation. Facilitation of nonconscious involvement.

As you remain deeply hypnotized you will notice that there is a warm numb feeling beginning to form all over your body. A comfortable feeling of heaviness and warmth spreading from the very, very top of your head down through your face, jaw, neck, and shoulders, becoming more and more limp and relaxed, all the muscles of your body, as this comfortable warmth, heaviness, and relaxation move down through your neck and your arms and chest and stomach muscles, down through your whole body, more and more comfortably heavy. Muscles limp and relaxed, feel this warmth, wonderful warmth, almost as though you were in a hot tub, so relaxed.

Utilization of positive transference via touching.

Now in a moment I am going to place my hands on your shoulders and this will allow you to go even more deeply into hypnosis, you will feel the heaviness coming over your entire body. As I press

down gently on your shoulders, you will
go deeper into hypnosis, comfortable
and relaxed. [Therapist places a hand
on each of the patient's shoulders and
very gently applies modest pressure].

PHASE 3: INTRODUCTORY SUGGESTIONS

In the initial hypnosis experience it is useful to follow the
induction and deepening procedures with three very simple suggestions which serve a twofold purpose. First, the patient gains
further experience with the hypnotic state, gauging if and how
this state is different from their normal state of consciousness.
Second, by noting the response to suggestions the therapist makes
a determination of the patient's general hypnotic ability which
may be important in treatment planning. We offer three examples of relatively neutral suggestions which can serve the purpose
of educating patient and therapist about how hypnosis is being
experienced.

Arm Lowering or Levitation. Here the procedures are almost identi-
cal to the arm lowering and arm levitation induction, but with
the difference that they are dramatically shortened. For instance,
an arm lowering suggestion might consist of:

> Now that you are deeply hypnotized, I would like you to hold out
> your right hand up in the air, straight out in front of you, palm
> facing down. As I have been talking, perhaps you have noticed a
> feeling of tension in your hand or in your arm or maybe you have
> noticed a tingling sensation . . . . . or a tendency for your fingers
> to twitch ever so slightly, or you have noticed something I have
> not mentioned. . . . . There may be a feeling of warmth or coolness
> in your hand or your arm or in both. Now, I would like you to
> continue to pay very close attention to your arm because some-
> thing interesting is about to happen to it. It is beginning to get
> heavy . . . . . heavier, and as I continue to talk you can be aware
> that thinking about this heaviness creates a tendency for your arm
> to become heavy, very heavy, and you will find that in a moment

your right hand and arm will become so heavy . . . . like lead, so heavy that your hand and arm will gradually very slowly begin to move down more and more down, as it becomes heavier and heavier, like lead. I am going to count from 1 to 10 and the hand and arm will become increasingly heavy and move down more and more. 1 . . . down. . . . 2, down more and more. . . . 3 . . . . down, 4 to 5 down more and more . . . . 6 down . . . . 7–8 down more and more . . . . like lead. 9 to 10 more and more down. [allow about 10 seconds of silence, then note if hand and arm have moved, and how much].

This is a relatively easy item which about 75 percent pass to some extent. Of course if the hand and arm have reached the patient's lap or the side of the chair before the count of 10, the therapist simply says: "that's fine, just relax, let your hand feel normal once again . . . . . as we move on to something else." If the patient's hand and arm move very little, the therapist might say at the end of the procedure: "You are doing fine, you felt the heaviness in your hand and arm . . . now you can put them back in their resting place and we will move on to something else."

Hands together. Another relatively innocuous suggestion is the hands together item from the Stanford Hypnotic Susceptibility Scale, Form A.

Now what I would like you to do is hold both hands straight out in front of you, palms facing toward each other. That's right arms out in front of you, palms facing inward . . . . about a foot apart. [if the patient has difficulty with these instructions the therapist positions the hands accordingly.] Now, I would like you to imagine a very strong force attracting your hands together. And as you think of this force attracting your hands together, they begin to move together. . . . it is a powerful force, like powerful magnets or maybe very very thick rubber bands around your hands. . . . pulling and moving your hands closer and closer. Moving, more and more closely together, that's right. . . . moving. . . . moving. . . . closer and closer. The force is so powerful, that your hands begin to move more and more . . . . . moving . . . moving . . . closer and closer [allow about 10 seconds of silence].

Here again, the procedure is terminated if the hands come together at some point: "Good, your hands have come together and are now touching. . . . now let the force dissipate." If the patient fails to respond to the suggestion, gentle reassurance is given as above. About 65 percent of patients will respond positively to this procedure.

The hypnotic dream. Another item fashioned from the Stanford family of susceptibility scales is the hypnotic dream. This item has the advantage of probing for the patient's ability to regress more substantially than the other items, but has the disadvantage of having an abreactive pull, which usually should be countered by the therapist at the very initial session of the relationship. But for some very fragile patients, no matter how the suggestion is worded, no matter how carefully the therapist emphasized a pleasant, or at least affect-neutral experience, a disturbing affect will emerge. Nevertheless, the item does merit inclusion for most patients.

> As you continue to remain very deeply hypnotized, I am going to count from 1 to 5, and as I do you will become sleepier and sleepier. . . . and when I reach the count of 5 you will sleep and have a dream. . . . but a special and pleasant dream . . . you will have a dream about what hypnosis means . . . you will have a dream, just like you might have when you sleep, and it will be a dream about hypnosis. You may dream directly about hypnosis, or you may have a dream which does not seem outwardly to be about hypnosis, but may very well be. Now I am going to count from 1 to 5 and you will get sleepier and sleepier . . . when I reach the count of 5 you will have a dream about hypnosis. After awhile I will speak again to ask you about the dream that you had, and you will remember everything very clearly . . . and you will be able to tell me all about it without it disturbing your relaxed state of hypnosis. Now, 1 . . . more and more sleepy . . . 2. . . . sleepier and sleepier, you are going to have a dream about hypnosis. . . . 3. . . . 4. . . . 5. . . . sleep and dream. . . . . deep asleep [therapist waits about a minute, noting any eye movements, or other bodily indications of private experience]. . . . . That's fine, deeply relaxed and hypnotized, but no longer dreaming. . . . tell me about your dream. . . . tell me all about it [therapist listens, asks open-ended question, etc.].

There is no question that this dream can provide important information about the patient's experience of the therapist as often the dream is explicitly interactive, with a person who is unmistakably a therapist equivalent. Thus this item not only probes for the patient's ability to regress in service of the ego, but offers a window into the nature of the transference. At the end of the dream, the therapist can ask how the patient experienced the dream: Was it like watching a movie? Or was it like being there? Was there actually a dreamlike story? Or were there just passing colors or shapes with no story or discernible objects. Of special note is how the patient manages affect under these circumstances: Is affect constricted in the dream? Is it present but fairly neutralized? Or is it overwhelming? Only about 20 to 30 percent of patients have a dream experience that approaches that of a routine night dream, most others report a daydreamlike experience. Rarely does a patient report nothing at all.

Phase 4: Instructions for Subsequent
Sessions: Abbreviated Hypnotic Inductions

An extremely simple but exceedingly important therapeutic maneuver during the latter portion of the initial hypnotic sessions is to structure a constellation of cues that will enable the patient to enter hypnosis quickly and easily on subsequent sessions. It is entirely unnecessary to employ lengthy hypnotic inductions each time hypnosis is used in therapy. Here is where we return to Bernheim's dictum that any hypnotic induction of over 30 seconds is a waste of time. For indeed, after one or two sessions of using the full litany of induction, there is normally no reason for the patient to take more than a minute to enter hypnosis, *if* he or she is properly prepared.

Normally instructions for rapid reestablishment of the hypnotic state are administered *during* the latter portion of the first or second hypnotic session. They are given in hypnosis as a posthypnotic suggestion. Here there is a premium on establishing salient cues (both verbal and nonverbal) which have become associated with the state of hypnosis and the person of the therapist. What follows is one example of such a procedure:

> As you remain deeply hypnotized I will now help you to learn how to enter hypnosis easily and quickly. Whenever you are in this

room, and in your chair, and whenever we want to use hypnosis in our work together, all you need do is to close your eyes and listen to me count from 1 to 5. . . . . and when we do this together you will find that by the count of 5 you will be as deeply relaxed and hypnotized as you are now. . . . perhaps even more so. When I reach the count of 5 you will be deeply relaxed, finding yourself walking down the spiral staircase that you liked so much today. Whenever we are in this room together, and we wish to use hypnosis in our work together, all you need do is close your eyes and listen comfortably to me count from 1 to 5. And by the time I reach the count of 5 you will be deeply relaxed and hypnotized. . . . . walking down that very special spiral staircase.

When the patient is brought out of hypnosis, and after the post-hypnotic interview, the therapist and patient might "practice" this abbreviated counting procedure. A second termination then follows. In the next session when hypnosis is used the patient and therapist can repeat the procedure. Sometimes it is helpful to follow the abbreviated induction with a brief and familiar deepening technique. In any event, subsequent induction of experienced hypnotic subjects need take no longer than one or two minutes.

PHASE 5: TERMINATION OF HYPNOSIS

The termination of hypnosis is very straightforward. For patients who have never before experienced hypnosis the therapist simply states:

In a little while I am going to count backwards from 10 to 1. And as I do you will become less and less hypnotized. When I reach the count of 1 your eyes will open and you will be fully awake and alert, in your normal state of awareness. When I reach the count of 1 you will be fully awake, and you will feel refreshed and relaxed, remembering everything you wish to remember. That's right, now I will begin to count backwards from 10 to 1, and you will become more and more awake and alert, and when I reach the count of 1 you will be fully alert. 10, 9. . . . less and less hypnotized. . . . . 8, 7 . . . less hypnotized, more awake . . . 6, 5, 4. . . . more and more awake. . . . . 3, 2, *1 . . . eyes open, wide awake* . . . Are you awake? [the therapist then proceeds with the posthypnotic interview].

For subsequent sessions in which hypnosis is used, the patient can be instructed: "Soon you will be ready to come out of hypnosis. . . . . when you are ready, take a deep breath in, open your eyes, and you will be wide awake [patient opens eyes]. That's it, wide awake."

The termination of hypnosis is an emotionally charged event as evidenced by the widespread, but completely inaccurate, belief that patients can "get stuck" in hypnosis. Patients are no more likely to "get stuck" in hypnosis than they are to "get stuck" in a traditional, intensive nonhypnotic therapy session. In both instances themes of separation and loss can render the transition away from the therapist difficult. Sometimes hypnosis patients enjoy their experience so much that they are reluctant to "come out" of hypnosis because it is so pleasant. On the *exceedingly* rare occasion when a hypnosis subject does not easily come "out" of hypnosis, the therapist can simply note: "I notice that you have chosen to remain in hypnosis for awhile. . . . tell me what is happening. . . . ." In the experience of the two authors, the mere act of asking for information provides the solution. Sometimes patients claim to have not heard the termination instructions; sometimes they are so wonderfully relaxed that they do not want to interrupt the experience; sometimes there is something they wish to share with the therapist before hypnosis ends; sometimes they are in fact asleep. On all counts there is the defensive avoidance of separation embedded in the transference. Attention to any unfinished material along with gentle and reassuringly direct suggestion for termination will suffice. It may be helpful for therapists to keep in mind that in research where the hypnotist abruptly left the room while the subject was still hypnotized, subjects were found to gradually and spontaneously arouse themselves from the hypnotic state, no worse for wear (Evans, 1966; Orne and Evans, 1966). While we certainly do not recommend this as good clinical technique, these findings can help the therapist keep an even perspective on the situation at hand, and thereby not internalize the patient's projected separation anxiety and abandonment fears.

PHASE 6: THE POSTHYPNOTIC INTERVIEW

It is helpful, especially in the initial hypnosis session, to allow for 5 or 10 minutes to discuss the patient's experience of hypnosis.

While the therapist has had an opportunity to observe the patient's behavioral response to hypnosis, it is important to assess the patient's subjective experience, and the patient's attitude about that experience. As in any such semistructured interview, the therapist begins with very open-ended, neutral questions, and then moves through a series of increasingly specific queries regarding the patient's experience. The therapist may begin with, "What was that like? . . . What else did you experience? What was it like being hypnotized. . . ." Then the therapist may move to questions regarding the patient's general phenomenological experience: "How deeply hypnotized did you feel? . . . How did you experience my voice? . . . . . How did time seem to go by? . . . . . Did you feel hypnotized more deeply at some times than at others? . . . . . How did your body feel during hypnosis? . . . . . ." Another series of questions addresses responses to specific suggestions. Here the therapist can listen for evidence of topographic regression, especially nonconscious involvement: "What was the staircase like? . . . . . What was it like for your arm to move down and get heavy? . . . . . What was it like when your hands moved together as they did?" The therapist can assess whether movement seemed to "happen by itself" or whether there was a more conscious participation ("I helped it along quite a bit"). The therapist can probe for the vividness of imagery and richness of fantasy: "What was the dream like? . . . . Was it like a real dream? . . . ." Finally the therapist can invite a frank discussion of technique: "Tell me, was there anything I did that helped you go more deeply into hypnosis, or anything I did that seemed to get in the way?"

Typically patients will be quite forthcoming about their experience, diminishing the need for formal questioning. Further, patients can be expected to be understandably curious about what the therapist thinks of their response and what that means about subsequent treatment. As we will discuss later, there are times when the patient's response is so problematic, or their hypnotic ability is so very limited, that nonhypnotic interventions are indicated. If this is the case, the therapist should discuss this with the patient in a way that avoids implying failure or poor prognosis. But since most patients will be moderately to highly hypnotizable, and since for some problems even low hypnotizables benefit from hypnotic intervention, the therapist can be justifiably encouraging about the patient's performance. In short, the posthypnosis interview is a time for the patient to debrief the therapist on how he or she experienced hypnosis. The information derived from this interview period is easily as valuable as any information the therapist gleans from the hypnosis phases proper. Similarly, the therapist informs the patient about treatment implications of this initial hypnotic experience, and in so doing underscores the joint nature of the therapeutic enterpise.

THREE KEY ASPECTS OF TREATMENT PLANNING

Beyond accurate case formulation and diagnosis, there are three clinical considerations which detemine whether and how hypnosis should be employed in a psychotherapy. These are: the patient's hypnotic ability as assessed in the initial hypnotic session; the presence of certain special clinical features which may contraindicate hypnosis; and the relative importance of uncovering versus supportive therapeutic aims.

THE RELEVANCE OF HYPNOTIC SUSCEPTIBILITY

A patient's ability to respond to hypnosis is multiply determined by the action and interaction of innate ability (perhaps genetically determined), capacity to regress in service of the ego, and a host of cultural, family, and individual attitudes and expectations about hypnosis (both conscious and unconscious). Even the most rigorous index of hypnotizability is no more capable of measuring pure innate hypnotic ability than is an IQ test capable of measuring pure brain capacity. In both cases, we must be satisfied that we are realiably measuring a constellation of factors among which innate ability figures prominently. Nevertheless, there is impressive evidence that for some types of disorders a person's gross responsiveness to hypnosis predicts positive outcome in therapies which employ hypnosis. Most notably this applies to psychological disorders and medical conditions related to pain. There is clear evidence across a number of studies, that patients with considerable hypnotic talent profit more from hypnosis interventions than do patients of limited hypnotic ability (Bates, 1994). In fact, for highly hypnotizable patients, hypnosis may provide more pain relief than does morphine, even in intrusive medical procedures such as nasal surgery, abdominal surgery, debridement after burns, and bone marrow aspiration. Similarly, among patients suffering from asthma and dermatological disease there is a clear relationship between initial behavioral responsiveness to hypnosis and successful treatment outcome (Collison, 1978). In short, if a therapist encounters highly hypnotizable patients with these specific types of problems, he or she might be remiss in not at least *trying* hypnosis.

Nevertheless, the relationship between hypnotizability and treatment outcome in hypnotic therapies remains unclear for many types of patient groups and intervention types. For the most part the relationship between hypnotic responsiveness and outcome in longer-term, expressive psychotherapies has not been examined empirically. For shorter-term, more circumscribed patient problems which lend themselves to traditional experimental control (e.g., smoking cessation, obesity treatment, alcoholism), there is some reason to believe that hypnotizability is unrelated to outcome in hypnotic treatments, though even here there are findings on both sides of the issue (see Wadden and Anderton, 1982 for reviews; Bates, 1994; Kirsch and Lynn, 1995).

Pending more systematic examination of this issue, especially in the realm of hypnosis as employed in uncovering, complex psychotherapies, we advise clinicians to be mindful that for about 5 to 10 percent of the population who are extremely hypnotizable, use of hypnosis can be associated with rapid and dramatic gain, both in supportive and expressive modes of therapy. For another 50 percent of patients who are high-medium in hypnotic ability, there is good reason to believe that hypnosis can be employed with reasonable success. For those subjects who are utterly unable to experience hypnosis (about 2% of the population), or for those who find it unappealing or troubling for other reasons, use of hypnosis may be contraindicated. But it is probable that even some very low hypnotizable subjects respond positively to hypnotic therapeutic intervention when it carries with it a special meaning, or a particularly compelling placebo effect.

Clinical Features Associated with Negative Effects
It is now abundantly clear that most patients benefit from psychotherapy (Beutler, Crago, and Machado, 1991 for review). But it is equally clear that in a small percentage of cases psychotherapy in general is associated with the patient getting "worse." In the groundbreaking meta-analytic review by Smith, Glass, and Miller (1980) 9 percent of effect size measures were negative. Jacobson and Edinger (1982) reported that 5 percent of patients were adversely affected by relaxation training. It is within this context that the negative effects of therapeutic applications of hypnosis should be assessed. As Frauman, Lynn, and Brentar (1994) point out: "These statistics (regarding psychotherapy in general) are a reasonable estimate of the frequency of negative effects during and after hypnosis. Hypnosis is neither more nor less hazardous than other psychotherapeutic procedures that are used because of their potential to influence and treat clients" (p. 116). Nevertheless, it is important for the therapist to understand and appreciate the conditions under which negative effects may occur when using hypnosis. In general, factors contributing to negative outcome are the same for hypnotic and nonhypnotic therapies, namely, therapist characteristics, patient characteristics, and technical characteristics.

Therapist Characteristics
As Strupp and his associates have demonstrated, negative effects are primarily a function of unexamined countertransference (Strupp, Hadley, and Henry, 1977). For instance, overly controlling, self-blaming therapists are far more likely to engender a poor interpersonal process in the therapeutic dyad. Therapists with harsh parental introjects are rated as least warm by observers, and engender the most hostility on the part of patients. We contend that, especially where hypnosis is employed in service of *expression*, there is a heightened potential for emergence of troubling unneutralized aggressive, erotic or narcissistic fantasies on the part of the therapist which may compromise therapeutic neutrality. Given the regressive pull of hypnosis, with attendant shifts in the patient's experience of self and boundary, countertransferential reactions can be amplified beyond optimal levels. There is thus a premium on the therapist's ability to recognize, neutralize,

and therapeutically utilize primitive material emerging during hypnosis. The technical implication of all this is clear: When a therapist who is considering using hypnosis is faced by material which he or she finds unmanageably jarring, it is prudent not to use hypnosis at that time, but rather, to employ techniques which afford the therapist sufficient time to clarify and reflect upon his or her emergent experience of the patient.

Patient characteristics. Several researchers and clinicians have suggested that certain patient characteristics may be associated with negative effects (Rosen, 1960; Spiegel and Spiegel, 1978; Kleinhauz, Dreyfuss, Beran, and Azikri, 1979; MacHovec, 1986). As one might expect, characteristics which place patients at risk for negative reactions to psychotherapy in general, are precisely the ones associated with risk in hypnotherapy. They include incipient borderline character structure, paranoia, and acute psychotic decompensation among others. Hypnosis can be used with all these conditions (see later chapters of this book), but we advise therapists who are just beginning to employ hypnosis with patients to refrain from using it in the above situations pending acquisition of more experience and training. Further, patients with dissociative disorders can pose problems initially. Though almost all are highly hypnotizable, these patients may come to associate the hypnotically induced disruption of the general reality orientation as a recapitulation of dissociative experiences previously only experienced during or after trauma. Again, while this poses a special challenge to immediate therapeutic management, significant benefit can accrue *if* the therapist is properly prepared to contain and utilize the resultant affect. In short, with only a few exceptions, negative effects occur in hypnosis, as in psychotherapy, when the therapist's clinical reach exceeds his or her conceptual grasp.

There are, however, a number of patient characteristics which, if not associated with iatrogenic effects per se, are signs that hypnosis is not likely to be helpful in the therapeutic enterprise. First and foremost of these is low motivation. Even patients who present specifically for hypnosis may in fact be exceedingly resistant to the procedure itself. Spouses, referring physicians, and even employers may mention hypnosis in the referral, but the patients themselves may have no wish to pursue this approach.

Beyond the usual primary and secondary gain serving to maintain the symptom cluster, patients may have been coerced by others to present clinically in the first place. The added approbation of hypnosis may then be experienced by the patient as just another untenable intrusion. Of course it is the therapist–patient interaction (and the hypnotic intervention itself) which becomes the stage on which the patient's protest will be enacted. If low motivation for hypnosis persists, even after being addressed in the initial consultation, then use of this technique is contraindicated. Second, in addition to low motivation, low hypnotizability may mitigate against use of an hypnotic intervention, especially if the patient depressively experiences his or her hypnotic performance as a failure. Further, if the low hypnotizable patient presents with no particularly dramatic expectations about hypnosis, which might otherwise lead the therapist to anticipate a dramatic placebo effect, then even the accoutrements of the hypnotic procedure would seem pointless.

Finally there are two disorders which traditionally have been viewed as resistant to hypnotic intervention: organic brain syndromes and manic–depressive disorder. Organic brain syndromes sometimes involve such drastic alterations in normal ego functioning, especially regarding attention, that hypnotic induction, with its emphasis on sustained focus, is hopelessly compromised. This, indeed, does seem to be the case in our clinical experience. Nevertheless there are a few isolated reports of successful application of hypnosis in brain-injured patients: with adult head trauma patients having attention-deficit disorder (Laidlaw, 1993) and with a $6^1/_2$-year-old girl with chronic pain, vomiting, and sleep disturbance secondary to malignant astrocytoma (LaClave and Blix, 1989). Expressive psychological interventions with manic–depressive patients are not fundamentally helpful, and hypnosis is no exception. The exaggerated, primitive overidealization that can transpire during hypnosis with bipolar patients can reach psychotic proportions, especially as themes of power and grandiosity are so figural for these patients. The clinical literature does contain one reference to the successful use of hypnosis with a series of five bipolar patients during the remission period (Feinstein and Morgan, 1986).

Technical characteristics. The way in which the hypnotic procedure is carried out and the specific nature of certain suggestions can also increase the risk of negative therapeutic outcome. Groundbreaking research examining the causes of negative outcomes in psychoanalytic psychotherapies (Henry and Strupp, 1992) has uncovered a paradox which we believe applies as well to hypnotic interventions. Therapists who were judged to be properly adhering to the treatment paradigm as operationalized in the time-limited dynamic psychotherapy training manual (Strupp and Binder, 1984) produced superior outcomes across measures of patient progress. However, a small subset of these therapists who closely adhered to the training model, appeared to do so mechanistically and countertransferentially, thereby evoking a substantial amount of disaffiliative countermeasures by patients. As Henry and Strupp point out: "This raises the provocative hypotheses that when therapists apply learned techniques in an unskilled manner training may actually have some negative effects" (Henry and Strupp, 1992, p. 172). We echo these sentiments regarding hypnosis. Imparting technical knowledge on one hand, and improving therapeutic skill on the other, may be two very different clinical training problems. It seems almost certain that one *does not* necessarily follow on the heels of the other. Thus, we once again remind the reader that mechanical application of hypnotic techniques, when divorced from conceptual understanding and a foundation of therapeutic presence, can lead to unfortunate and unnecessary negative outcomes for our patients.

In addition to the problem of technically "correct" but therapeutically mismanaged applications of hypnosis, there is the fact that some hypnotic techniques are simply prepotent in their capacity to pull for negative effects. Meares (1961) cites the failed posthypnotic suggestion as fertile ground for treatment complications. When patients are given a direct posthypnotic suggestion to respond in a certain way to a predetermined cue (e.g., "every time you see a cigarette you will gag and cough"), and when the patient fails to respond in this way, at home and between sessions the patient can become highly anxious and depressed. It is therefore prudent for therapists to refrain from employing such direct and specific posthypnotic suggestions, and thereby avoid the specter of patients concluding that they themselves have failed. Further, several clinicians have warned against *any* such authoritarian and direct "suggesting away" of symptoms, out of respect for the patient's need for the symptoms and in the knowledge that, without the presence of benign substitutes, other more virulent symptoms may emerge as replacements (Rosen, 1960; Orne, 1965).

Finally there are a number of perfectly acceptable hypnotic techniques which, though sometimes dramatically mutative, can involve precipitous regressions for which the therapist must be prepared. Hypnotic age regression is one of these procedures. Even when couched in the most preliminary, innocuous, and benevolent language (e.g., "return to a happy sunny day when things were very good") there is a dark cultural expectation that when people are hypnotized and regressed in this manner they will unfailingly encounter a traumatic event. Though this procedure can be immensely useful, clinicians are well advised to refrain from age regression procedures in initial phases of treatment, and when used in later phases, the therapist must be braced for the unexpected. Similarly, age progression (suggesting that the patient move *ahead* in time) can be a helpful technique in allowing the patient to visualize healthy coping and success, thereby strengthening the ego (e.g., "you will see yourself in five months working at home, without any great discomfort"). Misapplications of this technique are those which in any way imply that the patient is "exploring" the future. Suggestions for temporal alterations are inherently destabilizing to some extent, but at least with age *regression* the ensuing material is to some limited degree bounded by what actually did happen—it is an admixture of memory and fantasy. Unstructured age progression on the other hand offers no such constraints, and offers unrestrained license for the patient's fears and fantasies to become enshrined as destiny. The authors can think of no clinical situation which would justify this risk. Similarly, suggestions which require the patient to experience gross alterations in body boundary may be risky, though sometimes very useful. Direct suggestions to leave the body as a means of coping with a painful medical procedure would be an example of this type of suggestion. In a study by Nash, Lynn, and Stanley (1984) it was found that experimental subjects experienced marked negative effects during and after abrupt hypnotically suggested out-of-body experiences. As noted in chapter 2, when suggestions are given for a broad-based dissociation, it is best to frame this event as a temporary separation of the experiencing self and the observing self. The therapist prepares the ground for reintegration by allowing the patient to be pleasantly absorbed in some faraway place, while occasionally reminding the patient that when he or she is ready, return to the usual state will be easy and interesting.

The Relative Balance between Expression and Support
In terms of treatment planning, careful attention to case formulation should inform the therapist as to whether a primarily expressive or supportive therapy should be attempted. Of course, even the most expressive therapies have supportive components, for this is the flesh and blood of the working alliance. In planning a hypnotic intervention the characterological maturity of the patient, the presenting problem, and the aim of the therapeutic intervention determine technique. We will later discuss hypnotic interventions with borderline and psychotic patients, both types of patients requiring special attention to primitive aspects of support and affect modulation in the face of expression. In the present section we will discuss the ways in which support and expression can be utilized with ego syntonic conditions, medical problems, and neurotic spectrum difficulties.

The table on page 129 presents a framework for this discussion.

With ego syntonic disorders, habit disorders, and medical conditions or procedures, either a primarily supportive or expressive approach can be taken. In the former case hypnotic intervention is designed to modulate disruptive affect, reinforce ego syntonic adaptive defensive and coping strategies, and support mastery. This type of intervention is indicated where there is minimal conflictual material, when limited time is available, or where the patient's ability to tolerate regression is in question. Significant and important symptom amelioration can be achieved with relatively brief interventions (1–6 sessions), for problems ranging from chronic pain, smoking cessation, simple phobias, acute pain from medical procedures, skin disorders, to other psychophysiological disorders). Technical considerations in the use of hypnosis revolve around careful containment of any regression, active support throughout the hypnotic intervention, and deflection of undue dependence on the therapist through early training in self-hypnosis techniques.

Therapeutic Aim		
Pathology	Symptom Elimination	Insight/Expression
Ego Syntonic Disorders and Medical Conditions	Supportive techniques designed to modulate disruptive affect, reinforce ego syntonic adaptive defensive and coping strategies (e.g., pain relief, smoking cessation, weight loss).	Initial phases of hypnotic intervention designed to resolve and ameliorate clearly delimited and/or encapsulated symptoms which nonetheless have considerable dynamic underpinnings (e.g., some types of psychogenic pain, physiological, and other medical conditions).
Neurotic Spectrum Problems	Refinement of defenses with some expression. Some work on discharge of disruptive affect, and subsequent decrease in intensity of emotional arousal via imagery and direct cathartic techniques. But primary emphasis on ego mastery, along with containment and affect modulation.	Designed to provide insight and working through of significant arenas of conflict. Involves the use of hypnosis within the context of a traditional transference-mediated psychotherapy. Hypnosis is used to facilitate uncovering, regression, working through, and integration.

Other patients presenting with ego syntonic disorders and medical conditions who may have pronounced dynamic under-pinning to the symptomatology and who evidence appropriate motivation and resources, may achieve more lasting and general-izable benefit from a more expressive approach. Here hypnotic uncovering techniques are utilized to ameliorate clearly delimited symptoms, yielding not only relief from the symptoms per se, but some modest insight into the unconscious determinants of the problem, especially as they relate to repetition of maladaptive interpersonal scenarios. Here, work with psychophysiological dis-orders, smoking cessation, or simple phobias involves utilization of expressive hypnotic techniques to ascribe interpersonal mean-ing to what might (in the above strictly supportive mode) other-wise be labeled as mere chance, habit, or "stress." Self-hypnosis is still used with these patients, but the content is usually themati-cally more intimate, interpersonally richer, and emotionally charged.

Symptom relief with neurotic spectrum patients can sometimes be achieved via primarily supportive hypnotic techniques which facilitate ego mastery experiences and further support affect regulation. It is usual to pair this approach with some abreactive work, which, though expressive, may not yield well-articulated insight. Here symptom relief is achieved primarily via catharsis coupled with enhancement of defenses. In pursuit of the latter, hypnotic relaxation, imagery, ideomotor, and sensory focusing increase the capacity for self-observation, self-regulation, and related self-esteem. But tension reduction strategies and rehearsing "better alternatives" also play a role in the "shoring-up" of defenses. It is important to choose strategies that are consistent with the patient's character style and developmental maturity.

Hypnosis is well suited for traditional expressive work with neurotic spectrum patients. While not neglecting the therapeutic alliance and the real aspects of the patient–therapist relationship, the emphasis is on the use of hypnosis within the context of the on-going transference-mediated relationship. Hypnosis provides an avenue to regression in service of insight, especially in regards to the transferential relationship. Hypnosis then has a role in each phase of an uncovering therapy: instilling hope, enabling insight, facilitating the working through process, and imparting clarity to termination.

Instruction on Self-Hypnosis
In the course of supportive hypnotherapy with an aim of symptom alleviation, it is often quite essential for the therapist to teach the patient how to do self-hypnosis, so that coping techniques developed in the consulting room can be transferred to the patient's day-to-day life. Of course, patients should not be encouraged to use self-hypnosis for uncovering or expressive purposes, but only for self-soothing and symptom containment. Instructing patients on how to do self-hypnosis is very straightforward. Assuming the therapist has introduced the patient to the role of self-hypnosis in the treatment plan, the topic is addressed during a subsequent hypnosis session. When the patient is sufficiently hypnotized, and the supportive effect is obtained, the therapist

may directly instruct the patient as follows (this example is taken from a pain patient):

> Now that you are deeply relaxed and hypnotized, once again on your tranquil beach where no discomfort of any sort can reach you, listen to my words carefully. Whenever you wish to go into hypnosis, whenever you wish to take control of the sensations you have in this way, all you need to do is to find a reasonably comfortable place to be, shut your eyes, and count slowly to yourself from 1 to 5. As you count you will note that your breathing changes, the way your body feels changes, and you become transported once again onto this wonderful beach. So that by the time you reach the count of 5 you will always be deeply hypnotized, and in the wonderfully relaxed state you are now in. You may find that you actually go even more completely and deeply into hypnosis with practice.
>
> Whenever you wish to go into hypnosis, all you need do is find a comfortable place, close your eyes, and count silently to yourself from 1 to 5. You will find that your mind and body are effortlessly transformed back into this peaceful state of hypnosis, a state in which you have a different kind of control over your sensations. At the count of 5 you will always be right there on the beach, calm, tranquil, free of all undue discomfort. Once you are thus hypnotized, once you are again at the beach, you can stay for as long as you like. You need only stay there one or two minutes to obtain the benefit of hypnosis, or you may choose to stay longer. But whenever you wish to bring yourself out of self-hypnosis, all you need to do is take a deep breath in, and open your eyes, and you will be wide awake. . . . refreshed. . . . . . alert. . . . . . . and completely comfortable. You can be surprised how far this refreshed, comfortable, and alert feeling will extend in the remainder of the day. You will practice self-hypnosis in this way at least twice a day. For now, just remain hypnotized, as you listen to my voice.
>
> [Therapist repeats the general instructions of the second paragraph.]
>
> Now, in a little while you will come out of hypnosis. Soon you will take a deep breath . . . . open your eyes. . . . . and you will be wide awake. You will remember everything we did today. You will

find you are especially clear on how to do self-hypnosis. After you
have a chance to talk a bit about your experience today I will ask
you to practice self-hypnosis right here in the office.

After termination of the hypnosis the patient and therapist
discuss the work of the day. The therapist then reminds the patient of the self-hypnosis instructions, and asks the patient to practice hypnosis in the consulting room: "Now what I would like you
to do is to go ahead and use self-hypnosis right now with me here.
[Therapist reminds patient of instructions.] When you are there
on the island, comfortably hypnotized, just say the word *Now*, so
that I know you are there. When you do, I will speak to you, and
help you go even more deeply into hypnosis. Now I will be quiet
for awhile . . . go ahead and go into hypnosis. . . . . just saying
'Now' when you are on the island." When the patient signals that
he or she is hypnotized, the therapist probes for the patient's
experience, and repeats by now familiar phrases associated with
increased depth and/or symptom alleviation. It is once again
suggested that the patient will employ self-hypnosis at least twice
a day, more if needed. The sessions need be no more than one
or two minutes each, but they can be longer if the patient so
wishes. The patient is then asked to come out of hypnosis as he
or she would when doing self-hypnosis alone. The therapist then
queries the patient about the self-hypnosis experience, again reit-
erating the instruction to practice self-hypnosis at least twice a
day. The first order of business on the subsequent session is to
discuss how the patient found self-hypnosis to be.

For the most part, patients who respond well to traditional
heterohypnosis respond well to self-hypnosis. Patients who struggle with conflicts around autonomy will sometimes actually report
that they go deeper into hypnosis when they do it alone. On the
other hand, strikingly dependent patients may resist self-hypnosis
initially, but this is rarely unmanageable. There is, of course, nothing special about any of the specifics contained in the above example: Providing a cue is helpful; whether it is counting, a subtle
motor gesture, or some particular word is not important. Instructions on practice are probably important, but the specifics are
less so. Two authoritative texts on self-hypnosis are: Fromm and
Kahn (1990) and Fromm, Brown, Hurt, Oberlander, Boxer, and
Pfeifer (1981).

5

Symptom Alleviation in

Behavioral and Health-

Related Disorders

In the 1940s there was a great deal of excitement in the medical community regarding the contribution psychoanalysis might make to our understanding and treatment of what were then termed "psychosomatic disorders" (Dunbar, 1943; Alexander and French, 1948). But the attempt to link specific organ dysfunction (e.g., cardiovascular, gastrointestinal, pulmonary) to a specific conflictual theme (e.g., anger, fear, frustration) based on psychoanalytic metapsychology, though laudable, was misguided. Nor was there any credible evidence that certain "types" of people were prone to certain types of somatic difficulties. We consider it unfortunate that in the wake of these negative findings many psychoanalytically oriented clinicians and theorists abandoned the area and were quickly replaced by behaviorally oriented clinical researchers. To make matters worse, some psychoanalysts left in a bit of a "snit." Treatment of psychosomatic disorders was often vilified as "merely treating the symptom thus insuring symptom substitution," a charge that has proven to be untenable.

Interestingly, however, the same theorists who seized the field of psychosomatic medicine, applying behavior modification

and other behavioral change techniques developed from laboratory conditioning paradigms, have now become interested in the role of cognition, implicit learning, emotional disregulation, and interpersonal misattribution in the development of disorders of behavior and soma (Turk, Meichenbaum, and Genest, 1983; Melzack and Wall, 1988; Miller, 1992). This, coupled with the tragedy of overmedication, multiple surgeries, and the immense financial strain on the health care system has moved the field to reexamine constructs that are in fact quite core to psychoanalytic clinical theory, such as threat, unconscious processing, defensive coping, conflict, trauma, and repetition. We believe that the psychoanalytically informed clinician, steeped in a discipline which stresses careful and comprehensive case formulation, can make an important contribution to the alleviation of this type of human misery, even with fairly brief, problem-focused interventions. The remainder of this chapter outlines some of the current strategies employed by clinicians who use hypnosis to address behavioral and health-related disorders.

TREATMENT OF ACUTE AND CHRONIC
PAIN

With the advent of the gate theory of pain (Melzack and Wall, 1988) there has been an increasing acceptance of psychological interventions for the relief of not just psychogenic pain, but acute and chronic pain associated with physical trauma and disease process. There is a rather extensive research and clinical literature on the impact of hypnosis on the experience of pain (e.g., E. R. Hilgard and J. R. Hilgard, 1975; J. R. Hilgard and LeBaron, 1984; E. R. Hilgard, 1986; Spanos, 1989), and there is ample evidence that for patients who are experiencing serious pain, hypnosis can be very effective in reducing the extent of reported suffering, in some cases as much as does morphine (Stern, Brown, Ulett, and Sletten, 1977). Reduction in medication requirements and medical side effects are well documented (Wadden and Anderton, 1982). Further, the extent to which the pain patient experiences relief from pain is correlated with overall hypnotic susceptibility

(Wadden and Anderton, 1982; E. R. Hilgard, 1992), thus underscoring the fact that something specific about hypnosis is associated with symptom alleviation. Of course hypnosis should be used as part of an ongoing comprehensive treatment package which addresses the role of physical, factitious, depressive, and family factors.

In general, the strategy for management of pain with hypnosis is the same across most types of clinical situations, and the strategy is primarily, though not exclusively, supportive. Initial intake and history taking should reveal the ways in which the patient tries to cope with pain. As the treatment proceeds, the therapist capitalizes on these endogenous patterns by gaining more knowledge about the patient's experience of pain, its meanings, both primary and secondary gain issues related to the pain, and characteristic coping mechanisms. Early sessions further reveal the patient's responsiveness to initial attempts at hypnotic control, and thus inform development of new hypnotic procedures. The patient is then taught to use these same hypnotic strategies outside the consulting room via self-hypnosis (see chapter 4 regarding self-hypnosis), and encouraged to practice and refine these skills in a number of follow-up sessions. Here the aim is to facilitate maintenance and generalizability of these new coping mechanisms. This primarily supportive intervention nonetheless can involve dramatic abreactive experiences which, when properly contained, can be a source of enormous relief for the patient, and of immense value for the clinician as he or she seeks to fashion a treatment strategy rooted in the patient's conflictual thematic material and character style.

Chaves (1993) and others (E. R. Hilgard and J. R. Hilgard, 1975; Scott and Barber, 1977) offer several hypnotic strategies which can be used with pain patients once the meaning and phenomenology of the pain experience is explored. Essentially these hypnotic strategies fall into one of three categories: direct suggestion of complete symptom alleviation, alteration of the sensation of pain, and distraction. Again, it is incumbent upon the clinician to select an approach which is most compatible with the patient's own defensive proclivities (undoing, repression, denial, rationalization, externalization, primitive narcissistic defenses, schizoid defenses, perceptual defense, regression). Further, it is important to be mindful that the nature of the intrusive affect differs between chronic and acute conditions. Patients suffering from acute pain (e.g., dental and medical procedures) are most commonly quite anxious. Chronic pain patients are more often depressed and demoralized.

DIRECT SUGGESTION OF COMPLETE SYMPTOM ALLEVIATION

Reinstatement of Previous Chemical Anesthesia
Some highly hypnotizable subjects will respond quite well to direct suggestion for anesthesia: "You tell me that you remember a time when you were in outpatient surgery and the anesthesiologist began to inject the medication which gave you total relief from the pain. Now, in this deep hypnotic state I want you to picture this situation once again. . . . . [describe details of the remembered procedure with associated gradual relief of pain]." Sometimes having the patient count backwards (e.g., from 10 to 1) as the pain decreases can be helpful.

Numbness
Similarly, many highly hypnotizable subjects can experience hypnotic anesthesia on a noninvolved hand or arm. After demonstrating to the patient that this type of control of sensation is indeed possible in noninvolved portions of the body, the therapist proceeds to extend this numbness to the affected area: "Now that you have had a chance to experience how completely numb your left hand can feel. . . . how much it feels like a piece of wood, so profoundly and completely numb. . . . . even when I pinched that hand quite vigorously, you felt nothing. . . . . now I'd like you to move that numb hand of yours (as best you can) to your stomach, where you have been feeling so much discomfort. . . . . let the numbness spread from your hand to your stomach. . . . that's it. . . . . place your numb hand on your stomach, and feel the numbness sinking into your stomach. . . . . now your stomach is feeling numb . . . completely numb. . . . . "

SUGGESTING THE ALTERATION OF THE PAIN
EXPERIENCE

Transformation of the Painful Sensation
Patients in the mid to high range of hypnotic susceptibility often
respond well to suggestions which encourage a change in the way
the pain is experienced, rather than total ablation. A number of
possibilities are available. The "size" of the pained area can be
"shrunk." The pain can be moved to another, more benign loca-
tion. Or the quality of the sensation can be changed from one
involving suffering, to one involving a dull, tingling, warm (but
not aversive) sensation. For instance: "You describe your pain as
sharp knives sticking you in the arm. I'd like you to picture these
knives right now. . . . . . describe them to me. . . . . . Now as we
continue our work together you notice that the knives are changing. . . . they are actually becoming more and more blunt. . . . .
now they are less like knives and more like a ballpoint pen. . . . . . .
now like an unsharpened pencil. . . . . now like a pencil that has
never been used. Notice how the sensation has changed. . . . . like
being touched with the erasure end of number of pen-
cils. . . . . feel how the sensation has changed. . . . . . just a kind of
pressure that is increasingly unimportant. . . . blunt, soft,
pressure. . . . .

Transformation of the Painful Stimuli
Patients facing the acute pain of a medical procedure will sometimes respond to suggestions for an alteration in their perception
of the pain stimuli: A needle can be pictured as rubber, a scalpel
as a paint brush.

Performing a Cognitive Analysis
Chaves (1993) describes a clever intervention which might be well
suited to patients with obsessive–compulsive proclivities. Here the
patient is invited to analyze in exquisite lexical detail every component of the pain sensation, to cognitively distill the pain experience into its more manageable parts: heat, cold, pressure,
tingling, throbbing. The patient can then be encouraged to focus
upon one aspect of the pain (preferably a component involving
less suffering) so that it comes to dominate the phenomenal field.

Time Distortion

Another parameter of the pain sensation which can be addressed with hypnosis is its duration. Patients, especially those with considerable self-punitive or masochistic urges, can be given suggestions to heighten their pain by briefly making it worse, then allowing it to recede for longer and longer periods of time. Sometimes these patients spontaneously picture the pain as a container or balloon with a finite amount of pain inside. By purposely straining the container beyond its limits, it bursts, and is thus emptied completely . . . allowing for longer periods of pain-free functioning.

Focus on Reducing Catastrophizing Self-Statements and Imagery

Here suggestions are given to acknowledge the pain, to know it for what it is, and what it is not. If specific maladaptive self-statements are identified, hypnotic suggestions can be given for incompatible statements (e.g., "I am having a stroke, and I'm going to die," versus "I'm" having a headache and it will be over soon"). Alternatively, for some patients it is imagery, and not secondary process mentation, that drives the fear or suffering. A catastrophic image associated with the pain can be rendered less intrusive with an hypnotically induced image of calm, efficacious coping.

Thermal Imagery

A hybrid of alteration and distraction strategies is sometimes used with migraine headache sufferers. Diamond and Friedman (1983) have found that suggestions for peripheral (hand and foot) warming combined with suggestions for central (head) cooling may late influence patterns of peripheral and cerebral blood flow posited to play a role in the vascular pathology involved in migraines. These hypnotic suggestions are often employed with other types of pain disorders that have prominent vascular involvement (e.g., reflex sympathetic dystrophy).

DISTRACTION

Shifting Foci of Attention

Even low hypnotizable patients can derive some benefit from suggestion to refocus attention on another part of the body, some aspect of the environment, pleasantly absorbing fantasies, or just breathing. When the patient can tolerate therapeutic regression to the point where imagery is effortlessly experienced as fully absorbing, results are most positive. But patients differ in their imaging ability such that the therapist must attempt to find an environmental or somatic focus for attention. For example: "Now as the nurse prepares to remove the bandages from your burn remain deeply hypnotized and begin to pay exquisite attention to your breathing . . . . hold your breath a bit. . . . feel the pleasant tension . . . now exhale [etc.]. . . . You have never been so wonderfully aware of every nuance of your breathing. . . . . as your breathing remains slow and regular, and as you remain deeply hypnotized, you can feel every muscle, every nerve, every tendon, every part of your body that's involved in breathing. . . . . how elegant and how complex an experience it is . . . . and you know that nothing that happens around you can interrupt the ongoing inhale and exhale that permits you to go more deeply, more completely into hypnosis. . . ."

Cognitive Distraction

For some overideational patients effortful problem solving is the most absorbing phenomenal experience. For these patients the therapist can encourage a pattern of thought which leaves little attentional "space" for the experience of pain. Computational tasks, complex tasks of logic, arithmetic problems, or business inventories can serve as surprisingly effective distracters.

Gross Dissociation

For patients who are highly dissociative in their day-to-day lives, the therapist can use hypnotic suggestions to facilitate an out-of-body experience. These patients can sometimes "hover above" their bodies, describing with mechanistic detachment the procedures around them. Others are able to dissociate their awareness from the involved body part, such that the leg, or arm, or hand is simply "not mine." It is our experience that this type of gross dissociation is best used for coping with time-limited, but painful medical procedures, where the hypnotist is immediately present, or at least accessible. Suggesting that patients employ such broad dissociative techniques in the context of self-hypnosis seems ill-advised.

A relevant example in the area of obstetrics is as follows: a woman who is afraid of labor pain is seen in hypnotherapy three times during the last month or two of her pregnancy. Each time the hypnotherapist uses imagery and a dissociation technique to give her the posthypnotic suggestion that she will not suffer pain during labor by saying to her:

> Imagine that this is the day or night when your baby will be born . . . Twice now, you have felt some vague, light, momentary pains in your abdomen . . . You wonder whether these are the beginnings of labor pains . . . You decide to watch the time . . . to see whether they come at regular intervals . . . You call or wake up your husband so he can drive you to the hospital. As you step out of the car . . . in front of the hospital, something interesting is going to happen: a woman who looks very much like you is going to step out of your body and walk just ahead of you into the hospital . . . She is being put in a wheelchair and taken to a hospital room . . . while you and your husband walk behind her, into the elevator, and to the hospital room. A nurse makes her comfortable in the hospital bed, and you are allowed to sit over there in the corner of the room, watching that woman go through labor pains which come at closer and closer intervals. You see the resident and the doctor come in and talk to her . . . Then there comes the time when she is being wheeled into the delivery room and put on the delivery table while you sit in the corner of the delivery room and watch that woman in labor. And then, toward the end of her labor, something strange is happening. Just before the baby is fully being born, a strong pull, like a powerful magnetic pull, moves you back into the body of that woman and you become one with her again . . . The baby is being born, your baby is being born. The doctor hands you the baby to look at, to feel, to put on your chest. You feel all of the joy and the great happiness of having a new baby.

The technique can be embellished by giving a good deal of information in the beginning about the various sensations and stages of labor pain that the dissociated "I," the subject, is watching and thus the object, "that woman lying on the delivery table," is going through. Knowledge of what will happen in labor naturally relieves some of the fear and the tensing which contribute to increased labor pain by tensing abdominal muscles. It is of utmost importance that the hypnotist in his "spiel" address the woman who in the fantasy sits in the corner and observes, as "you" in order to keep the self in the dissociated person who does *not* feel labor pain. It is equally important, in the last few minutes of labor, to reunite the self with "that person who is giving birth to the baby," in order to avoid the risk that the new mother for the first few days after the birth will doubt that the baby is hers. This happened to one of the authors (E.F.) when she used the technique for the first time and did not know that one needs to undo the dissociation.

Age Progression or Regression
Another hypnotic technique that can be used in service of distraction is age progression or age regression. Here the patient imagines activities, places, and people before the onset of pain occurred. Alternatively, they can project themselves into the future, imagining how it will be when they are feeling less pain.

In sum, hypnosis can be an effective intervention for both chronic and acute pain. Further, hypnosis appears to be as effective with "organic" as "psychogenic" pain. Practically every medical specialty encounters pain in some way, and there is a legitimate role for hypnosis in medical practice ranging across oncology, obstetrics, dentistry, trauma medicine, surgery, anesthesiology, pediatrics, and internal medicine. The deteminants of hypnosis' effectiveness are the extent to which the patient is able to experience hypnosis, and the skill of the clinician in fashioning an intervention which is personally relevant, emotionally tolerable, and interpersonally empowering. Indeed, we believe that for highly hypnotizable patients who are suffering intractable pain, hypnosis is the treatment of choice.

TREATMENT OF BEHAVIOR AND HABIT
CONTROL DISORDERS

Hypnosis can be applied to a host of behavior and health-related difficulties. For purposes of illustration we have chosen three disorders for which hypnosis is particularly relevant: obesity, nicotine addiction, and eating disorders. As is the case with pain disorders, there is now sufficient empirical evidence to support the notion that hypnotic interventions are reasonably effective in treating these three problem areas (Levitt, 1993; Lynn, Neufeld, Rhue, and Matorin, 1993; Nash and Baker, 1993; Crawford and Barabasz, 1993). However, the relationship between hypnotizability and treatment outcome for behavior and habit control is less clear than is the case with pain disorders. Several authors note that outcome in hypnotic treatment of self-initiated disorders is unrelated, or only minimally related to hypnotizability. These theorists question whether there is any unique contribution to outcome attributable to suggestion alone for these disorders (Perry, Gelfand, and Marcovitch, 1979; Wadden and Anderton, 1982; Spinhoven, 1987). Others disagree, pointing to studies which do demonstrate that being more hypnotizable increases the chances of positive outcome (Levitt, 1993; Barabasz and Spiegel, 1989). Every credible researcher and clinical theorist agrees, however, that treatment of such serious (and sometimes life-threatening disorders) should be thorough, comprehensive, and multimodal. Hypnosis, if used at all, is then only one aspect of a broad-based treatment approach.

HYPNOSIS IN THE TREATMENT OF OBESITY

Though there is a good deal of controversy surrounding the area, most theorists agree that obesity has multiple causes including metabolic, genetic, neurological, socioeconomic, and interpersonal (Rodin, 1982; Levitt, 1993). They also agree that the probability of achieving and maintaining weight loss, even under the most ideal treatment circumstances, is very grim. Stunkard (1972) states: "most obese persons will not remain in treatment. Of those who do remain in treatment, most will not lose weight, and of those who do lose weight, most will regain it" (p. v).

When used, hypnosis is usually incorporated into a medical–behavioral modification paradigm (Kroger, 1970; Bolocofsky, Spinler, and Coulthard-Morris, 1985), but this is not at all necessary. Several theorists instead approach the problem from a cognitive–behavioral or psychodynamic perspective (H. Spiegel and D.

Spiegel, 1978; Fromm, 1987). Whatever the theoretical orientation, if the target symptom is eating behavior, the initial assessment must include specific content. First, it is important to gauge
the extent of the overweight problem. Patients who are less than
40 percent overweight (this constitutes 90 percent of patients
presenting with a desire to lose weight) are more likely to respond
to psychological intervention than are patients who are over 40
percent overweight. In the upper ranges of the latter case, surgical
procedures must be considered, in concert with supportive coun-
seling. Second, a thorough weight and diet history must be taken,
including the onset of the weight problem, past attempts to lose
weight, reasons for diet success or failure, relationship of weight
to major life-change events, and unusual responses to diet. Third,
the general psychological status of the patient must be evaluated;
Are there indications that weight is associated with depressive,
anxiety, sexual, or characterological symptomatology? With or
without serious psychopathology, we believe it is essential for the
clinician to fashion a thorough formulation of what food and
eating *means* for each patient. We find it helpful to remember
that people do not just eat. . . . they are fed, even when they are
alone. In other words, there is always an interpersonal quality to
our relationship with food, whether it involved soothing, abase-
ment, surrender, humiliation, shame, guilt, or disavowed passive–dependent yearnings. Without a sharp understanding of the
patient's unique experience of eating, resistance and therapeutic
misalliance may proceed unattended. Fourth, the patient's characteristic defenses must be assessed. This knowledge is then useful
in tailoring an hypnotic intervention to the patient's adaptive
strengths. Finally, it is probable that an initial assessment of hypnotic susceptibility is helpful in determining whether the planned
intervention should include hypnosis. As mentioned above, it is
not at all clear that medium to high hypnotizability is a prerequisite to treatment success for these disorders. What may be relevant
is the patient's overall reaction to hypnotic procedures: Does he
or she find it credible, comfortable, relaxing, hope inducing?

There is a wide variety of hypnotic procedures which can be
used to support weight loss. In almost all programs which use
hypnosis, self-hypnosis is actively encouraged to reinforce eating
behavior changes (see the end of chapter 4 for a description of

self-hypnosis training). The number of sessions ranges from 4 to 16 once-a-week sessions. Further, hypnosis is typically used in conjunction with a number of procedures which have been shown to be associated with successful weight loss (Levitt, 1993): keeping an eating diary, standardizing daily eating events (the where, when, and what of meals and snacks), slowing down of hand to mouth movements during a meal, significant periods of rest during a meal, and vividly and regularly imagining desired weight outcome and effective diet behaviors.

Specific hypnotic suggestions for treatment of obesity fall into three general categories: direct authoritarian suggestion, imagery suggestions, and ego enhancing suggestions. Of course most practitioners employ a combination of the above, according to patient need. All approaches teach self-hypnosis. Authoritarian approaches are championed by a number of clinicians including Crasilneck and Hall (1975) and H. Spiegel and D. Spiegel (1978). These procedures include such content as: "Everyday you will find that your craving for foods like (e.g., candy, sweets, etc.) will decrease. You will find it easy to avoid those foods and to maintain your diet. Every day it will become easier and easier. Whenever you feel a hunger pang you will say to yourself 'it will pass in just a minute'. . . . and it will. As your craving becomes less and less, soon there will simply be no craving. You can and will become slender and graceful. . . ." A very direct, cognitively based standard hypnotic protocol is used by H. Spiegel and D. Spiegel (1978) for weight reduction. In one to three sessions patients are hypnotized and instructed to recognize that while the food they eat supports their body functions, excess eating is damaging. Direct suggestions are given to concentrate on the concept of eating "like a gourmet": slowly, relishing the taste, color, and texture of the food. Emphasis is placed on eating less but enjoying it more. The Spiegels devote a great deal of time to restructuring the patient's approach to a balanced diet, experiencing this as self-respect rather than deprivation. Three key points are made throughout the procedure, and eventually incorporated into the self-hypnosis training: (1) "For my body, smoking is a poison" (or alternatively, "is damaging" or "disfiguring"); (2) "I need my body to live"; (3) "I owe my body this respect and protection."

Patients within 20 percent of their ideal weight seem to respond to this very brief and direct approach.

Another approach to suggestions for weight loss, is use of imagery, preferably generated by the patient before or during hypnosis. The range of images is practically limitless: The "red balloon" technique can be used with suggestions that the patient fill up the gondola of a helium balloon with all the cravings that trouble them most. They can then watch as the balloon and gondola float far out of sight. Age regression or progression can be used. If the patient was not overweight as a child age regression suggestions can help the patient focus on the somatic/kinesthetic sense of being at an acceptable weight. For example, "It's good to be back in junior high school. Look at yourself in the mirror. . . . how good you look, slender and just right for you. Now feel the sensation of health in your entire body. Your stomach is flat, your body is efficient, and you feel quite good. . . . ." In the case of age progression, the therapist encourages mastery and self-efficacy:

> In a little while I am going to count from 1 to 5. As I do you will move ahead in time. So that by the time I reach the count of 5 you will have progressed 12 months into the future. You will find yourself slim and graceful in the bathroom, feeling good. . . . 1, You are moving ahead in time, it's no longer March or April, but moving ahead; 2. . . . 3. . . . . and it's no longer June or July or even August. . . . you are moving ahead in time. . . . . . 4. . . . . September, October always moving ahead in time. At the next count it will be March (next year), and you will be at your ideal weight, near your scales in the bathroom. . . . . . 5.

The therapist can then follow the patient's associations or guide the patient to notice how slender and healthy he or she looks. Further, suggestions can be given to experience the joy, satisfaction, and relief of taking control of a problem that has been so distressingly unresponsive to previous effort. These robust feelings of self-efficacy (with their associated image) can then be incorporated into a self-hypnosis procedure.

Though rarely used in isolation, administering aversive hypnotic suggestions in regards to food can be helpful for some patients. These suggestions usually take one of two forms: imaging aversive food-related stimuli, imaging aversive consequences of overeating. An example of the former case is as follows:

> Right now I would like you to pay particular attention to your sense of smell, because as I am talking you notice a most repulsive, vile smell of greasy, fatty, corrupted food. It is so disgustingly repulsive that you feel your whole body responding. Your stomach is getting quite queasy. Feel your whole body rejecting this horrible smell of corruption and decay. [Inquire of the patient how he or she is experiencing these sensations. When the effect is as fully realized as can be expected, the therapist makes the following suggestion] Yes, it is really disgusting. . . . . let this sickening smell and feeling continue as you now picture [the type of food that is most problematic]. Look at this food, and feel the nausea. . . . . how utterly sickened you are right now. . . . the food *is* this smell, this unspeakably repulsive feeling. Whenever you encounter something that is not on your diet, you will immediately reexperience this disagreeable smell and feeling. This awful and disgusting smell and taste will arise whenever you have an urge to eat something not on your diet.

Imaging aversive consequences of overeating involves adapting hypnotic techniques to an implosive behavioral procedure. Prehypnotically patients are asked to describe their worse fears about overeating: Some patients report health concerns like diabetes, gout, hypertension, and heart disease. Others focus on appearance: a double or triple chin, gross flaps of excess fat, etc. During hypnosis then the therapist can suggest that the patient picture him- or herself eating and becoming increasingly and visibly engorged. These suggestions can be carried to the extreme. For instance:

> As you eat more and more food you can see your body filling up . . . and you can feel it too. Keep on eating. . . . . becoming engorged and bloated as the food immediately turns to fat. . . . . What do you see happening to your body now? [patient answers]. That's right, your eyes are sunken into a face which is now bloated with fat tissue. . . . your shirt is straining at the buttons as flabs of fat poke out between them. . . . . look at your legs. . . . . how thick and flabby they are. . . . . What's happening now? [patient answers]. Your entire vascular system is beginning to become more and more

clogged with all this food, your heart has to work so hard. . . . feel your body weighted down and burdened, strained by all this greasy, yellow adipose tissue . . . that's right, you can hardly even recognize yourself. . . . . . Whenever you experience an urge to eat something not on your diet, this image will return, helping you be mindful of what you want, and what you do not want, to become.

Finally, a third approach to suggestions for weight loss involves ego strengthening techniques. Here the therapist gives direct and general suggestions for well-being, relaxation, serenity, and calm. In some sense these suggestions, when incorporated into a self-hypnosis procedure, can operate (like food) as a self-soothing technique: a way in which the patient can gratify passive–dependent yearnings without compromising the weight-loss program, a source of emotional supply that does not directly involve food.

Hypnosis in Smoking Cessation Programs

There is an enormous health benefit for smokers who can successfully quit smoking. One out of four regular smokers dies of cancer, lung disease, heart disease, and pregnancy complications. As is the case with the use of hypnosis in weight control programs, hypnotic interventions for smoking cessation are commonly embedded in comprehensive treatment programs which may include aversive conditioning, pharmacology, nicotine replacement, education, group support, behavior modification, and role-playing. Because the treatment context in which hypnosis is incorporated varies so widely, and because the specific technique of hypnosis employed is often imprecisely defined, it is no surprise that research findings report a broad range of abstinence rates following treatment with hypnosis: Lynn et al. (1993) report a range from 4 to 90 percent abstinence across studies. Holroyd (1980) suggested in her review that there were four characteristics of smoking cessation programs using hypnosis that were associated with higher levels of abstinence: (1) Length of treatment: Single-session treatments may be less efficacious than multiple-session programs of at least four or five session). (2) Intense interpersonal interaction: the quality of the working alliance, and the perceived interest of the therapist supports better outcomes. (3) Individualized procedures: Hypnotic procedures that are not "canned," but instead are generated from thorough case formulation, increase the chance of abstinence. (4) Follow-up treatment such as telephone calls or "booster sessions."

Before we offer an example of a single session and a multiple session model of hypnotic intervention for smoking cessation, it is important to note the characteristics of almost all responsible interventions using hypnosis. In all these programs hypnosis, followed by training in self-hypnosis, is one of several ways in which the therapist encourages attitudes and behaviors which are associated with successful abstinence. These include enhanced control of behavior: Hypnosis, and especially self-hypnosis, is a potent communication that the patient can learn and hone a skill that will increase the ability to control their body, cravings, and behavior.

1. *Cognitive reframing.* Overideational patients sometimes respond well to hypnotic interventions which stress autonomy, and elimination of "negative self-talk." Hypnosis can provide constructive, "positive self-talk" which emphasizes strength and perseverance, and deflects unconscious yearnings for oral supply.

2. *Self-hypnosis as a self-soothing technique.* In almost all forms of hypnotic intervention some attempt is made to enable the patient to utilize self-hypnosis as a benign substitute for the self-soothing function of smoking. This is particularly relevant for patients who are predisposed to acknowledge the wish to be soothed.

3. *Abstinence, not tapering-off.* In most programs a target date is set for complete abstinence. Until then, the patient is learning and practicing skills that will enable him or her to remain abstinent. The smoking cessation research literature in general supports the notion that a "cold turkey" approach is superior to a gradual decrease in smoking frequency (Marlatt and Gordon, 1985).

4. *Identity as a nonsmoker.* All programs help the patient forge a new identity as a nonsmoker. This helps soften the natural tendency for nicotine addicted individuals to experience not

smoking as a deprivation. Hypnosis is employed in various ways to help patients image themselves doing things they could not do before, tasting foods in new ways, and experiencing their body more fully and joyfully.

5. *Inoculation against relapse.* Hypnosis can be employed to help the patient anticipate high-risk situations in which impulsive smoking may occur, and plan responses (both hypnotic and nonhypnotic) which will prevent relapse.

Example of a Single-Session Intervention for Smoking Cessation
The Spiegels developed (H. Spiegel and D. Spiegel, 1978) and refined (D. Spiegel, Frischholz, Fleiss, and H. Spiegel, 1993) a single-session intervention hypnotic approach to smoking cessation. It involves a direct attempt to impact cognitive structures which support the identity of becoming a nonsmoker. In content this approach is quite similar to the same authors' approach to weight reduction. The patient is hypnotized and presented with three self-statements: (1) For my body smoking is a poison; (2) I need my body to live; (3) I owe my body this respect and attention. Each statement is elaborated upon in great detail, and repeated many times during the one-hour session. During hypnosis patients are instructed to use self-hypnosis every one or two hours in the day, or whenever they have an urge to smoke. Throughout, the emphasis is on restructuring the smoking problem by concentrating on an affirmation experience (protecting the body) rather than fighting an urge. A recent well-designed study (D. Spiegel et al., 1993) reported a modest 23 percent abstinence rate at two-year follow-up.

An Example of a Five-Session Hypnotic Intervention for Smoking Cessation
We favor a five- or six-session approach which allows us to capitalize on some of Holroyd's (1980) previously cited observations concerning individualized treatment and the importance of the therapeutic alliance. A typical treatment protocol is as follows:

Session 1. An initial intake and interview is carried out during which special attention is given to smoking history, previous attempts at quitting, health factors, other psychological difficulties (especially affective disorder), current life problems, motivation for becoming a nonsmoker, and typical defense style. In this same session a rationale for the treatment is presented. The patient and therapist agree on a target date for quitting, which will also be the fifth session. Patients are encouraged to tell loved ones about their intent to quit, along with the target date. The patient is instructed to smoke at whatever pace he or she wants until that day. It is explained to the patient that on the following session he or she will be administered an hypnotic procedure which will help the therapist in treatment planning. Further, the patient is either referred to a physician or asked to contact his or her own physician for pharmacological support (nicotine replacement or patches). Of course these pharmacological interventions will not be implemented until the target date.

Session 2. The patient is briefly asked about whether the appropriate steps have been taken in preparation for the target date. Sometimes the patient will note spontaneous changes in smoking behavior during the preceding week. These are noted carefully. About half an hour is devoted to the initial hypnosis session, which is conducted according to our description in chapter 4. The patient's responsiveness is noted, and the patient is encouraged to elaborate on what the experience was like for him or her. The patient is reminded that the next session will begin the work on helping him or her to become a nonsmoker.

Session 3. The patient is once again hypnotized. During this phase of the work the therapist attempts to uncover more information about the patient's conscious and unconscious motivation. Carefully contained uncovering techniques can be used here such as the hypnotic dream ("in a moment you will have a dream about what smoking means . . . you may dream directly about smoking, or you may dream about something that does not seem outwardly to be related to smoking, but may very well be. . . .). The patient is further helped to deepen the hypnotic state via deepening techniques described previously in this book. Near the end of the session the patient is instructed that he or she will always be able to enter hypnosis very rapidly in the therapist's office by merely closing his or her eyes and listening to the therapist count from 1 to 5. At the count of 5 the patient is told that he or she will be comfortably hypnotized.

Session 4. The aim of this session is twofold. First some further exploration is conducted during hypnosis in service of fashioning a compelling experience. Sometimes the emergent content involves images associated with health, appearance, parental figures, athletic prowess, self-efficacy, deep contentment. For other patients the suggestions are of a more cognitive nature: H. Spiegel's (1978) three-statement, rational reminders that smoking is (after all) dirty, hearing the word *stop* following an urge, etc. Whatever material emerges is then incorporated into the instructions for self-hypnosis. The patient practices self-hypnosis in the consulting room, and is told to practice it at least twice a day for the next week. The patient is reminded that the next session is the target date. All smoking paraphernalia should be out of the house, and the last cigarette will have been smoked before the next session.

Session 5 (the target date). The patient is asked about the self-hypnosis during the week. Self-hypnosis is again carried out in the consulting room, with the therapist joining in only when the patient indicates that he or she is reasonably comfortable and hypnotized. The therapist elaborates further on the smoking cessation images, words, and metaphors. This can be a time to strengthen and consolidate the patient's intent by offering ego supportive suggestions in combination with age progression. After hypnosis the patient is reminded to use any pharmacological aides that have been arranged. A midweek follow-up telephone call is scheduled for the patient to report smoking status. Usually a sixth session is scheduled.

Session 6 (follow-up). The patient updates the therapist on events since the phone call. Any set-backs are discussed and addressed, not as failures, but as opportunities to "fine-tune" the patient's skills. Hypnosis is again employed to support continued abstinence.

Though definitive empirical evidence is not yet available, among well-designed research studies, multiple session approaches to smoking cessation are associated with higher abstinence rates (33 to 60%) than are single-session approaches (Cornwell, Burrows, and McMurray, 1981; Hyman, Stanley, Burrows, and Horne, 1986).

HYPNOSIS IN THE TREATMENT OF
EATING DISORDERS

When used in the treatment of eating disorders hypnosis is typically introduced as part of a multifaceted intervention based on the proposition that the eating disorder had become a metaphor to symbolize a variety of intrapsychic and interpersonal struggles. Many of the struggles center around self-pathology, control, and power conflicts, and difficulties with the adequate differentiation and integration of a cohesive sense of mature identity. These structural and dynamic difficulties operate with differing valences for different patients. Those who present with anorexia nervosa are a relatively heterogeneous group. Therefore, different aspects of the treatment approach are emphasized more or less with different patients depending on their individual needs and specific treatment responses. This treatment approach is explicated in Baker and Nash (1987).

1. *Hypnosis is introduced to patients as a means for gaining enhanced self-control associated with various opportunities for increased security and mastery.* It is not introduced as an opportunity to gain control over eating habits or to restore patients' weight. Most patients are more responsive to this specific conscious introduction of hypnosis as an adjunct to the therapeutic regimen because they are ambivalent about mutually participating in activities designed to alter their eating habits or increase their weight level. Most of the patients readily verbalize feelings of being anxious, apprehensive, and out of control, and are generally willing to participate reciprocally in a program designed to facilitate an increased sense of potency and security.

2. *Structured and permissive induction techniques are used with anorexic patients.* A structured rather than purely permissive induction is indicated to help modulate the regressive experiences that often accompany the trance and that may be frightening or even retraumatizing for many anorexic patients. This permissive approach helps to avoid control struggles and associated resistance around power dynamics and competition. Most patients respond well to an induction that combines relaxation and fantasy, which is also useful for early instruction in self-hypnosis.

3. *Early applications of hypnosis are specifically designed to enhance the patients' sense of personal power, to increase their capacity for autonomous functioning, to support the working alliance, and to provide a generalized sense of ego support leading to increased mastery and positive expectations for behavioral success.* For this reason, instruction in self-hypnosis is introduced early in the treatment, and patients are taught to use self-hypnotic strategies to manage feelings of anxiety or insecurity between sessions. Hypnosis is also used for tension reduction, with specific suggestions being made to help patients to become increasingly aware of their generalized tension level and to learn to manage this through a variety of relaxation strategies. Direct and indirect suggestions are used to provide the patients with a sense of comfort, thereby supporting the ego's emerging capacity for mastery. Directed and structured imagery and fantasies are often useful in indirectly suggesting to patients improved functioning and to support most positive attitudes regarding capacities for self-control and adaptation.

4. *Once patients learn to use self-hypnosis for relaxation and once hypnotic suggestions and imagery have been established to stabilize and support the working alliance between the therapist and the patient, hypnotherapeutic interventions are directed more specifically at a number of arenas of difficulty that are more directly associated with core pathological features of anorexia nervosa.* Many patients have a good deal of difficulty with accurately perceiving sensory stimulation from their bodies. For this reason, many of them are unaware of sensory cues typically associated with physiological functioning. For some patients who present with more severe forms of preoedipal structural pathology, this defect appears to be related to a more generalized problem with boundary management and maintenance. They defensively avoid awareness of sensory stimulation because this evokes insecurity and anxiety associated at a primitive level with a lack of adequate boundary differentiation and integration. For many of these more borderline-level patients, attention to physical functioning begins to arouse concerns about the deterioration of body boundaries and merger with the external environment. For these patients, sensory focusing is preceded by general work on boundary support and management. Both guided imagery and specific sensory exercises are used during

hypnosis to support the integrity of boundaries and to communicate through indirect and direct suggestions that body and ego boundaries are constant and dependable.

In addition, many patients have learned to defensively dissociate body and body-related experiences from the conscious perception of self and their intellectualized phenomenological experience of the world. The patients often describe either directly or symbolically, a sense of a split between their "body selves" and their "mind or spiritual selves." When this is the case, the hypnotherapeutic work also needs to address the reintegration of these various phenomenological arenas. Imagery and suggestion are used to reestablish a sense of communication between the mind and the body that cannot be interrupted by anxiety. When anxiety begins to intrude on this work, suggestions for calm and relaxation, as well as fantasy designed to reestablish a soothing and comfortable environment, are interspersed with work directed at reintegration until patients are able to maintain a sense of comfort and continuing security while attempting to reconnect physical and mental representations of self and others.

This approach relies on the therapeutic action of a relaxation-based desensitization paradigm. When this work is successful or for patients who are less severely disturbed and therefore not in need of attention to boundaries and unmodulated dissociative experiences, the hypnotherapeutic work directly supports patients' improved awareness of their body-based sensory phenomenology. They are taught during hypnosis to more accurately label and attend to muscle tension and related skeletal and visceral sensations. This is related to their experiences of hunger as well as to the careful differentiation of a variety of affective experiences. Patients are encouraged in the trance to recapture the affect associated with being in a variety of different fantasized situations and to learn to deal with this emotional experience adaptively.

Frequently, patients report that they begin to find themselves unable to eat or to experience hunger situations that are emotionally charged (i.e., with anger and anxiety). These situations are revivified in the trance, and patients are taught to differentially recognize their affective responses to these situations and to reduce the associated tension. Patients then manage these feelings through more adaptive coping strategies rather than via the restriction of food intake, withdrawal, or dissociation accompanied by distortions in body experience and body image. This pattern of affective differentiation and abreaction is often accompanied by a generalized decrease in tension and improvement in the symptoms associated with distorted eating behaviors and body image.

5. *Body image distortions are also addressed more directly in hypnotherapy.* Patients are asked to represent their conscious and preconscious body images in hypnosis by projecting them onto screens or drawing them on blackboards. Age regression techniques are used to uncover the roots of these distortions in malevolent interactions with family members and the associated development of distorted self and object representations. We have found that the distortions are often related to split-off aspects of the self representation that cannot be integrated into a conscious sense of self because they evoke a negative sense of vulnerability and associated negative affect. Once the roots of these distortions have been explicated and explored, interpretative work can be done regarding them in the trance and during nontrance verbal, insight-oriented psychotherapy sessions.

We use directed imagery and fantasy in hypnosis to confront these distortions, to help patients to become increasingly aware of them, and to suggest their amelioration. For instance, distortions in body image drawn on an imagery blackboard during the trance can be corrected by erasing and redrawing the aspects of the image of the physical self that are particularly distorted. Frequently, patients become anxious and uncomfortable, but relaxation is introduced to restore a sense of comfort and calm. When this is accomplished, patients can then return to working on correcting distortions in the represented self-image without the intrusion of undue anxiety.

It appears that this work results in some generalization of an improved self-image external to the trance. However, more important, patients seem to be able to learn to think about their physical self and to begin to explore their representations of their body without the same degree of defensiveness and anxiety that characterized attempts at this work prior to the specific use of hypnotic imagery and exploration. Age progression is used to suggest the eventual integration of an adequate and reality-based self representation and the incorporation of this integrated, accurate, physical representation into the conscious sense of self. This is represented through progressive physical changes or, more symbolically, through natural images of differentiation, integration, and growth, structured through evolving hypnotic fantasy.

6. *This work on distortions in body image and the correction of these is closely associated with a more generalized consideration of the integration of an appropriate and mature sense of personal identity.* Because many anorexic patients experience considerable conflicts around individuation and independence because of their prolonged enmeshment in their families, severe generalized distortions in identity maturation are frequently seen. These are explored in hypnosis and corrected through the use of direct or indirect suggestions and through the use of specific images and fantasies. It is often useful to suggest specific hypnotically induced dreams during the trance to help clarify, for the therapist and the patient, the conflicts that are associated with defects in identity integration. Once these had been clarified, they are further explored in regular psychotherapy sessions and addressed via hypnotic imagery.

7. *Hypnotic work is also used to explore the relation between negative affect expression and distorted attitudes toward eating food, and unusual eating behaviors.* The relation between these eating behaviors and their role in controlling or avoiding unacceptable affective experiences are established and connected during the trance through suggestion and imagery. Once this has been done, the unacceptable affect was ventilated and abreacted, resulting in an emerging sense of mastery over those feelings. Dreams and imagery are often useful for this, as are more direct hypnotic abreaction techniques.

8. *As aspects of body imagery and general identity integration were corrected, patients' general capacity for mastery was enhanced.* Work in hypnosis is used to further address concerns related to separation, individuation, integration, and adaptation. Rehearsal in fantasy, age progression, and guided imagery are used to provide patients with a more positive sense of their ability to tolerate the affect associated with maturation and to deal with their increasing stability and individuated integrated identity.

The use of directed hypnotic experience, imagery, and fantasy, as well as specific suggestions, does not necessarily correct defects in patients' internal representational world, nor does it resolve all aspects of the dynamic conflicts seen in patients who present with anorexia nervosa. However, it does provide an opportunity to address some of the issues that interfere with successful, traditional psychotherapeutic work with these patients, particularly the defensive use of denial and dissociation, which are central to distortions in body image and general self-concept. Until these have been addressed, successful psychotherapeutic work with these patients is significantly compromised.

Our work suggests that this sort of hypnotherapeutic approach, when used in conjunction with insight-oriented individual and group therapy and occasional conjoint sessions with families (when the patients are still living at home), is a successful treatment approach. Patients' experiential participation, with an emerging sense of mastery and self-control, avoids many of the struggles that emerge around control issues when patients project parental transferences onto their therapist and attempt to maintain their distorted eating behaviors in an effort to maintain some sense of personal control through manipulating the environment.

This hypnotherapeutic paradigm provides a more direct avenue for addressing the problems in identity formation that are so frequently encountered with patients with anorexia nervosa. More than simply providing an opportunity for learning adaptive behaviors or for exploring and interpreting the structural and dynamic etiologies of core conflicts, the hypnotherapeutic approach described engages patients experientially in examining, exploring, modulating, and correcting these areas of difficulty. This experimentally based use of hypnosis appears to be particularly important in dealing with arenas of structural defect and is also useful in circumventing the extreme defensive denial and control struggles that form the basis for resistance to both behavioral and psychodynamic approaches to psychotherapeutic intervention. For this reason, it appears to augment the patients' ability to use psychotherapy and benefit from treatment in a fashion that is generalized and maintained at a significant level of success.

TREATMENT OF
PSYCHOPHYSIOLOGICAL DISORDERS

When patients present with somatic symptoms which persist
in the absence of demonstrable pathophysiology, the diagnosis
of somatization disorder must be considered. Estimates are that
over 50 percent of patients visiting a primary care physician are
somatizers (Barsky and Klerman, 1983), but most somatizers do
not display gross forms of psychopathology (Jencks, 1985). The
difficulty appears to be systemic, constitutional, and stylistic. Hypnosis has been used adjunctively to support treatment of a host
of psychophysiological disorders including hypertension, upper
and lower gastrointestinal disorders, dermatological disorders,
asthma, seasonal allergies, hiccups, urinary retention, extensive
hemorrhaging, and some aspects of chronic diseases. It is abundantly clear now that hypnosis alone can actually have a mutative
effect on physiological processes once thought to be entirely inde-
pendent of conscious control. And at least for some disorders,
the extent of treatment success is dependent on the patient's
general hypnotizability—a fairly certain indication that it is the
specific effect of suggestion (not some nonspecific aspect of treatment) that accounts for the change. For example, there is no
simple intuitive explanation for why hypnotic suggestions for the
resolution of disabling skin lesions should be effective, especially
when symptom relief is not systemic, but specific to the side of
the body for which the curative suggestions were given (Mason,
1955). Nor is it at all clear why and how hypnosis impacts allergic
response or asthma, yet it does, sometimes dramatically so (Collison, 1978). Indeed one of the enduring conundrums for scientific
hypnosis is to explain the mechanisms for this action. We have
chosen two physiological processes which figure prominently in
general medical and mental health practice, and which have been
shown empirically to be responsive to hypnotic intervention: skin
disorders and gastrointestinal disorders. Below we discuss conceptual and technical considerations for incorporating hypnosis into
a comprehensive treatment of these disorders. The same principles and similar techniques apply to hypnotic treatment of other
psychophysiological disorders noted above.

SKIN DISORDERS

There is a fairly extensive research and clinical literature on hypnotic interventions for alleviation of skin disorders (DuBreuil and Spanos, 1993). One of the earliest and most astonishing clinical reports was presented in detail in the mid-1950s by Mason (1955): A boy suffering from a debilitating congenital case of ichthyosiform erythrodermis of Brocq (or "fish skin disease") was rendered bed-ridden and chronically infected by severe lesions covering over 90 percent of his body. The lesions were nonresponsive to various medical and surgical treatments. Mason carefully documented a systematic intervention with hypnosis. What is particularly fascinating about this case is that Mason gave hypnotic suggestions for symptom resolution "one portion of the body at a time" (e.g., first there was a suggestion for symptoms to clear on one arm. This was followed by a period of evaluation to note any effect; then another limb would be addressed by an intervention etc.). What Mason observed was an orderly site-specific resolution of symptoms which lawfully followed the suggestions given. Overall the treatment was a dramatic success, enabling the boy to be essentially symptom-free.

But there is also ample evidence that hypnosis can impact a number of far more common dermatological disorders such as psoriasis (Frankel and Misch, 1973), genital herpes (Longo, Clum, and Yaeger, 1988), and viral warts (Spanos, Stenstrom, and Johnston, 1988; Spanos, Williams, and Gwynn, 1990). If we generalize from the area most thoroughly researched (that of warts), there appear to be several conclusions from clinical research: First, hypnotic suggestions produce wart removal that cannot be explained by spontaneous remission; second, the effect of hypnotic intervention is different from and superior to placebo response; third, site-specific response to suggestion is sometimes, but not always, obtained.

Perhaps as in no other disorder discussed in this book, hypnotic intervention for skin disorders is direct, authoritarian, and brief—the actual content of the suggestion (e.g., suggesting warmth versus coolness; increased blood flow versus decreased blood flow; relaxing imagery versus direct demand for resolution) seems irrelevant. Typically treatment duration is six weeks, with early training in self-hynosis and daily use of self-hypnosis by the patient between sessions. What follows are a number of protocols used by prominent researchers and clinicians in the field.

> Notice that the skin on and around the (lesion) on your hand is beginning to feel warm and a little tingly. The skin around the lesion on your hand is beginning to tingle. Notice the sensations around the (lesion). You can feel the tingling, prickling sensation around the (lesions) on your hand, you know that this sensation will cause the (lesions) on your hand to disappear. . . . As you feel these sensations you can see the (lesions) on your hand shrinking in size and dissolving away, shrinking in size and dissolving [Spanos et al., 1988, p. 628].

> Nothing is beyond the power of the unconscious mind and these warts are going to leave completely and your skin will be void of them. . . . . the area of warts now begins to feel very cool. . . . cool. . . . slightly cold. . . . . As you feel this, nod your head. . . . . good. . . . Think the thought as I continue talking. . . . the area is cool. . . . . . The area is cool, and the warts will leave my body because of the power of my mind over my body. . . . These warts are going to leave. . . . We have demonstrated the control of your mind over your body, and these warts will be gone very shortly [Crasilneck and Hall, 1990, p. 224].

> The water in one of the ponds is only for drinking and it has very special properties that allow your anti-viral and immune system to work at its best, to maintain and support your healing process so that you can remain free from illness and the vaginal warts. . . . .

> If any warts ever appear, your body will automatically search and find them, and will activate your anti-viral mechanism in your brain, along with decreasing the blood supply to any wart, any-where on your body. Lastly you will permit yourself to feel the warmth of the sun and its heat in any area where the warts may appear and the warmth of the sun will dry out immediately [Stoler, 1990, pp. 225].

While the content of these suggestions is indeed eclectic, some common elements of treatment programs include: initial

hypnosis and training sessions, daily self-hypnosis, direct suggestion of resolution, suggested changes in skin sensation or imagery,
posthypnotic suggestion for sensation change, and follow-up.

GASTROINTESTINAL DISORDERS

Gastrointestinal disorders are often roughly categorized into
two classes: upper GI disorders (e.g., esophageal spasm, reflux
esophagitis, and peptic ulcer disease [PUD]) and lower GI disorders (irritable bowel syndrome and inflammatory bowel disease).
Of these two broad classes of GI disorders, lower tract disorders
seem most responsive to suggestive techniques. Interestingly, patients with irritable bowel syndrome in particular display a high
incidence of neuroticism, with depression and anxiety (both generalized and phobic) being quite prominent. For these reasons
we will focus this section on how hypnosis can be incorporated
into medical treatment of patients with irritable bowel syndrome
and inflammatory bowel disease. But, given the prevalence of
peptic ulcer disease, it is important to make some note of how
hypnosis might be used in this regard.

Far more common forms of psychosocial intervention for
peptic ulcer disease (PUD) are electrogastrogram (EGG) biofeedback, relaxation training, along with medical regimes of diet and
medication. Though systematic clinical studies are lacking, it appears that whatever effect hypnosis may have on peptic ulcer disease, it is mediated not by the hypnosis per se, but by relaxation
itself. While patients can learn voluntary control over gastric muscle activity (Walker, 1983) and gastric secretion (Welgan, 1974)
via nonhypnotic EGG biofeedback, there is only modest evidence
that hypnotic suggestions enable patients to gain control over
these functions (see Colgan, Faragher, and Whorwell, 1988; Klein
and Spiegel, 1989). Nor, for that matter, is it at all clear that
gaining control over these functions results in clinical improvement in the first place. Thus, if hypnosis is to be used at all in
the treatment of PUD, it would be to support general relaxation,
and encourage compliance with diet and medication regimes.

The picture is quite different for irritable bowl syndrome
(IBS) and inflammatory bowel disease (IBD). Both diseases can

involve abdominal distention, rectal bleeding, mucus in the stool, frequent bowel movements, nausea, and pain. Irritable bowel syndrome also involves serious inflammation of the bowel and ulceration. Some serious psychological difficulties attend both these disorders, though it is unclear whether the psychological distress is secondary to the strain of having a chronic disease, or causal. But two points do seem quite certain: For over 40 percent of these patients emotional stress and associated high levels of catecholamines precede the onset of acute episodes; and second, hypnotic interventions can significantly reduce abdominal pain, distention, and disturbance in bowel habit, especially for those patients who are younger than 50, who present with fairly "classical" IBS (Whorwell, Prior, and Colgan, 1987).

Technique can be guided by three characteristics of IBS and IBD patients. First, these patients have very little capacity to accurately perceive sensation and change in the gut in part because untoward anxiety in response to triggering situations inteferes with interoceptive awareness. Thus hypnotic suggestions can be given that enhance interoceptive awareness by directing attention to visceral cues in the context of safety and support. The goal is to familiarize the patient with bowel sensations and thereby minimize the chance of gross misperception. For example, after the usual initial experience with hypnosis, and following suggestions for relaxation and support, the therapist might suggest: "Now pay very close attention to your lower abdomen . . . every sensation you are having right now. . . . . you are relaxed, comfortable, and hypnotized, and you are able in this state to feel every sensation. . . . what is there and what is not there. . . . . what is your bowels and what is not. . . . . tell me what you feel right now. . . . ." Following some elaboration of this work, the therapist can begin to offer metaphors of automatic regulation, for instance: "You are becoming better and better able to know what your gut is doing. . . . better able to distinguish what has to do with your bowel and what does not. . . . You will become increasingly able to just relax and experience the security that your bowel will take care of itself. . . . You trust your body and its sensation. . . . your body will resume its normal functioning . . . like a clock. . . . effortless and easy regulation. . . ."

Second, these patients can sometimes become quite passively demoralized by a body which seems to be out of control. Here, hypnotic technique resembles that applied in cases of pain management, in that IBS and IBD patients who are moderately to highly hypnotizable can be encouraged to hypnoticaly manipulate the sensations they are experiencing in their gut. The emphasis here is not automaticity (as above), but mastery. The therapist exploits the patient's hypnotic ability to transform sensation thereby convincing the patient that control over physical processes is possible. This can be done in a number of ways; for example:

> In a moment I am going to count from 1 to 5, and as I do your left hand will become quite numb. . . . . [the therapist gives standard suggestions for glove anesthesia. When the anesthesia appears to be complete the therapist proceeds.] Now in a moment I am going to reach over and pinch your completely numb hand. . . . you will feel no discomfit. . . . you may feel a kind of pressure. . . . or you may feel nothing at all. . . . . here I go, I am pinching your hand right now [therapist pinches hand with some vigor]. There, did you feel anything? [answer]. . . . Now I would like you to take your hand and place it on your lower abdomen where you sometimes feel distress. You will note that the numbness that you have established in your hand will spread into your abdomen, so that your abdomen begins to feel like your hand. . . . . numb, comfortable. . . . ." Suggestions for warmth, coolness, tingling, and abiding immobility can also be used. These suggestions can be paired with imagery of the gut, slowing down and becoming quiescent.

Finally, these patients sometimes become so overreactive to conditioned triggering situations (e.g., being in a car on the interstate with no bathroom nearby) that the physiological concomitants of fear actually induce bowel activity. Here a desensitization approach can be taken, with or without hypnosis. Patients construct a hierarchy of increasingly distressing triggering situations. Then, during deep hypnotic relaxation they are asked to imagine a triggering situation while nonetheless remaining profoundly relaxed. Slowly and carefully moving up the hierarchy over several sessions deconditions the autonomic response and affords the patient an opportunity to fashion an emergent sense of self-efficacy.

Though the mechanisms are still not fully understood, hypnosis can expedite symptomatic relief with disorders of pain, habit, and disrupted physiology. We are emphatic that it is not necessary for psychoanalytically oriented therapists to abandon the principles of psychoanalytic metapsychology and comprehensive case formulation when addressing these disorders which are so often construed by others as merely products of "faulty learning." On the contrary, it is the conceptual richness of analytic theory which enables informed clinicians to tailor hypnotic interventions to the unique dynamic, thematic, and characterological status of each patient. In this chapter we have only touched on some of the possible applications of hypnosis in medicine and psychiatry. In so doing we have passed over a clinical hypnosis literature which also includes applications in dentistry, surgery, oncology, autoimmune disease, opthalmological disease, sleep disorders, obstetrics, sexual dysfunction, and childhood disorders. For further description of how hypnosis can be used with health-related problems we recommend the following books: Rhue, Lynn, and Kirsch (1993) *The Handbook of Clinical Hypnosis*; Brown and Fromm (1987) *Hypnosis and Behavioral Medicine*; J. R. Hilgard and LeBaron (1984) *Hypnotherapy of Pain in Children with Cancer*.

6

The Four Classic

Psychoanalytic Techniques

and Their Uses and

Extensions in

Hypnoanalysis

There are four classic psychoanalytic techniques:

1. Free Association
2. Transference Analysis
3. Interpretation of Resistances and Other Defenses
4. Dream Interpretation

All of these techniques are employed also in hypnoanalysis. Some are used more, some less frequently than they are when the patient is on the couch in the waking state; and still others are extended in hypnosis in ways which are characteristic for hypnosis and made possible only by the hypnotic state.

FREE ASSOCIATION AND IMAGERY

Breuer's and Freud's early (1883–1885), and perhaps most important patient, Anna O (Bertha Pappenheim, who later became the first social worker in Germany), called psychoanalysis the "talking cure," and indeed it is. Free association is its most basic tool.

Free association can be used, and sometimes is used with the hypnotized patient, in the same way in which it is employed with waking patients in psychoanalysis or in psychodynamically oriented psychotherapy. However, in hypnosis, free association most frequently appears in the form of imagery. A string of images, usually visual images, may appear before the patient's eyes. In nonvisual patients they may be auditory, tactile, or olfactory images such as the smell of roses or garbage dumps. Some images, at first glance, may seem unrelated to each other and unrelated to what the patient has just said. As in verbal free association the unconscious connections should be uncovered in the interpretive process. The reason for imagery appearing in trance much more frequently than in the waking state is that hypnosis is an altered state of consciousness in which the patient's thinking is much more in primary process terms. And the language of primary process is visual, while that of secondary process is verbal.

TRANSFERENCE ANALYSIS

In hypnotherapy and hypnoanalysis tranferences develop faster and usually are at least as intense as in psychoanalysis. This is so because hypnosis tends to activate the unconscious object representations and bring them into focus more rapidly than traditional approaches. In addition, conflicts and repressed affects that are associated with these internalized object representations, come into awareness. These phenomena occur because the patient in trance is in closer contact with his or her unconscious than is the case during the waking state.

NEUROTIC TRANSFERENCES

Frequently patients come to us with the hope that hypnotherapists can look straight through them and solve all of their problems. Partially this attitude is due to the mystique and the sensationalism that have surrounded hypnosis from the time of the ancient tribal shamans until the middle of the twentieth century when we, the scientific researchers in hypnosis, started to fight the sensationalism and to dispel the mystique that surrounded hypnosis. Hypnosis is and can be explained as a perfectly natural phenomenon. Partly, the wish for an omniscient healer is also due to the fact that patients often come to the hypnotherapist only after having tried many other therapies unsuccessfully. They are desperate, and think of hypnosis with its nimbus of mystique as a last hope. Third and most important, it represents a parent transference, that of the small child, the 2- or 3-year-old who believes that his or her parents are omnipotent and omniscient, and that they can fulfill immediately every wish of the child's or solve every problem that causes emotional pain and suffering.

When faced with such a patient the senior author invariably will say: "Look here, I am not God. Nor even a relative of His." This usually leads to an insightful laugh on the patient's part and she then can explain to the patient that in hypnosis, just as in psychoanalysis or in any other psychotherapy, the patient must do his part, too: collaborate with the therapist, and find the solutions that are just right for him. The therapist can do no more than facilitate this process.

Besides the omniscient parent transference, all the other types of parent and sibling transferences well known to psychoanalysts can and do develop in patients in hypnoanalysis. They can be interpreted in trance in the same way as in psychoanalysis. But most hypnoanalysts nowadays do not use transference analysis as the central organizing principle in therapy. With neurotic patients they put somewhat less emphasis on transference analysis than do orthodox psychoanalysts. Hypnosis is more commonly employed to support the problem-focused aims characteristic of psychoanalytically oriented brief psychotherapy, with special emphasis on integration, coping, and mastery.

DEFENSES AND RESISTANCES

By tactful wording and careful timing of his suggestions, the hypnotherapist can often resolve resistances.

The hypnoanalyst must always be aware of the fact that defenses are protective mechanisms the patient has erected and is maintaining in order to protect himself from becoming aware of emotional pain he has suffered. Because hypnosis is a regression in the service of the ego (Gill and Brenman, 1959; Fromm, Oberlander, and Gruenewald, 1970; Fromm, 1977, 1979; Fromm and Nash, 1992), defenses are attenuated in trance relative to the waking state. Not infrequently patients become aware in trance of material that in the waking state is below the threshold of conscious awareness. It has been relegated to the unconscious, below the repression barrier. The more deeply hypnotized they are, the more likely this is to happen. The fact that not infrequently a patient can recall traumatic events he or she cannot remember in the waking state demonstrates this. It happened to Freud (Breuer and Freud, 1893–1895) whose hysterical patients told him in trance about incestuous experiences they had had in early childhood. But when he woke them up, they vigorously denied ever having had the experiences about which they had just told him in trance. In part, this led Freud to infer that these patient reports were fantasies, oedipal fantasies (Freud, 1900, 1905a,c) rather than fact.

DEALING WITH RESISTANCE AND OTHER DEFENSES

In psychoanalysis, defenses and resistances are most frequently expressed by coming too late to the hour, blocking, consciously withholding material, or filling up the hour with innocuous small talk in order to avoid getting to the real problem. In hypnoanalysis the most common forms of resistance are avoidance or refusal to go into trance, not allowing oneself to "let go," lightening the trance, blocking on imagery, or producing imagery that symbolizes resistance (such as an impenetrable wall rising up that prevents the patient from seeing anything beyond that wall; or a heavy curtain falling down, also preventing further uncovering). If this happens, the therapist has a number of choices: She or he can either interpret the resistance as such, or divert the patient's attention temporarily to something else that is less conflictual. After a while the hypnoanalyst brings the patient back to the original topic in the hope that now he or she will be ready to face it. The hypnotherapist can also suggest then that as the patient has had a restful, fortifying time, she or he will be ready to let the wall crumble so that progress can be made. Or, perhaps the analyst can suggest that the patient can now drill a little hole into that wall and put his eye to the hole to look at the landscape beyond, while at the same time he is protected from any harm by the strength of the wall. As dissociation is an easy, naturally occurring mechanism in hypnosis, the hypnotherapist may also suggest that the patient really has two parts within himself, one that is afraid and resists further uncovering, while the other, the more mature and stronger part, is curious and would like to find out more about the conflict. The frightened part can sit "over there" in a corner surrounded by a safety bubble, while the other, the stronger, more mature part of the ego forges ahead in order to find out more about how the patient can solve the problem that is frightening the weaker part.

However, let it be said that one of the great dangers the beginning therapist faces when using hypnosis, is that he or she might too quickly pierce a defense, when the patient is not ready to do so. As the patient in hypnosis is so much closer to his unconscious than in the waking state, he may, for instance, produce a drawing, or the dissociated hand may make a drawing, that clearly expresses a forgotten memory. The therapist then may think the patient is ready for major interpretation, while actually he or she is not. In a case of severe repressed trauma, a patient dissociated her writing hand in trance which then rapidly drew a sharply detailed depiction of a small child being sexually violated. To interpret the drawing to her at this point would have been a serious mistake; she would have fragmented. The patient was not, at that time, ready to face this stark trauma in the waking state. So the hypnotherapist had to wait several months until the ego strength of the patient had improved so much that she could become aware of the trauma, first in hypnosis and much later in the waking state. In psychoanalysis, an interpretation made too early will usually roll off the patient's back like rainwater rolls off the back of a duck. In the hypnotic state, an interpretation made too early may more often "soak in," deeply traumatizing the patient. The hypnoanalyst must have genuine respect for the protective function of defenses, particularly in cases in which severe traumas have occurred in a patient's life.

Because we cannot always know whether a patient is ready to deal in a waking state with memories and affects that have been uncovered in the hypnotic state, the hypnoanalyst should routinely say to the patient before he wakes him up: "You will be able to bring up with you into the waking state as much of what you have experienced in trance now as you know deep inside of yourself you can face in the waking state." That encourages the patient to bring up the uncovered material, and at the same time gives him full permission to keep some or all of it repressed, if it upsets his emotional balance too much and he is not ready for it yet. The decision is left up to the patient's unconscious.

HYPNOTIC PRODUCTION AND
UTILIZATION OF DREAMS

In the areas of producing and remembering dreams, hypnoanalysis as a technique has some advantages over psychoanalysis. Laboratory research on rapid eye movements (REM) and dreams (Dement and Kleitman, 1957) has shown that the human being dreams four to six times every night. How many people remember four to six dreams every morning, or even any morning? Many dreams are not remembered because, regardless of whether they are conflictful dreams or not, they have a tendency to fade from memory with the passage of time. Thus dreams occurring during the early part of the night are rarely remembered. However, sleep laboratory research has also demonstrated that dreams are almost always remembered when the dreamer is woken up right after the cessation of REMs, which indicates that dreaming has stopped. The sleep lab researchers' work has been done under normal, nocturnal sleeping conditions in the laboratory. Much the same can be done in hypnosis with hypnotic dreams, except for the fact that if the patient is in light trance, the dream will have the qualities of a non-REM (NREM) or daydream only. Non-REM and daydreams lie on the primary process/secondary process continuum quite close to the secondary process end; nocturnal dreams lie close to the primary process end. Hypnotic dreams appear to involve more primary process than daydreams, but less than night dreams.

Figure 6.1

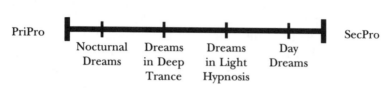

PriPro ⊢———┼———————┼———————┼———————┼———┤ SecPro

Nocturnal	Dreams	Dreams	Day
Dreams	in Deep	in Light	Dreams
	Trance	Hypnosis	

A number of patients come to the psychoanalyst insisting that they do not dream at all, or reporting that they cannot remember their dreams after awakening. Some come to their psychoanalytic hour saying that they know they had one or two "important" dreams during a preceding night, but cannot remember them. Or they can remember only minor fragments of the dream. What is the psychoanalyst going to do? He can interpret the resistance, but he cannot interpret a dream the patient cannot tell him. Hypnosis affords the therapist five different options for recalling, producing, and interpretively utilizing dreams as a vehicle toward therapeutic progress.

POSTHYPNOTIC SUGGESTIONS TO REMEMBER
FORGOTTEN NOCTURNAL DREAMS

A simple straightforward way to remember forgotten dreams is to give the patient a posthypnotic suggestion tying the return of the repressed dream to his seeing the hypnoanalyst the next time. While the patient is in trance the therapist says:

> When you sit down on this chair the next time, an important
> nocturnal dream you will have had between now and then will
> suddenly pop up in your mind, and you will be able to tell me that
> dream. But you will have forgotten that I told you so.

The last sentence is usually added in order to make the posthypnotic suggestion operable through the unconscious. Like all direct suggestions, this suggestion works better with highly
hypnotizable people. With some people, particularly those in the
grip of a negative transference, the suggestion works better when
they do not realize that the therapist gave it as a suggestion.

To refine the posthypnotic suggestion and make it somewhat
more indirect and more permissive, the hypnotherapist may put
two chairs for the patient close to each other and designate one
of the chairs as the one which will bring back the dream if the
patient consciously or unconsciously chooses to sit on that chair.
Through this chaining, the patient is given the chance to make
his own unconscious or conscious decision as to whether or not
he will recall the dream. If the patient sits down on the "I don't
remember" chair, the hypnotherapist can simply accept it as indicating that the patient is not yet ready to drop his resistance. Or
he helps the patient to go into trance and relax for a while, and
then invites him, in hypnosis, to dream the same dream he dreamt
during the night; or he points out that the patient resisted the
posthypnotic suggestion and helps him to analyze the resistance.

HYPNOTICALLY INDUCING DREAMS IN THE
THERAPY HOUR

A great advantage the hypnoanalyst has over the psychoanalyst is that she or he can induce a dream during the therapy hour
while the patient is in hypnosis. When the dream is ended, the
hypnoanalyst can immediately ask the patient to tell him the
dream, which, as has been shown in laboratory research on nonhypnotic night dreams, prevents forgetting them. He can ask for
associations while the patient still is in trance and thus closer to
his unconscious than in the waking state. Usually the hypnoanalyst interprets the dream together with the patient in, as well as

out of, hypnosis. Inducing a dream in trance is done by means of the following permissive and open-ended suggestion:

> You are in trance now, but you can go even deeper into a state that is more like sleep. When you are deep enough to have a dream like dreams that you dream at night, a finger on your hand will lift up by itself. When the dream is finished, the finger will sink down by itself indicating to me that the dream is ended.

In order not to interrupt a dream which, after all, is dreamt like all real dreams, mostly in primary process language, the hypnoanalyst keeps absolutely quiet and says no more until she or he gets the ideomotor sign of the patient's finger sinking down indicating that the dream is finished. Immediately upon completion of the dream the therapist asks the patient to report the dream, and to give associations. Together with the patient the therapist interprets the dream while the patient is still in trance. After the therapist has woken up the patient, she or he goes over the same three steps again and notices differences, if there are any. They could indicate additional specific conflict areas.

By hypnotically inducing dreams in the therapy hour and asking the patient as soon as the dream is ended to report it, the hypnoanalyst counteracts the patient's forgetting of dreams as well a secondary elaboration.

TYPES OF HYPNOTIC DREAMS

Some hypnotically induced dreams show the characteristics and have the structure of nocturnal dreams. Others present more as daydreams. Still others cannot be distinguished with absolute certainty from more or less elaborate fantasy productions. We discovered this in our self-hypnosis research (Fromm and Kahn, 1990). Our subjects had been told that while practicing self-hypnosis for an hour daily during a four-week period, they should at some time during that hour give themselves a suggestion to dream a dream about hypnosis and write it down right after waking up. Here is the journal entry of one of our experimental subjects, S-003, on day 1:

I was breathing deeply, falling slowly through blue warm water, deeper and deeper. Everything moved in an easy slow motion. The set lights were granulated and diffuse.

I decided to melt my body. In my breathing rhythms, I instructed myself to sink deeper with every breath, to lose my anger and frustration with every exhalation, thus becoming lighter. As I was breathing, I centered in on my head, watching the revolving light of a lighthouse swing through the thick blackness. It lulled me and took all my concentration away from my limbs. Limbo-like [Reader, note the wordplay!], I transferred the lighthouse pulsations to my own body, turning it off and on. Slowly my light got brighter. The deeper I dove, the brighter my lights glowed.

At this point—I decided to fly. So I detached my light bulbs and centered on becoming a bird, strong and condorlike. . . . My head jerked back and forth tilting to one side. My nose became my beak; I preened my feathers and quivered my arms as wings. Soon, I was sailing above some mountain, tense-winged and flapping every once in a while. I landed quite cleanly, I believe, and rather jubilantly preened again. I make a good bird.

[Up to here, all is imagery. Then the dream begins:]

I am walking toward a plateau with three oily black trees gawking at me. The sky is black. It is a world of shadows. So, I turn back and begin trudging down the mountain.

Slowly at first, the light thins, the cliff I am circling becomes more pleasant. The lower I climb the brighter and happier the scenery becomes. Suddenly, there are profusions of flowers by the path; I look to a maze of gardens below—and reach a grassy field. A woman meets me in a gauze dress and flowers. She leads me toward the Monarch. I mention that the sky is grim above them. She smiles slowly and agrees, but adds that her people are slowly, steadily clearing the black pollution away and someday there will be clear blue skies again. "But we are happy anyway," she laughs. "Everything here generates its own light." At this point, I am glowing brighter than before.

The Monarch is a young woman with grace (beauty), an old woman as earth mother (wisdom), a man as authority, and a gargoyle. Beside it stands a Phoenix breath-takingly beautiful, wild, strong, brilliant, and virile. The Monarch absent-mindedly shakes it. The Monarch talks to me kindly and offers that I stay; that perhaps I can find a way to clean her (she is a woman) kingdom. I agree.

[Here the hypnotic dreaming ends]

> My left leg is asleep—as it tingles awake, I make my body repeat the performance.
> I am so relaxed I begin to fall asleep. So I sit up and try to imagine a lady-ghost I have seen before—twice while tripping, twice without. She does not appear. I close my eyes. She appears and walks with me silently for a while. I open my eyes again and watch a shadow-play on my wall. By blinking quickly, I make it appear like a silent film. Amusing.
> I become a mountain for a while, a gray, soft, pulpy mountain. I decide it is time to rise. [Subject wakes herself up.]

This hypnotic dream clearly has the qualities of a nocturnal dream.

Here is a journal entry from another subject, S-061, day 8:

> Strange hypnotic dream. I must have the travel bug. Dream started with painted masks (people behind them) dancing and parading by. At first I thought it was Mardi Gras, then realized I was in some ancient South American culture. All of a sudden this village where I was began filling up with lava. The people were all buried. My feelings as I stood there were "this probably happened centuries ago and I'm far enough removed from it that it shouldn't bother me." Then their different parts were floating in the air and crying. This being my dream, I walked away from the sadness, insisting, to myself, on only observing and not feeling. I walked into a cool garden area. This garden or patio was very peaceful and I felt like I was walking through a page in a book and yet everything seemed abstract and sort of disconnected. Lovely. There were marble benches and the flooring was colorful mosaic tile. There were lovely plants and lovely quiet women just sitting around. They were dressed in beautiful flowing robes. I was embarrassed because I was wearing Levis and a shirt. I hoped they didn't notice me. I stood back in order to remain inconspicuous. I noticed that red smoke was trying to arise and surround us. I knew that whatever this was, it wasn't good. I allowed the dream to fade. I had no desire to watch more destruction which I felt was coming.

Is this a dream or is it vivid imagery? That is an important question to ask in the context of hypnosis research and often difficult to decide. But whether it is fantasy/imagery or a dream actually does not matter too much in hypnotherapy. Both can be used in hypnoanalysis for the purposes of uncovering, working through, or integrating, and both should and can be interpreted.

While it is often difficult to make a distinction between vivid hypnotic imagery and hypnotic nocturnal-like dreams, it is quite easy to judge whether material produced in hypnosis with the suggestion that the patient dream a dream is like a daydream or whether it is a nocturnal-like dream. Here is an example of an hypnotic dream resembling a daydream, daydream S 062, day 15:

> I let my mind be sort of blank except for colors and let it all flow out. I sat like this for a while—it was so relaxing I didn't want to stop. Eventually a dream crept up on me, all sneaky and subtle.
>
> I was in a large green field, sort of ambling along, feeling peaceful. The sky was rather gray/blue, but I knew it wouldn't rain on me. It was good to be alone, with no one else around for miles. A path—coblestoned, but smooth and worn into the ground with time—appeared and I started walking. Soon the entire area misted over. I couldn't see more than two feet in any direction. I kept on walking, unafraid and feeling good. Trees appeared on either side of the path—tall green leafy trees. First irregularly, then often; finally along the entire path. I felt so good I stopped, lay down, and went to sleep. When I woke I was no longer there—in fact I woke out of the dream back into hypnosis.

This dream contains much less primary process than the other two. It is like a daydream and does not stem from as deep an unconscious source as the other two dreams.

Free association (which is closer to the secondary process end of the continuum) and nocturnal dreams and imagery (which are closer to the primary process end) can be employed for uncovering in hypnoanalysis as well as in psychoanalysis. Freud (1900) called the dream the "Royal road to the unconscious." It is not the only one. Hypnosis is another; and so are various other altered states of consciousness. Freud (1900) conceived of the dream as expressing the unconscious wishes of the id, and the superego's attempts to censor and quell them. French and Fromm (1964) have conceived of the dream as an ego function, an attempt to find solutions to unconscious or partly conscious conflicts. However, Fromm no longer believes that every dream expresses conflict. Since laboratory research on dreaming (see, e.g., Dement and Kleitman, 1957) has demonstrated that every human being dreams four to six times a night, such a position, she feels, is no longer tenable. Life is hard, but it is not so hard that we would need to attempt to solve a conflict every single night of our lives! Some dreaming serves the function of uncovering and solving an unconscious conflict. Being psychoanalysts, we simply have assumed that this is the case with every dream people produce. But dreaming must have other functions, too. We are inclined to assume now that dreaming also can have the purpose of maintaining the ego as functioning while one is asleep by providing the chance to think more in primary process terms than is possible in the waking state, in which we need to be more reality oriented. Because Fromm now feels that perhaps not all nocturnal dreams deal with conflict, suggesting that the patient have a dream about a conflict provides a good safeguard that the dream indeed deals with conflict and is not just the expression of a primary process exercise.

Cartwright's (1972) finding, that schizophrenics (who think so much in primary process during their waking hours) have fewer REM and more non-REM nocturnal dreams than healthy people, would support the idea that the human being needs to spend a certain amount of time every twenty-four hours in each of the two cognitive modalities, primary process and secondary process.

THE HYPNOTIST'S SUGGESTIONS WITH REGARD
TO DREAMS ABOUT A PARTICULAR CONFLICT

Because during hypnosis, people are more ego receptive (Fromm, 1977) than they are during the waking state, the hypnoanalyst must be very careful not to suggest what the patient could do or what the solution could be. The patient can best be helped if he finds his own solutions, not those of the therapist, which may not fit him. The hypnoanalyst must be extremely careful with regard to the wording of the suggestion for dreams. She or he can suggest that the patient have a dream about a particular conflict on which they are currently working. The hypnotherapist can suggest that in the weeks to come the patient will develop more and more of an ability to understand the meaning of his dreams, and that the patient will produce consecutive dreams that will improve the dream function of conflict solution. But the hypnotherapist must never suggest what the solution(s) will be.

7

Alternative Hypnoanalytic
Techniques

TALKING TO THE PATIENT IN PRIMARY
PROCESS LANGUAGE

As we have said in chapter 6, the hypnotic state is an altered state of consciousness characterized by what Kris (1936) has called a "regression in the service of the ego." The regression brings with it a change in the prevalent cognitive mode. While in the waking state we think mostly logically and sequentially (i.e., in the secondary process mode), in hypnosis, as well as in nocturnal dreams, we think mostly in imagery, that is, in primary process language, the mode of early childhood cognition. Because the patient in trance operates in this mode, it is incumbent upon the therapist to talk to him or her in the same mode, namely, to use a great deal of imagery in the evocative communications and suggestions he gives to the patient. In speaking to the hypnotized patient in the primary process language, the hypnoanalyst is making use of symbolism.

Symbolism is employed in hypnosis for indirect suggestions, indirect ways of uncovering, indirect or symbolic ways of talking to our patients' unconscious, and for helping them gain self-confidence, coping strength, and mastery in real life. By means of indirect suggestions one can often circumvent resistances or prevent them from arising.

IMAGERY TECHNIQUES

CLOUD IMAGES

In the 1920s, Hermann Rorschach, a Swiss psychiatrist, invented the first projective technique used in psychology, the Rorschach Ink Blot (Rorschach, 1921). The same technique can be employed using imagined clouds as unstructured stimuli rather than spots of ink on paper. The hypnoanalyst says to the patient: "Perhaps you would like to imagine that you are lying on your back in a beautiful meadow on a mountaintop, looking up into the sky. The sky is blue and there are a few clouds floating in the sky. Look at the clouds. What do they look like? What can you see in them?"

The patient may see (i.e., project onto the imagined cloud) whose human beings in interaction, faces, animals, inanimate objects, or landscapes. The animals, people, or faces he sees may be aggressive or tender, happy, demanding, satisfied, angry, or aloof, expressing the patient's current unconscious drive tensions and needs as well as the defenses against them.

The great majority of patients keep their eyes closed during trance. With them, the image of the cloud can be used diagnostically in roughly the same way as the Rorschach ink blots are used with patients who are awake or with those hypnotized patients who are able to open their eyes and stay in trance.

In a slightly different way the cloud image can be used in the therapeutic process. For instance, a patient who feels abandoned by a love object may be told to imagine that while he is lying there on the mountain meadow staring up into the blue sky a nice, big, white, fluffy cloud is rising over the horizon, moving in the sky until it is right above him. Then, the hypnoanalyst says, it is coming down to envelope him "like a warm, fluffy blanket, making you feel very comfortable and good all over." The cloud here is used in the sense of the comforting childhood blanket, the transitional object.

A cloud image can also be employed in the process of uncovering repressed material. The hypnoanalyst may suggest that the patient look at an earlier time in his life as if he were looking through a heavy cloud which slowly and gradually lifts so that he can see more and more of the still hidden landscape of his childhood. For variation one can replace the picture of the cloud by the image of a dense fog that becomes thinner and thinner, and more and more transparent.

SPLIT MIRROR AND TV SCREEN IMAGES

Split mirror and TV screen images are used in supportive hypnoanalysis when one wants to help the patient correct a faulty body image, lose or gain weight, or see himself the way he will look when he is happier and healthier and therapy is finished. That is, with these methods one encourages the patient to set a healthy goal for himself and to strive to reach it. Here are some examples:

An anorexic patient, 5 feet 5 inches tall and weighing 90 pounds, was helped into trance and then asked to imagine that she was looking at the left side of a mirror or TV screen that was split into two halves. She chose a mirror. She was asked how she saw herself in that left-hand side of the mirror and described herself as being fat, much too fat. We then asked her to look at the right part of the mirror, and said that while this half of the mirror at the moment looked foggy or as if there was some water condensation on it, it soon would clear up as she was staring at it and she would see herself the way she wanted to look, having the *appropriate weight* for her height. The patient in trance stared at the mirror image and after a while said, "Oh, I can see myself now in the right side of that mirror. I really look quite nice. I wish I would look that way." The hypnoanalyst said, "How much do you weigh there in that right side of the mirror?" And the patient said, "Well, about 120 pounds." The patient then was told to look again at the left-hand side of the mirror, and to become aware that slowly the reflection on the left-hand side would move over toward the right part of the mirror. As this was happening, her picture of herself was going to change to the right reflection. She also was told that in the weeks to come, in reality as well as in her own view, all the curves of her body would come to fit into the curves of the body image that she now was seeing in the right side of the mirror. Thus we indirectly suggested to her that she would gain weight and that her body image would change. Direct suggestions would have been likely to evoke resistance.

On account of the double meaning that the word *right* can have, it is important to designate the right (and not the left) side of the mirror or TV screen as the one that will reflect the appropriate body weight and body image.

For patients who really are obese and should or want to lose weight the split mirror technique would be worded about as follows:

> In the left half of the mirror you can see yourself as you really look now; in the right-hand side as you want to look, much thinner. Your figure in the left side of the mirror is now changing, it is shrinking in width and moving into the picture in the right side of the mirror. As you watch how this left side picture, seemingly by magnetic force, is being pulled into the much thinner figure on the right side of the mirror, the thought comes up in your mind that you, too, can shrink in width and that over the next few weeks you can shed the extra pounds you have, until you just exactly fit into the picture on the right side of the mirror. As the right side of the mirror attracts you more and more . . . . . more and more . . . . . you can shed those pounds. You feel proud of being able to do this for yourself and to remain at this lower weight.

Here we employ a variation of a technique that women frequently use consciously when they want to lose weight: they buy a new dress a size or two smaller than the ones they are currently wearing, hoping to lose weight by picturing themselves as fitting into the new dress. When done in hypnosis, a state in which the unconscious is more available, it works much better than in the waking state.

The split screen and the split mirror techniques can also be used to help patients make (other) good self-fulfilling prophecies. For instance, the patient is told that on the left side of the screen he will see himself the way he feels now, anxious, depressed, isolated (or whatever the case may be), while on the right side he will see himself as he will be when his therapy will be completed:

comfortable, relaxed, happy within himself, surrounded by friends, and leading a productive life. He can then be asked *when* he thinks this will have happened. The hypnoanalyst may say:

> Now look over there to that wall, the wall opposite the window (patient imagines looking at a wall of the room but does not open his eyes). There is a calendar which has a leaf for every month. The wind is blowing in through the open window, ruffling up the leaves of the calendar and then holding them so that the leaf for one month this year or next year will be held open. On that leaf all days of that month will appear in red because that is the month in which your therapy will be completed.

It is wise not to say "in that month your therapy will be terminated or in that month you will terminate." People in hypnotic trance easily can misunderstand a word that has two meanings. They may misunderstand "you will terminate" as meaning "you will die." And that needs to be avoided, so that it does not become a self-fulfilling, bad prophecy the patient feels he needs to fulfill. We want him to understand clearly and unmistakably that we are talking about the end of therapy and *that* self-made prophecy we hope he will fulfill. Therefore, it is important to say "completed" not "finished" or "terminated."

THE THEATER TECHNIQUE

The Theater Technique is a frequently used hypnotherapeutic technique. The patient projects onto the stage and the actors his own problems and attitudes and those of the important others around him, as he sees them. The hypnoanalyst may say to the patient:

> You are going to the theater now to see an important play about [name patient's symptom or problem]. At first you may not see how the play relates to your problem, but it does. You will be able to watch the play with great interest and to describe to me what is happening on the stage. [*By saying this, the hypnoanalyst helps the patient to become the author and producer of the play who naturally structures the unstructured stimulus ("a play"), according to the laws of his,*

the patient's, own personality.] You are excited about the play, eagerly looking forward to seeing it. The lights in the audience are being dimmed now and the curtain will rise. There, it is rising. Look! Now describe what is happening as the play unfolds.

Frequently, it is good to state the problem. For instance, if the patient is suffering from insomnia, the hypnotherapist may say, "It is a play about a man who has trouble falling asleep." Or if the patient is a person who has difficulties with interpersonal relationships, the hypnoanalyst may introduce the play by saying: "This is a play about a woman who always gets herself in trouble with other people."

A play usually has several acts. Thus, the therapist can suggest to the patient that the first act will show the problem, the second act the working through, and that in the third act a solution will be reached. Frequently, the patient does that on his own. Sometimes it takes more than three acts. Rarely is there time in one hour to go through all acts. The hypnoanalyst can say that the viewing of the play will stretch over several weeks. As long as no (part-) solution to the Focal Conflict (French and Fromm, 1964) is reached in the play, the hypnoanalyst can have the patient view the same play over and over again until in this projective way a possible solution is seen or experienced.

Sometimes the patient may not see anyone coming onto the stage. That is a manifestation of resistance. The hypnoanalyst can either interpret the resistance or try to circumvent it by attempting to work with some other hypnoanalytic technique. We have had a few patients who, at the beginning, when the curtain was rising, suddenly said, "Oh, oh! The curtain is falling down." That, of course, is also the expression of a defense, and shows that the patient is not ready yet to face the problem. It is also a beautiful teaching example to show that (1) defenses really exist in hypnosis, and (2) that they, as well as unconscious wishes and thoughts, express themselves in hypnosis in primary process language. The wise therapist accepts the defense for a while and says, "Oh! yes; one of the ropes on which the curtain is being pulled up has broken. The producer has to have some stage hands come and fix it. Let's just wait and talk while the rope is being repaired." He or she then makes some small talk with the patient for the next few minutes, after which she or he says: "There, the lights are being dimmed again in the theater and the curtain has been fixed. Watch it rising." If the patient says that the same thing has happened again or that an even heavier curtain (an "iron" curtain) has fallen down, then the hypnoanalyst knows that this particular topic should be avoided for a while until in the ascending spiral of therapy it becomes focal again but somewhat less threatening to the patient.

The second act does not necessarily begin the working through. It often is used by the patient to explore more of the problem.

The theater technique, in a way, is an equivalent to the production of dreams. The hypnoanalyst skillfully produces a situation (going to the theater) that will give the patient's unconscious or preconscious a chance to communicate to the hypnoanalyst the dynamic meaning of the patient's problem as well as his unconscious resources for coping with the conflict.

ANAGRAMS (IMAGINARY PLAY WITH SCRABBLE LETTERS)

This is another technique used for uncovering of repressed material. The hypnoanalyst says to the hypnotized person:

> Imagine that in front of you there stands a box with Scrabble letters. Keep your eyes closed, grab a handful, and throw them up into the air. Some of the letters will fall down on this table blank side up, others with the letter showing. Move the letters so that they will form a line. Out of that line your hand will take those that will form a word that will give us a clue as to what the root of the problem is on which we are working now. Perhaps at first the letters that form the word are still scrambled up. You can move them around until they form a word that is a real word.

This technique appeals to the unconscious to deliver up some of the secrets it holds. The patient is given a chance to play around with the repressed material, arrange and rearrange the letters until they form a word that he is ready to recognize as what it was that he had to defend himself against. Sometimes this imaginary play leads to an insight right in the hour in which it is first used. Sometimes the game has to be repeated several times before the patient's unconscious will allow letters to fall down that, arranged and rearranged, make a sensible word giving a clue to the origins of the conflict. The time it takes for the full word to come to the surface of consciousness indicates the strength of the defense and of the affect involved.

AUTOMATIC DRAWING AND WRITING

Janet (1893) was one of the early clinician-researchers who recognized that dissociation plays a great role in hypnosis. He based his whole theory of hypnosis on dissociation.

Nearly a century later, E. R. Hilgard (1974, 1977) anchored his theory of hypnosis, the neodissociation theory, also on dissociation. Dissociation plays an important role in hypnosis, giving rise to the technique of dissociating the hand from the rest of the patient's body, and designating the hand as "the part that knows" about the patient's unconscious. The patient can then be told that the hand will write out information which the patient has, but of which he is still unaware. The two main techniques developed for this purpose are automatic drawing and writing.

Many severely disturbed patients, as well as many creative artists, find themselves at times voluntarily or involuntarily experiencing an altered state of consciousness, a self-hypnotic state, in which their hand produces a drawing or a composition without their being aware of more than that "the" hand produces something on paper (see, e.g., Fromm [1992] for the case of the composer; or Brown and Fromm [1986, pp. 290–292], for the case of the woman who was incestually raped at age 3 or 4, a fact that was deeply repressed and of which she was totally unaware before and even for half a year after her hand made the drawing). In both the creative process and the confession-out-of-awareness, the hand is dissociated from the conscious and goes into the service of the unconscious ego. What the hand draws in this state of unawareness is often so clear-cut and revealing to the psychoanalytically oriented therapist, that, particularly if he is a novice with hypnosis, he thinks it must be near-conscious to the patient, too, and interprets the material to the patient then and there. That is a severe mistake. Eventually he will learn that in cases of post-traumatic stress disorder (PTSD), what to him is utterly obvious from the patient's drawing, is by no means clear to the patient. In fact in cases of PTSD, for quite a while the patient typically vigorously defends him- or herself against understanding such a preconscious interpretation. Thus, it is wiser to wait for some months before interpreting such production to patients suffering from posttraumatic stress.

Here is an example:

A married woman in her thirties, who slept in the same bed with her husband but never allowed him to have intercourse with her, found herself sitting at her desk one day staring at a piece of paper in what she described as "a funny, dreamy state." "Then," she said, "my hand suddenly picked up all kinds of crayons and pencils lying on the desk and furiously drew pictures." One was a clear-cut fellatio representation, the other a cunnilingus. In both pictures the female was a little girl, the male a full-grown adult. The patient was not an artist and had never done any drawing before. She stated that she had no idea why her hand had drawn these pictures, and that she did not know what they possibly could mean. To the hypnoanalyst it was perfectly obvious, but no interpretation was attempted until half a year later when much more material had come up in her hypnotic sessions that made her wonder whether she had not been abused by an adult as a little girl.

Similarly we have found that severely traumatized Vietnam War veterans who do not remember having committed any atrocities themselves, at times in trance find their hand doodling or drawing violent scenes of atrocities in which they are the perpetrator of the crime. But it takes months before they can recognize that they have committed the aggressive act which the drawing hand says they have done.

Automatic writing is usually employed for the purpose of unblocking and uncovering. The therapist finds out with which hand the patient writes, and when the patient is in a sufficiently deep trance he says: "This hand will now separate itself from the arm. It will move away from the wrist and become a being by itself that knows things about you that you consciously do not know yourself. I am going to ask you some questions now, and no matter what your mouth answers, the hand will write down the real truth." Or the hypnoanalyst may say, "Whenever I put a pencil into your hand, the hand will write down something about you that you yourself may not even know." The writing hand, here again, becomes the spokesman of the unconscious.

IDEOMOTOR SIGNALING

Unconscious motivation can be expressed via fantasy and imagery, and also via the motor system. Through involuntary facial expressions, through our posture and in the way we walk, we communicate to others how we feel, usually without knowing that we do so. Because the involuntary motor system is one of the communicators of the unconscious and the preconscious, hypnoanalysts use ideomotor techniques to help patients communicate to them thoughts, affects, and memories of which the patients may not yet be aware.

One of the most widely used techniques in the hypnotic state is finger signaling. The technique of finger signaling was mentioned earlier, as a technique, in connection with the patient's signaling to the therapist the end of an hypnotically induced dream. In that case, it does not matter whether the patient's finger lifts involuntarily or whether he or she lifts it voluntarily. Voluntary lifting is a smooth, rather quick movement, involuntary levitation is slow and jerky. Voluntary lifting of the finger is an intentional, conscious act, while involuntary levitation of the finger is a communication from the unconscious. Thus, if the hypnotherapist wants to get a communication from the unconscious, he must carefully watch *how* the finger lifts. In order to facilitate the involuntary response, the hypnoanalyst must be careful to dissociate the finger by saying "*the* finger will lift," and not "you will lift your finger." If notwithstanding his correct wording he sees a straight and relatively fast movement of the finger upwards, his suggestion has not really worked and the patient's answer has been a perfectly conscious, voluntary one. In the involuntary response coming from the unconscious, the finger moves slowly and jerkily.

Finger signaling can be used hypnotically as a simple answering device whenever the therapist suspects that the patient is consciously not aware of how he really feels about something; or that he denies, represses, or in any other way defends himself against a thought, a feeling, or an upcoming memory. Finger signaling can also be used to answer any question a hypnoanalyst may ask. Because of its simplicity, it is one of the most useful and most frequently employed hypnotic devices. To work, it does not require more than a light trance.

AGE REGRESSION AND THE AFFECT BRIDGE

Age regression is perhaps the most fascinating of all hypnoanalytic uncovering methods. It can be done in a number of different ways. Using the simplest, least artful technique, the hypnotist may say to the hypnotized patient: "You will now be getting younger and smaller. . . . Your body is getting smaller. Your limbs are getting shorter. You are getting younger and smaller. . . . smaller and younger. Soon you will be 8 years old." (The hypnotist names the age about which he wants to find out more.) In another, more imaginative version the hypnoanalyst describes to the patient that he is sitting at a table turning the pages of a book or a calendar backwards. With each page that he turns, he gets younger and younger until he comes to an age where something very important happened to him that caused some of his problems. Once the patient has relived that event, the hypnoanalyst lets him go further back to other events that helped shape his problem.

In the authors' opinion the best technique for producing age regression is Watkins' (1971) "affect bridge." To start it, the hypnoanalyst first suggests that the patient experience a particular affect or sensation currently figuring in the therapy (sadness, anxiety, joy, or an itch) and that this affect increase more and more. She or he suggests the feeling that most characteristically accompanies the patient's troubles. For instance, if the patient suffers from an anxiety neurosis or phobias, the therapist would suggest mounting fear; if he is a depressive, the therapist suggests rapidly increasing depressive feelings to the hypnotized patient. Then the therapist says: "Now you can take this strong feeling and walk back over it—like over a bridge or like along a rope you hold onto—until you come to an earlier time in your life when you felt just like this."

As an example, let us give you an actual case. In this case we used a happy affect in order to retrieve a repressed childhood language. There was no need to make it an unpleasant affect.

THE CASE OF DON

In July 1967, I (the senior author) went to Japan for the Convention of the International Society for Clinical and Experimental Hypnosis. While there, I learned a couple of dozen Japanese words and phrases.

Shortly after my return to the United States, one of my assistants asked me to watch a session in which she was hypnotizing a young man whom we shall name Don. He was an excellent subject; he had scored 12 on the Weitzenhoffer and Hilgard (1959) Stanford Hypnotic Susceptibility Scales, Form A (SHSS:A).

When I entered my assistant's office, the subject was in deep trance, age-regressed to 7 years. He looked Japanese. I knew nothing of his background except that he was a graduate student. The assistant introduced me to him and asked him whether it would be all right if I talked to him, too. He eagerly agreed saying he knew I was a good hypnotist.

Thinking that he was a Japanese student, and also perhaps wanting to show off my newly acquired, meager Japanese vocabulary, I addressed him in Japanese:

"Ika gade suka?" (How are you?)
No response.
"Anata wa nano shobu gotowo asobe mashoka?" (What game would you like to play?—a sentence I had found on our trip in one of those Japanese language guides for tourists, and thought I would never have any use for.)
No response.
Then I said: *"Hai"* (Yes). *"Domo arigato"* (Thank you very much) and a dozen other words I knew in Japanese.

None of them seemed to strike a spark. Don sat intently listening, but seemed not to understand. In the age-regressed state, as well as later in the normal waking state, he said—upon being questioned—that he had not understood what I said. He only knew the word *arigato*—that meant "thank you"—but even the word *domo* (which means "very much"), he said he had never heard. When asked to speak some Japanese, he said he only knew the words for *grandmother, good food,* and *Is it okay if I eat now?* polite phrases he was required to say whenever his family ate at his grandmother's house. That, he said, was the sum total of his Japanese vocabulary.

Don was a second generation American, in his twenties, a Sansei. He was born in California. Both his parents were Nisei, born in the United States, and at home spoke English only. English was his mother tongue.

A few months after initially meeting Don, I started a new class of students in hypnosis and used Don as a subject for demonstrating some of the phenomena of hypnosis: arm levitation, limb catalepsy, hypnotic dreams, and positive and negative hallucinations. It occurred to me also to demonstrate age regression. So I age regressed him along the affect bridge of feeling very happy, to an age which he described as being 7 years old. We talked (in English) and played a board game together on the floor, for which he opened his eyes while remaining in deep trance. Then I told him to close his eyes again and to go back further in time, to age 3, to a day on which he felt equally happy and good. For a few moments there was silence. Then, suddenly, in a high child's voice, Don broke into a stream of rapid Japanese. He talked on and on in Japanese for about fifteen to twenty minutes. He seemed to want to involve me in his Japanese talk, and so again I threw in what Japanese words I knew. But from his puzzled, or at times irritated, expression when I spoke, it was clear that my words did not fit into the context of what he was talking about. When I progressed him to age 7, he flipped back into speaking English again.

I was more than surprised when this flood of Japanese came out of his mouth. The students in my class crowded around Don, gaping. From the experience with the original age regression, I had been convinced that he talked no, or as good as no, Japanese.

How come he did now? I was puzzled. Certainly this could not be due to experimenter bias, because my bias had been that he did not speak Japanese.

In addition, why did Don talk English when age regressed to the 7-year level, but suddenly come up with Japanese at age 3? I had a hunch: He was a young man apparently in his midtwenties; it was the late sixties. He must have been born on the West Coast in the early 1940s, of Japanese extraction. Perhaps during World War II, when he was a small child, he and his family had been sent to a Japanese relocation camp, where he learned to speak Japanese. I age progressed Don back to the then current date, the date of the experiment, and then asked him when he was born. His answer: December 2, 1941.

That was five days before Pearl Harbor! The picture was abundantly clear to me now. Californians had panicked after Pearl Harbor and feared that Japanese invaders would soon land on the West Coast. In every Japanese, Nisei and Sansei, they saw a potentially dangerous spy of the Country of the Rising Sun. In 1942 all people of Japanese extraction who lived on the West Coast were rounded up and shipped inland, to Minnesota and other Midwestern states, away from the West Coast. There, all the displaced Japanese lived in camps together. Japanese, of course, was spoken a good deal in these camps. Only after the end of World War II did our government allow people with Japanese backgrounds to return to the West Coast. Don and his family must have been put into a relocation camp with many other Japanese shortly after he was born, and released when he was less than 4 years old, at the end of World War II in 1945.

When I age progressed Don from age 3 to age 7, he started to talk English again. After termination of the trance he had a spontaneous posthypnotic amnesia. He was astonished to hear that he had spoken apparently fluent Japanese during the trance. He was not told to what age he had been regressed then.

Unfortunately, during that dramatic class session we had no tape recorder in the room.

Four months later Don asked me to take him on in psychotherapy to help him concentrate, so he could finish his dissertation within the next six months.

After a few weeks, I decided to age regress him again, for therapeutic as well as for experimental reasons—with tape recorder at hand. As an experimenter, I was still very curious to find out whether my hypothesis about his having spoken Japanese as a child, perhaps even as a first language amidst the Japanese population in a relocation camp, was correct. As a therapist, I wanted to help Don lift the repression and make available to himself—in the conflict-free sphere of the ego—his bilinguality. Here follows the verbatim transcript of that session. I induced hypnosis by saying:

Perhaps, you want to imagine now . . . that you are lying in a boat . . . floating down a river, gently. . . . You can see the banks of the river on both sides. There are some woods over there and then a wide open field. Corn is growing on it. And over there you see a barn . . . a red barn. . . . . The sun is shining onto the left side of your face as you are lying in your boat, drifting . . . drifting down the river . . . gently, comfortably, very relaxedly. You don't need to row. You don't need to do anything. You can just let yourself float . . . floating, floating into deeper and deeper trance. Deep. Gently. . . . comfortably, relaxedly. You're becoming sleepy, very sleepy. With every breath you take, you go down deeper into the state of trance. . . . Deeper and deeper. Just let yourself float. There is no worry. It's comfortable, relaxed, floating there, floating comfortably. . . . . Sleepily, dreamily floating. Just let yourself float. (Pause) Just let yourself float . . . even deeper . . . deeper . . . as deep or deeper as you have ever been . . . Pretty soon everything in the outside will feel nebulous. . . . will fade away . . . you are in a state where the outside world of reality has faded so far away that only your inner world is real to you now . . . deep . . . very deep . . . deep. And now, I would like you to imagine that . . . I am . . . putting a string around your wrist, and at the other end of that string there is a balloon, it's not blown up yet, it's kind of wrinkled. . . . .

Pt:	*How can it stay up then?*
T:	*It isn't up yet. Can you see it? It's lying there on the ground. . . . That's right . . . What color is it?*
Pt:	*It's red.*
T:	*It's red.*
Pt:	*But it doesn't look red, it looks dark, sort of almost purple because it's all squinched up and it's nothing but shadow . . .*

T: *That's right. . . . And now this balloon is being filled with helium.*
        Helium is being pumped into it. . . . . , and you know how light, how
        very light helium is . . . Yes, what are you seeing?

Pt: *The balloon, getting filled up, and the color is getting lighter because*
        it's not all squinched, and it floats, the balloon . . .

T: *It starts to rise. That's right, that's right.*

Pt: *My hand is going up. . . . .*

T: *Yes, it is pulling your hand up . . . there it is pulling your hand*
        higher and higher. And now the wind is catching it . . . the wind is
        blowing to your left side and slightly behind you . . . way up in the
        air, left and behind you . . . and your hand is coming closer and closer
        to your head . . . and you know that when your hand touches your
        head, you are falling into an even deeper trance . . . There . . . that's
        right. Now let me cut the string. . . . very good. . . . that's right. . . .
        that's right, and now, Don, you will find that a feeling of deep happi-
        ness is going all through you. [Here the hypnoanalyst begins to
        induce the age regression via the Affect Bridge.] *You are doing*
        something that you are enjoying . . . very, very much. . . . What are
        you doing now? Or thinking, or feeling?

Pt: *I'm hearing the slow section of the Schubert Impromptu. The second*
        section of the Schubert Impromptu. [Don loved music.]

T: *And you are feeling so happy?*

Pt: *Yes.*

T: *Can you sing along with it?*

Pt: *No, because I just . . . uh . . . . I just am playing it. . . . I just . . . if*
        I sing I wouldn't be as happy.

T: *Hu-um . . . And this feeling of happiness when you are playing goes*
        all through you. Your face looks happy and smiling . . . your body
        looks happy and relaxed . . . [Therapist simply reflects to patient
        here what she sees; which, in turn, makes the patient feel that
        the hypnotic process is working.] *There . . . this strong feeling of*
        happiness goes all through you . . . a very strong feeling of happi-
        ness. . . . And now, I would like you to go back, back, back in time
        along this feeling of happiness. You pass through other experiences
        than just play Schubert—take this feeling of happiness—it's like a
        rope which you can hold onto, let yourself slide back along this rope
        till you come to a time when you were about 7 years old, feeling just
        that happy. Go back, back, back, back in time . . . Where are you now?

Pt: *I'm in the cl—I'm—I'm in the class with Miss X* [Patient suddenly speaks in a high childlike voice, a clear indication of age regression].

T: *What are you doing?*

Pt: *Well, we're going to sing a song with Miss X. She's going to play "My Country 'Tis of Thee," and we're going to sing, too.*

T: *Let's all sing it.*

Pt: *Well, she has to play it first.*

T: *Can you hear her play it?*

Pt: *Yes! Well, that's the introduction. We're not supposed to sing during the introduction. Only when she—only* [Sings "My Country 'Tis of Thee" loudly and lustily. At this point the therapist became aware of the fact that the patient had an identity problem in relation to his being or not being an American. Of all the songs this highly musical boy must have known when he was 7 years old, why would he choose unconsciously to hear and sing "My Country 'Tis of Thee"?]

T: *Very good, very good—the whole class sang it?*

Pt: *Yeah.*

T: *Yes, good. And what is the class doing now?*

Pt: *Well . . . well, they're just waiting to see what the teacher is going to say to do next.*

T: *What is she saying?*

Pt: *Well . . .*

T: *Who am I? Do you know me?*

Pt: *You're, ... no.*

T: *I'm just a visitor in the classroom.*
    [As the therapist was not known to the patient when he was 7 years old, she had to find out who he saw her as now. Or she had to introduce herself as somebody who could have been in the same place as he was when he was the age he felt he was in the age regression.]

Pt: *Oh, did you come to hear us sing?*

T: *Yes, I did!*

Pt: *Did you see how good our teacher plays the piano?*

[Reader, please note faulty grammar: "how *good* she plays the piano." The patient is a graduate student, and at his current age, as an adult would never use an adjective in place of an adverb. But 7-year-old children often do. This again clearly indicates he is in an age regression, not a hypermnesia.]

T: *Yes, she plays the piano very, very well.*

Pt: *I wish I could play the piano too, like Miss X.*

T: *Well, someday when you grow up, you can play it that well. How old are you, Don?*

Pt: *I'm only 7.*

T: *"Only" 7?*

Pt: *Well, it's not only 7, I mean, it's—I mean 7 is nice, it's good to be 7 . . .*

T: *Seven going-on-eight maybe?*

Pt: *Well, no, I won't be 8 until next year.*

T: *What day is it today? Do you know?*

Pt: *Well it's a Friday, I think.* [In reality it was Monday.]

T: *What's the month?*

Pt: *It's April, I think . . .* [In reality it was February.]

T: *Yes, . . . uh, huh . . . yes. What can you see when you look out of the window?*

Pt: *Well, I can see, oh, I see the school . . . the roof and the bricks, and I can see the sky and the trees, and I can see Fourth Street . . .*

T: *You can see Fourth Street?* [There is no Fourth Street in Chicago, where the patient was treated.]

Pt: *Yeah, and the Safety Sally that's standing up, and my mommy knocked over the Safety Sally one time, when she was driving . . .* [Patient laughs gleefully.]

T: *She did?*

Pt: *Yes. And then I had to run out and I had to pick it up.* [Patient laughs heartily.]

T: *Mh . . . hm.*

Pt: *That's Fourth Street over there.*

T: *Yes, over there is Fourth Street . . .*

Pt: *Up by the wall, you know where you look out of the window, that's where it is. . . . . And I can see the roof of the school.*

T: *How can you see the roof of the school when you are in the school?*

Pt: *Because it curves over there.*

T: *Oh, yes, of course.*

Pt: *It's like that . . .* [Patient gestures]

T: *It's like at, at a right angle . . . What is the color of the roof over there?*
Pt: *Oh, well, it's the color, well, I can't really see the top of the roof. Well—*
T: *Well, what's the color of the wall over there?*
Pt: *Well, it's brick.*
T: *Hm . . . hm.*
Pt: *So it's red.*
T: *Yes, it's kind of red.*
Pt: *But it's sort of orange.*
T: *Who is sitting next to you? Over there?*
Pt: *You mean in front of me, behind me, or over here, or over here? I'm by the blackboard.*
T: *Well, over there to your left.*
Pt: *Oh, that's M.*
T: *And what is his last name?*
Pt: *Well, B.*
T: *Hm-hm . . . and who is sitting in back of you?*
Pt: *Oh, well, it used to be N, but it isn't anymore . . .*
T: *Well, who is it right now? Look behind you.*
Pt: *Well, I know . . . . I don't want to look at her.*
T: *You don't like her?*
Pt: *No, I wanted P to be sitting there, but the teacher made her move.*
T: *Uh, huh . . . and where does she sit now?*
Pt: *Well, now she sits, now she sits at the back over there, over in the corner, because the teacher said that well, . . . well . . . I don't know why she had to move back there . . . it's . . . I think she talked too much. . . .*
T: *Did she talk with you?*
Pt: *No . . . no, she talked to T . . . and . . . the teacher said that if you were going to be at the front of the class when other people came in, like visitors, that you had to give a good impression for the whole class—that's why I get to sit in the front of the class 'cause I—I—I don't talk, and I give a good impression.*
T: *Uh, huh . . . now what is the teacher saying—I think she wants to say something.*
Pt: *Oh! I was. . . . Miss X is saying I shouldn't have talked to you. I'm not going to talk to you anymore . . . I've got to listen. (Long silence) Oh, good . . .*
        [Both the patient and the therapist are quiet for a while now.]

T: *Now you are feeling very happy again, . . . very, very, happy . . . You can take that feeling of happiness and go back, back, back, even further, to a time when you felt just as happy. Go back, back, back, along that rope of happiness . . . to a much earlier time. You can feel yourself getting younger and smaller, your head is getting smaller, your body is getting smaller, going back, back . . . Where are you now?*

Pt: *Oh! I'm—I'm—I'm in Y, and, and Mommy and Daddy's friends are going to bring me my new tricycle.* [Patient is so happily excited that he has trouble getting the words out.]

T: *How old are you?*

Pt: *Oh! I'm only 5 years old and I don't go to school, yet.*

T: *They are coming.*

Pt: (In a very happy, excited small child's voice with slight Japanese accent) *Oh, yes! The G's are bringing me my, oh! well, oh—it's got big blue wheels, and it's got . . . and oh, I get to ride it, and I get to ride it on the front porch, and I'm not going to fall off the front porch . . . Oh! Oh! I love my blue tricycle. Oh! I can go fast . . . oh! Oh, yes, oh yes, thank you, thank you Mrs. G yes, oh, yes, oh, oh, you . . .*

T: *Now you feel very, very happy.*

Pt: *Yes!*

T: *And you can take that happiness again like a rope or a bridge to go back further and further along . . . further and further back . . . to a time when you are 3 years old . . . 3 years old . . .*

Pt: *Oh! I . . . oh . . . oh . . . I . . . oh . . . I . . . oh! Bet he won't bite me . . . grrr . . . no, no . . . he's a puppy . . . a puppy . . . (clap hands) . . . he's my puppy . . .*
[This was the moment at which the therapist had hoped the patient again would spontaneously lapse into Japanese. But he didn't. Actually he had said two Japanese words here, then he reverted back to English; but the therapist had not heard the Japanese words nor understood them. She was in a quandary. . . . What could she do? Obviously she could not suggest to the patient that he should speak Japanese now. That would have spoiled the whole experiment. She thought for a moment; and suddenly remembered that in Japanese and in English there are two words that sound very much alike though they have different meanings in the two languages, the words

"Hai" and "Hi." They are words that in either language a 3-year-old would know. In Japanese "Hai" means "yes." The patient could understand it either as an English or a Japanese word. So she said:]

T: *Hi!*

Pt: *Hi! . . . oh, oh, oh, . . . Hi! . . . . Hi!*

        [*Japanese starts. Patient excitedly and happily talks in Japanese*]

Bo Hai bo bo hai bo bo bo	*M yes mmm yes m m m*
Boku no inu yo	*it is my dog*
Hai	*yes*
Hontoni ii desu	*really very good*
Hontoni ii desu ne	*it is really very good*
Boku no inu yo	*it is my dog*
Boku no	*mine*
Boku no inu yo	*it is my dog*
Boku no	*mine*
Ii yo, hontoni ii yo	*very good, really very good*
Hontoni ii yo, hai	*really very good, yes*
Hontoni ii yo	*really very good*
Arigato okaasan ne	*thank you mother*
Arigato okaasan	*thank you mother*
Boku hontoni in suki	*I really like the dog*
Koko ne—koko	*here—here*
Boku no homai yo	*this is my (homai—probably dialect)*
Boku no homai	*my (homai—probably dialect)*
Asuko wa boku no inu yo	*over there is my dog*
Boku no inu	*my dog*
Hontoni kashikoi kawaii inu	*really smart cute dog*
Ita su ya	*(probably dialect)*
kawai	*cute*
hontoni ano wa	*really that is*
Hontoni okii me de	*with really big eyes*
Hontoni kawaii okii menme	*really cute big eyes*
ne	*(memne = baby talk for eyes)*
Boku wa totemo	*I am quite*
Totemo belu	*quite (cannot understand meaning)*
Beruni ne	*(must be dialect)*
Beteni ne, hai	*(must be dialect) yes*

Hontoni ii de su	really very good
Hontoni ii desu ne	really very very good
Asuko boku no inu	over there is my dog
Asuko wa inu wa	over there the dog the
Inu wa nima	the dog (nima—meant for what is probably)
Name wa nani de su	what is the name
Nani	what
Inu no namae wa nani yo	what is the dog name anyway
Hai, boku wa	yes, I am
Hai, boku wa	yes, I am
Hai, boku wa	yes, I am
No, boku wa	no, I am
Boku wa wakari masu	I can understand
Hai, hai, hai	yes, yes, yes
Boku no	mine
Boku no inu ne	my dog huh
Hai, hai	yes, yes
Boku wa totemo ii yo	I am quite well
Boku ii, hai	I good, yes
Asukono inu wa boku no yo	over there, that dog is mine
Boku no inu, hai	my dog, yes
Boku no	mine
Watashi no inu asuko yo	My dog is over there
Watashi no	mine
Sayonara [*said by therapist*]	goodbye
Doshite anta wa	why don't you
koko wa	this place is
Doshite wa anta wa	why don't you
Koko no hari masen	come in to this place

T: *Don, now you are going to grow up again, you're going back along that rope of happiness. You can feel yourself getting bigger and bigger . . . bigger and bigger . . . your body is growing larger, your head is growing larger, you as a whole person are going back, back up again, until you come back to* [the date this age regression was done] *. . . and you're back again in the Psychology Building, in Dr. Fromm's office, lying in a deep chair, very happy, very comfortable . . . When you are there, a finger on your right hand will lift.* [After a

while Don's finger levitates.] *You are no longer 3 years old . . . .
you're 26 years old . . . not really, you are 27, aren't you . . . no, you
are 26 years and 3 months. When were you born?* [The therapist
here made a mistake, figuring that there were twenty-seven
years between 1941 and February 1968, the date of this session.
She quickly corrected it. It is very important after an age regression to age-progress the patient to his correct chronological age.]

Pt: *December 2nd, 1941.*

T: *How old are you?*

Pt: *Twenty-six.*

T: *That's right, that's right . . . how are you feeling?*

Pt: *Happy and relaxed . . .*

T: *Very good. With your permission I'm going to wake you up now . . . by
counting from 10 to 1 . . .*

Pt: *Yes.*

T: *By the count of 5, your eyes will open, by the count of 1 you will be
fully awake, feeling good all over . . . 10, 9, 8, 7, 6, 5, 4, 3, 2, 1 . . .
Wide awake. . . !*

Pt: *Hello.*

T: *Hai!* [Therapist tests whether the no-longer-age-regressed patient would start to talk in Japanese when he heard the stimulus word "Hai."]

Pt: *Hi! (laughs)*

T: *(laughs) Fine. How are you?*

Pt: *Good, fine, thank you.*

T: *Hi!*

Pt: *(laughs)*

T: *What are you thinking of now?*

Pt: *Well, I am trying to remember what happened.*

T: *Yes?*

Pt: *And . . . and yet . . . at the same time not wanting to . . .*

T: *Uh, huh.*

Pt: *I mean if I think really hard . . . I can remember what happened . . .*

T: *Uh, huh . . . yes. Now . . . you say you can, if you want to, remember
what has happened in the last half hour or so. You can remember,
but you don't want to.*

Pt: *Yes.*

T: *Can you tell me some more about that?*

Pt: *Well . . . I guess it's because if I think I can remember, then I wasn't that deeply hypnotized . . .*

T: *Why is it so important whether you were deeply hypnotized or not?*

Pt: *Because I want to be a good hypnotic subject.*

T: *(laughs) Well, let's see whether you can remember. . . . . What do you remember? Do you remember anything?*

Pt: *Well, I remember trying hard to think. . . .*

T: *To think?*

Pt: *Yes.*

T: *Can you tell me some more about* that*?*

Pt: *Well . . . it was, . . . well, it was, . . . when I was . . . um . . . 3 . . . I remember, I mean. I remember it was hard because . . .*

T: *What was so hard?*

Pt: *Trying to think. I mean trying to . . . I mean . . . all of a sudden I was saying words, and I wasn't sure if they were words or not . . .*

T: *I see . . . Can you describe that a little more?*

Pt: *Well . . . I mean, . . . it was like my lips all of a sudden would move into these funny shapes and I (laughs) and then I would want to say something, and you know (laughs) and wouldn't know. I mean, they would just come out and I wasn't sure if they were real or not. (Laughs).*

T: *You wanted to say something . . . which you had thought of, or how was it that you wanted to say something, and then words would come out of your mouth, but you wouldn't recognize them? Is that it?*

Pt: *Well, it's like, it was, there were certain words that I would say that, you know, I knew were words, that I knew were words.*

T: *What kind of words were they?*

Pt: *Like, they were Japanese words.*

T: *They were Japanese words?*

Pt: *Yes, I mean they were Japanese words.*

T: *How come that you would even want to say Japanese words? Or how come that they came out?*

Pt: *Well . . . because when I was little, you know, I didn't really speak English until I was, well, I spoke some, but at some point I didn't really speak English.*

T: *Uh, huh.*

Pt: *So I just spoke Japanese because we moved into a relocation camp right after I was born. I don't know why but they never. . . . . I spoke Japanese more at the end of World War II than English . . . I remember*

*that when I moved to California, I had trouble because the kids that
I grew up with there couldn't understand Japanese.*

[Later in the therapy it turned out that the reason why he
stopped speaking Japanese was not so much that the other
kids could not understand him, but it was that the family
strictly forbade him to talk Japanese so that he had to repress
it. The parents were American citizens and wanted the family
to be thought of as being American. They themselves suffered
from the animosity against the Japanese which hung on for
quite a while after World War II.]

T: *You* had *to speak Japanese?*

Pt: *Yes.*

T: *Suddenly? You mean in the trance?*

Pt: *Yes.*

T: *Tell me a little more about that.*

Pt: *And the thing was, you know, . . . part of me said, well, I mean . . .
       what, do you know, what . . . what is Japanese? I mean you don't
       know Japanese.*

T: *Uh, huh . . . yes, yes, go on . . .*

Pt: *And, um . . . but then other parts kept saying, but you have to speak
       Japanese and you're on this rope of happiness, and so . . . talk about
       what was happy, what made you happy in Japanese . . . and so I, I
       started talking, but then, then, it seemed as though, I didn't really
       know what the Japanese word was . . .*

T: *But they came out?*

Pt: *But then all of a sudden, I mean, it would pop into my mind, and
       then I would, I mean I knew what that word meant, I really knew
       what it meant. But there were other times when I would just sort of
       say things, and* my mouth would form into funny shapes and
       the word would come out.

T: *Uh, huh . . .*

Pt: *And I didn't know if that was. . . . . , and I wasn't sure if I knew
       what the word meant. I mean,* I wasn't sure if that was a real word
       or not.

T: *I see. Now at that first moment when you kind of said to yourself. . . .
       I'm 3 and I talk Japanese, did you have a choice whether you were
       going to talk Japanese or whether you were going to talk in English . . .*

Pt: *Well, see what happened was then . . . it was like when you said "hi,"
       like it was sort of like . . . I mean, I stopped understanding it as "hi"
       then, but "yes" . . .*

T: *You stopped understanding it like the American "hi," and you under-*
          stood it as the Japanese "hai," which means yes.
Pt: *Yeah, and so then, then, I . . . then . . . once I started thinking that*
          "hai," meant yeah, then it seemed as though, I mean, I thought then
          in Japanese. But the trouble is that I really have trouble thinking in
          Japanese, uh . . . I mean I wasn't sure that what I was saying was
          real or not.
T: *It came out without your always knowing whether it was correct or not?*
Pt: *That's right, or even if the words were words. I mean, I didn't even*
          know. . . . sometimes I thought I don't know what's happening . . . no
          really, my mouth would form these funny shapes, and a sound
          would come out, but I really didn't know if that was a real
          word or not.

The patient was now asked, in the waking state, to listen
to the Japanese he had spoken when in trance. He could not
understand more than two words of roughly ten minutes of the
flow of Japanese, the words for *puppy* and the masculine form of
the word for *I.* A Nisei who had not forgotten her Japanese translated the material for me. It turned out that the patient talked
most happily and most excitedly about a cute puppy dog with
great big eyes, a present his mother had just given to him. A
couple of times he used some words which the translator described as being Japanese baby talk. Toward the end, when the
experimenter said "Sayonara," in order to indicate that her visit
with him was now over, and in order to terminate the 3-year-old
state, the patient said in Japanese, "Why don't you come and stay
here with us for a while?" kindly inviting her to stay with the
family in the camp.

By a lucky coincidence, David McNeill, a well-known psy-
cholinguist, is a member of our Department of Psychology at the
University of Chicago. His wife, Nobuko, is Japanese. Together,
they had done a great deal of research on the development of
grammar in the language of small children, both in English and
in Japanese. They had found that grammatically, children do not
just learn to speak as adults do; they do not take over the grammar
of adults. They form their own grammar which changes from half-
year to half-year until it is the same as that of the adults around
them. For instance, at a certain age small children will say, "I

bringed you something" a conjugation none of them has ever heard an adult use. So I gave the Japanese part of the tape to the McNeills and asked them to tell me how old the child was who had spoken on the tape. I did not tell them anything about Don or about his chronological age, and fortunately in the age regression he had not talked in the voice of a 26-year-old man, but in a high, childlike voice. The psycholinguists said: "This child is 3½ years old." Within a range of three to four months, that was indeed the age at which the patient left the relocation camp and returned with his family to a fully English-speaking environment. The relocation camps were swiftly dissolved at the end of the War in 1945, and the Japanese American population returned to the West coast and their ordinary lives again. I found out in a later therapy hour that the patient's parents had strictly forbidden him to talk Japanese after they left the camp. They were Americans (of Japanese descent) and had been born in the United States. The Japanese, even after the war for some years, were considered to be "enemies." Don's parents so strictly forbade him to talk Japanese that he had to repress it.

There has been a long and heated controversy among hypnosis researchers as to whether in age regression the hypnotic subject *relives* the earlier times of his life or only behaves as he thinks a child of that age acts and thinks. The senior author believes this experiment demonstrates that the age regressed subject indeed brings up into full awareness what really happend at the earlier age: that he reactivates and *relives* the early memory traces.[1]

Do we have memory traces for everything that we have ever experienced in our lives and can we in age regression get in touch with each one of them? That is still an unanswered question. The authors of this book cannot imagine that our brain has enough cells to store in memory every experience we have ever had in our lives and every word we have ever uttered. But they find it possible to believe that perhaps in a sort of Zeigarnik effect (Zeigarnik, 1927) for unfinished actions, anything that has to do with yet unresolved conflicts (i.e., materials against which the ego continues to defend itself) is conserved in the brain in unconscious

---

[1]The two authors have different opinions about age regression. The senior author believes that one can have age regression; the case of Don has become a classic case that many hypnosis researchers think proves that there is real age regression.

memory traces that in age regression can be brought into awareness. Nevertheless, this in no way assumes the historical authenticity of all material elicited during hypnotic age regression.

HYPERMNESIA

Hypermnesia, *heightened* memory, is a phenomenon typical for hypnosis. It is the ability in trance to bring into awareness and to remember events, thoughts, and affects that in the waking state are not available to conscious awareness. It has led hypnotherapists to feel that the patient in trance is in closer contact with his or her unconscious than in the waking state.

Not infrequently when one tries to help the patient to go into an age regression, what one gets is hypermnesia. Hypermnesia, too, is a valuable tool in the uncovering process and may at times result in uncovering forgotten memories and affect. Hypermnesia helps the patient to recover more deeply buried material than can be reached psychoanalytically in the waking state; but not quite as much material, and not as vividly, as what can be uncovered by means of age regression.

How do we judge whether what the patient produces is an age regression or a hypermnesia? In age regression the patient talks in the present tense ("my parents' friends bring me my new tricycle") because experientially to him it is really happening now. In hypermnesia the patient talks in the past tense ("my parents' friends brought me my new tricycle") because he is not reliving but remembering it. In addition, in age regression the patient frequently, though not necessarily, talks in a childlike voice and talks in the way a child would talk. In hypermnesia he does neither.

THE PAINTING IN THE ANTIQUE FRAME

Another method for reaching repressed and otherwise defended-against material is that of "The Picture in the Antique Frame." As an induction or deepening technique, the hypnoanalyst suggests that the patient is walking down a staircase; and that with every step he is going down, he will go down into deeper and deeper trance. At the bottom of the staircase he will find a "Room of his Own," which looks very much like a room he would like to have or has had at some time. (This is where the uncovering technique starts.) It is a very special room. A room in which perhaps he can see things that ordinarily he does not see. The hypnoanalyst lets the patient walk down the staircase, step over the threshold into this room of his own, and look around. On one wall, he suggests, the patient may see a painting hanging. It is a contemporary painting, but it is in an antique frame, and full of dust and spider webs. He further suggests that the patient may want to walk over to that painting, and look at it more closely, become curious to see what it represents. (Notice that all of these are permissive, open-ended suggestions.) The therapist, still in a permissive but more directive way then may say: "There is a table close to the painting near the wall with a bottle of turpentine, some Kleenex, and rags. Perhaps you would like to clean the dust and spider webs off the painting so that you can see what it represents. Symbolically it relates in some way to your problem or represents your conflict."

After the patient has described what he sees in the contemporary picture (the current conflict representation) the hypnoanalyst says: "And now you will notice something interesting about the picture. Look at the lower right hand corner of it. The oil paint seems to have come loose there. If you pull carefully where the paint has come loose and roll it back, you can see that on the canvas there is another painting underneath this one. It was painted at an earlier time. Put some turpentine on one of the rags, remove the top layer carefully, and look at the picture underneath. What does it show? (again an open-ended question). This procedure may be repeated as often as necessary to get at deeper and deeper layers of the conflict. To promote insight free association is usually combined with this technique.

AMNESIA

Hypnotic amnesia, lack of memory, is posthypnotic forgetting of what has happened in trance. It can occur spontaneously when the material that has come up in the hypnotic state cannot be tolerated in conscious awareness by the patient. This is what happened to Breuer and Freud's (1893–1895) early hysteria cases when in trance patients talked about incestuous abuse, but upon awakening denied ever having experienced (or said) anything like that. Amnesia also can be induced by direct or indirect suggestion. In therapy, the only advantage we can see in inducing an amnesia is to help a patient whose ego is not yet strong enough to protect him against the danger of being overwhelmed by material that has come up in the hypnotic state.

While as psychoanalysts, in general, we are against repression, and attempt to help our patients to facilitate the return of the repressed, there are special cases in which it is wise, or at least not unwise, to help them continue to keep the repressed trauma in the unconscious. The types of cases we are referring to here are survivors of concentration camps and of other kinds of inhuman torture; or adult patients who in childhood witnessed horrible events (e.g., saw their father murder their mother in front of their eyes). What happened in the concentration camps under the Nazis was so terrible, so much beyond the realm of the average expectable environment (Hartmann, 1939), that it is often better for such patients to protect themselves and repress it than to face these traumas in conscious awareness day in, day out, for the rest of their lives. Keeping such experiences out of awareness is a merciful repression, a needed protection to start a new life again. We would advise the hypnoanalyst not to tamper with that.

DISSOCIATING THE OBSERVING EGO
FROM THE EXPERIENCING EGO

In psychoanalysis we do not accept a patient for treatment unless he has the ability to observe his own feelings as they occur, that is, the ability to dissociate the observing part of the ego from the experiencing part. Hypnosis is an altered state of consciousness in which this ability is naturally greatly enhanced (Fromm, 1992b). In fact, two major theorists of hypnosis, Janet (1893) and E. R. Hilgard (1974, 1977) conceive of dissociation as the essence of hypnosis—though not in an ego psychological sense. Fromm

(1968a), with her background in psychoanalysis, has emphasized the aspect of dissociating the observing from the experiencing ego as a naturally strong and important factor in hypnotherapy.

Dissociation can be achieved in various ways. Most frequently one will employ imagery. For instance, the hypnotherapist may give a severely burned patient, who daily has to endure the very painful procedure of having his dressings changed, the following posthypnotic suggestion:

> Whenever the doctor comes to change your dressings, or whenever you feel too much pain from your burns, you can let yourself float out of your bed and body into that comfortable chair over there and watch what the doctors are doing to that person here on the bed who looks somewhat like you. You may find it interesting to watch. Or you may prefer to read a book, or just to sleep for a while in that comfortable chair over there.

It is important to construct the wording of the suggestion so that the "I," the self, remains within the observing ego and the experiencing ego becomes the object.

In cases of posttraumatic stress disorder (PTSD) it is usually wiser to titrate the return of the repressed than to let it come back into awareness and be reexperienced all at once together with the overwhelming affect that was connected with it originally. In such cases the hypnoanalyst may figuratively (in imagery) put the patient's observing ego behind a safe thick glass wall from behind of which at first the "I" need not yet affectively participate, but only watch, observe, and uncover what has happend to the child in the past.

Not infrequently dissociation of the observing ego from the experiencing ego, or dissociation of the mature adult ego from the childhood ego, occurs spontaneously in trance; particularly in age regression. We remember an experimental subject who was age regressed to age 4 and who described in a high childish voice how he was playing with his little friends in the sandbox. Suddenly his voice became his adult voice again and half-puzzled, but with great delight, he said to the experimenter: "You know, something strange is happening now. I feel I *am* that child who plays down there in the sandbox. But at the same time I am also the adult me sitting up here in a deep chair in your laboratory watching that child down there who is playing in the sandbox.''

EGO STRENGTHENING

The English hypnotherapist John Hartland (1965, 1971) was the first one to write about ego strengthening suggestive methods. While seemingly simplistic, they work quite well with many different kinds of patients. They are designed to encourage the patient to stand on his own feet, and to gain trust in his inner coping resources.

We differentiate three kinds of these ego strengthening suggestions: (1) general ego strengthening suggestions; (2) specific ego strengthening suggestions to facilitate the discovery and effectiveness of the patient's inner coping strategies; (3) specific suggestions to foster the patient's sense of self-efficacy (Brown and Fromm, 1986, p. 194).

The purpose of the general ego strengthening suggestions is to strengthen the patient's feeling of well-being and self-confidence. It is usually given as a graded posthypnotic suggestion:

> With every passing week (or passing day) you will find yourself getting less and less anxious, discouraged etc.; or you will find yourself getting more and more cheerful . . . more and more confident that you will be able to handle your problems. You will find yourself being more content with yourself . . . feeling more sure of yourself . . . and much more accepting of yourself than you have ever been before.

These very direct, simplistic suggestions work more frequently than one would assume. In particular, they work with the highly hypnotizables and with relatively simple-minded people of a not too complicated character structure. With more sophisticated patients it is better to use symbolic and imaginative ego-strengthening procedures. For instance one might say to the more sophisticated hypnotized patient:

> Perhaps you would like to imagine that you are in a beautiful park. It's Springtime. The grass under your feet is bright green and

soft . . . and there are many trees about. Young trees and old trees. Over there you see an old tree that has weathered many a storm. It has a heavy, big trunk, and its branches with bright young leaves stretch toward the sky like arms that are stretched up joyfully. You walk over toward the tree . . . you are attracted by it. You wonder whether you could span that tree with your arms. You move close to the tree . . . so close that the front of your body touches it. You put your arms around the tree. . . . You find that you can hug that tree and that your fingertips just touch each other on the other side. You can feel the bark of the tree. You put your feet close to the tree. And suddenly something very strange happens. Your feet sink into the good earth next to the tree and seem to become roots among the roots of the tree. . . . And you notice the sap rising in that strong tree that has weathered many a storm.

And another strange thing is happening now: As you are encompassing the tree, pressing your body against it and encircling it with your arms, some of the strong, good sap that is rising in the tree is flowing into you. . . . Some of it is also flowing into your roots, directly from the Good Earth. Notice how good that makes you feel. Notice how much stronger you feel now. . . . And perhaps the thought comes to your mind. . . . that in the weeks to come. . . . you will be able to stand up for yourself and to cope with your problems. . . . You may find that from week to week it will get easier and easier to do that as your own confidence in yourself keeps growing.

Now perhaps you want to loosen your fingers and your hands and arms from encircling the tree. . . . As you pull your legs up, the roots that your feet had become will change back to being your feet again; and you'll walk away from that strong tree that has been able to weather so many storms and you feel very differently about yourself, much better than you did before. Strong and hopeful. You can take that feeling up with you into the waking state, and every time you think about or picture it in your mind, you feel that strong, healthy sap rising in you again.

Ego strengthening here is attempted through symbolic imagery and by helping the patient to internalize the healthy strength of the hypnoanalyst. Symbols of the healthy strengths of the therapist and of his willingness to give of it to the patient, as well as to let the patient internalize him or her are: the tree that has weathered many a storm, the "Good Earth" into which the patient's feet sink and become roots, the sap that by osmosis flows from the tree into the patient. This is a much more artful, more psychoanalytically oriented method (the imaginary internalization of the hypnoanalyst). We believe it is a more effective method of ego stengthening than the direct suggestion techniques of Hartland (1965, 1971), though they, too, are valuable.

THE IDEAL SELF TECHNIQUE

The ideal self technique is based on the psychoanalytic concept of the ego ideal. In contrast to the superego, which represents that which we feel we ought to be or ought to do, the ego ideal is the inner representation of ourselves as we would *want* to be. The ego ideal must always be somewhat higher than the level of achievement we have reached at any age; but not too much higher.

If a patient comes to us, let's say with a phobia, one of the techniques that we would use in hypnoanalysis is the ideal self technique.

Here is the case of a flying phobia that was cured in two sessions: The patient, John, was a graduate student, who was afraid of flying. He was close to graduating from business school and had been offered a job in which he would have to fly at least once a month from the Midwest to the East coast. In the hypnotic hour the hypnoanalyst asked him to sit at one end of the couch, then helped him into hypnosis, and suggested that the door was opening now and a person would enter who looked very much like him and who was the person he really wanted to be. That person would come in and sit down at the other end of the couch. After a little while John said that this young man had come in. We called him Jonathan. John said Jonathan looked very much like him and was the kind of person he, John, wanted to be: He had no fear of flying. Flying to Jonathan, I (E.F.) confirmed, was just another, ordinary thing he did whenever he needed or wanted to do it. I then suggested that John would feel as if he were pulled into the body of Jonathan, as if by a magnetic force. After a few minutes I asked him where he was in Jonathan's body and how he felt in it. John said that he was not as big as Jonathan, in fact he felt quite small. But he could look out through Jonathan's eyes. I told John that as now he was inside of Jonathan he could also feel what Jonathan felt. There was a little silence and then John said again that Jonathan wasn't afraid of flying. I asked John when Jonathan would take his next flight. His answer was: later this afternoon, from Chicago to Philadelphia. I encouraged John to stay inside of Jonathan today and feel the same affects that Jonathan felt; over the weeks to come he could grow fully into Jonathan's body and fill out every curve of it. I described how Jonathan was taking a taxi to go to the airport, and how he was entering the plane and making himself comfortable in his seat with John inside himself; that the plane was taking off and John was looking out through Jonathan's eyes seeing the clouds in the sky and reading a book with him. After a while they would look down on the ground and see interesting things such as streams and fields and cities on the ground. From time to time, as the two were on the (imaginary) journey in our office I asked how John felt inside of Jonathan. In the beginning he said he felt a little bit queasy, but as time went on he relaxed more and more. We then discussed the descent of the plane during which John felt a little more uncomfortable but not really phobic, and the good time they were having in Philadelphia. Then I said that a few days had passed and they were now returning to Chicago by air. John described that he was now feeling a good deal bigger in Jonathan, really fitting relatively well into Jonathan's body. He also reported very little anxiety. We had made a tape of this session and I asked John to listen to it every day until I would see him again. A week later I went with him through a similar imaginary procedure in hypnosis in which he flew to another town sitting next to Jonathan, no longer inside of him. After that I urged him to take a short flight by himself in reality not just in fantasy. If he wished to, he could imagine that Jonathan was on the same plane as he was.

John did take a one-hour flight and reported triumphantly that, while at times he had felt a little queasy he had been able to do it, take a flight by himself. I warmly congratulated him and asked him to take another flight a week later and report to me afterwards by telephone how comfortable he had felt. It is important in such cases to say that he should report how comfortable he had felt and not to say he should report whether or not he had been afraid or uncomfortable. (We want to avoid even a minor suggestion of fear.) John again found that he could fly without fear, particularly if he involved himself in a very interesting book, or if he imagined that Jonathan was sitting on the plane behind him. He had successfully overcome his phobia, and I urged him to be proud of that. Follow-up telephone calls at three months, six months, and one year showed that he was cured of his phobia by using the ideal self technique.

Sometimes one needs to use additional techniques. The same technique does not always work with everyone. But the ideal self technique, helping a person to grow more closely into his own ego ideal, is a relatively powerful technique for overcoming fears, phobias, and lack of self-confidence. It helps the patient to cope with problems he has not been able to master before. Does it lead to a total character restructuring? Sometimes it does, sometimes it does not, but total character restructuring, anyhow, is not always the goal in hypnoanalysis. Where it is necessary, of course, it must be done by employing in addition some of the other hypnotic methods that have been described in this book and in Brown and Fromm (1986).

CREATIVITY

Kris (1936) was the first psychoanalyst to propose the concept of "regression in the service of the ego" for creative activities. A regression in the service of the ego is a healthy regression. The ego initiates and terminates it for its own benefit. It constitutes going backwards one step in order to be able to go forward two steps. Hartmann (1939) called it an "adaptive regression." Other adaptive regressions are going to sleep at night instead of working for twenty-four hours, letting oneself be nursed when one is sick, relaxing, or just "letting go." Frequently regression in the service of the ego is accompanied by an increase in primary process thinking, as for instance in dreaming during sleep, or in the creative act.

Gill and Brenman (1959) and Fromm (1979, 1992a) conceive of hypnosis as a regression in the service of the ego, because in hypnosis the individual regresses from logical, reality-bound, verbal secondary process thinking, to developmentally earlier, prelogical, primary process thinking in imagery. He or she makes constructive use of the ability "to let go" for a while or of what Patricia Bowers (1978) has called "effortless experiencing." The regression can voluntarily be terminated by the patient (or by the therapist). Usually it is of short duration, for just a few minutes or for an hour. In the altered state of hypnosis, the patient makes contact with his or her unconscious faster and more deeply than in the waking state, which is the reason why people often are more creative in trance (Fromm, 1988).

The creative forces not only express themselves in the fact that the patient gets better much faster than in the waking state in psychoanalysis, but we have also seen many a patient who in hypnosis or self-hypnosis produced highly artistic paintings, writings or other works of art who never had produced any before hypnotherapy in the waking state or whose productions were better in a (self) hypnotic than in the waking state (Bowers, 1978, 1982–1983). Some kept this artistic productivity after hypnotherapy ended; some only used it to express themselves during the time of their treatment.

In a pathological regression the overall ego regresses to an earlier, disorganized level of functioning and thinking. In hypnosis a subsystem of the ego is "triggered into action. . . . In the established hypnotic state the subsystem becomes reorganized into a temporarily stable structure that not only regains control of the 'deautomatized' apparatuses, but also is put into the service of the overall ego. . . . The overall ego never loses contact with reality totally" (Gruenewald, Fromm, and Oberlander, 1979, p. 625). Reality—and with it secondary process thinking—just fades into the background of awareness and unconscious processes fill the resulting void with effortless, often playful cognitive activity.

COPING, COMPETENCE, MASTERY, AND THE JOY OF FUNCTIONING

The goal of hypnotherapy, and in particular that of hypnoanalysis, is to enable the patient to cope with his or her problems and to master them competently. But coping does not only refer to dealing with conflict, it also refers to a person's dealing with novel situations and with challenges in the environment (Murphy, 1962). The person who copes successfully meets challenges, and in the process of attempting to meet these challenges acquires mastery and competence. Competence and mastery are always accompanied by highly pleasurable feelings, the joy of functioning at higher and higher levels. It is this pleasure in competence and mastery—an ego function—that the hypnoanalyst attempts to stimulate in the patient during the integration phase of therapy.

Let me reaffirm what was stated in Brown and Fromm (1986):

> Part of the therapist's task consists of helping the patient to allevi-
> ate anxiety, tension, and conflict. However, not all tension in life
> is undesirable. Quite the contrary. Tension can be joyful, as is the
> tension in foreplay and in the sexual act. And joyful tension is at
> least part of what one experiences in the creative process, the
> ecstasy part of the "agony and the ecstasy." Any theory of personal-
> ity that leaves out the concept of the pleasure of functioning, the
> joy of being able to do something well, ignores a multitude of
> processes that are characteristically experienced by children and
> by dedicated adults. One may teach, do research, climb mountains,
> ski, play a strenuous and hard game of tennis, or row in a race—not
> because it is one's job and one is paid to do it, or because one
> thinks one ought to do it for one's health; but because it is fun,
> because it is exciting, because one passionately *wants* to do it.
> There is joy in ego-functioning at increasingly higher levels of
> competence [Brown and Fromm, 1986, pp. 222–223].

TOUCH

Touch is a controversial topic. We all know that it gives comfort to those in distress. We all have a natural tendency to put an arm around a person who is grieving; or to put a steadying hand on the arm of a person who is very anxious or suffers pain. Infants need the maternal and paternal touch more than anything else. In ordinary life people touch each other naturally to express love, empathy, and warm affect.

But here lies the catch when it comes to therapy. Just because touch plays such a great role in love and sexuality, and because patients often have sexual longings for and sexual fantasies about the therapist, psychoanalysts have always been very careful about touching and made it a rule not to touch their patients. The patient in an oedipal transference might interpret the therapist's touch as a seductive gesture.

Unfortunately there are some therapists who have touched and seduced some of their patients. That is an unethical and totally inappropriate way of using touch in the healing arts. Therapists should never touch patients for whom they have sexual feeling, particularly if they are the kind of person who might be carried away and forget what their responsibilities toward the patient are. But that does not mean that patients toward whom the therapist has no sexual feelings should be denied the soothing, calming, and supporting effect touching can have. Touch is the earliest preverbal communication between the infant and its caretaker; and it remains a needed and very expressive form of communication between people throughout the life span.

Gentle touch with a focused intent on helping has been known for many centuries as a frequently effective method of healing. It has been used in primitive societies as well as in the Western world where it is usually referred to as "the laying on of hands." Nurses have used it for ages and are currently doing some interesting scientific research on it which shows that touch works best therapeutically when the therapist and the patient go into a sort of altered state of consciousness; and that touch not only can soothe and comfort the ill person but that it also can produce objectively measurable physiological changes (Meehan, 1990).

Most hypnotherapists and hypnoanalysts feel that nonseductive touch, used when the hypnotized patient is in danger of being overwhelmed by strong affect, is an effective technique when given with the clear intent of wanting to soothe, comfort, and help the patient to integrate. Many hypnoanalysts do use it in this way, successfully. Others shy away from it either because they have detected sexual feelings within themselves toward the patient, or because they are afraid that a patient might misunderstand their intention and start a lawsuit against them. The decision of whether or not to use touch as a therapeutic tool must be made on an individual basis and with great caution.

8

Treatment of Dissociative

Disorders and

Developmental Deficit

PART I: MEMORY, TRAUMA, AND
DISSOCIATION

A HYPNOANALYTIC PERSPECTIVE ON
DISSOCIATION

Perhaps for historical reasons dating back to the turn of the century controversy between Freud and Janet, psychoanalysis has largely ignored the problem of dissociative disorders. Frankel (1990) cautioned professionals treating multiple personality disorder (MPD) and dissociative disorders that the construct of dissociation may become the late twentieth century counterpart to what hysteria was in the late nineteenth century. That is, its boundaries may become so overinclusive that it will eventually mean everything and therefore nothing. Indeed, reliance on only descriptive features of dissociation, without a broad theoretical framework, may not lead to development of the precise and discriminating measures we need.

Lerner (Lerner, 1992; Tillman, Nash, and Lerner, 1994) discusses dissociation from the vantage point of psychoanalytic ego psychology and seeks to outline a comprehensive theory of dissociation from four perspectives: (1) defense, (2) memory, (3) consciousness, and (4) self. Integrating these four domains, Lerner defines dissociation as a defensive process in which experiences are split off and kept unintegrated through alterations in memory and consciousness with a resulting impairment of the self. It is Lerner's model which serves as our working definition of dissociation.

Lerner notes that dissociation can be distinguished from other defenses such as repression, splitting, and denial. Both splitting and dissociation separate mental contents, are used to deflect anxiety, and are involved in identity disturbance. But in splitting, the separation is really a polarization of self and object representations into "good" or "bad." In contrast, the division in dissociation is far broader, and rarely corresponds to "pure culture" manifestations of "good" and "bad."

In dissociation, disturbances of memory are prominent. Different theorists have speculated as to how dissociation affects the process of memory storage and retrieval. Examining the effects of psychic trauma on the mind, Horowitz (1992) has suggested that memories of the trauma are registered and retained but are difficult to integrate with existing meaning structures and the self schema. In terms of Klein's model, Horowitz postulates that in psychic trauma, the memory structure as a whole is not impaired, but the subfunction of categorization within existing schemas is impeded.

Almost all contemporary descriptions of dissociation include a disturbance in self cohesion. Concerns with self are also prominent in contemporary psychoanalytic literature. Dissociation theorists tend not to approach the disturbance of self from a psychoanalytic perspective, meaning that although a disruption in self or identity is a descriptive characteristic of dissociative disorders, contemporary investigators often fail to elaborate what they mean when speaking of self. By transposing current dissociation theorists' writings onto the various psychoanalytic conceptions of self, we can examine the various disturbances of self from several structural concepts.

Following Lerner's model, two functions of the self are impaired by dissociation: the function of immediate experiencing and the function of self observation (i.e., what in other chapters of this book we refer to as the experiencing and the observing ego). During trauma, when the individual experiences the painful event as happening to a different self, the experiencing self seems especially separate and estranged from the observing self. Or when an individual is absorbed in a special state such as an hypnot-iclike trance, in an effort to protect the self from memories of a traumatic experience, the observing self seems to all but diminish with the experiencing self's increasing absorption. While the functions of the self usually operate in a harmonious and inte-grated manner, in dissociation the experiencing and observing functions are split and operate separately. Most commonly this is reported as the experiencing self becoming distant and estranged while there is an acute awareness of the observing self.

HYPNOSIS, MEMORY, AND HISTORICAL EVENT

Most contemporary clinical theorists studying the psychologi-cal effects of trauma have adopted models similar to that of Breuer and Freud (Breuer and Freud, 1893–1895), contending that early childhood trauma leads to repeated overuse of dissocia-tion until it becomes the individual's primary psychological de-fense, manifesting itself in dramatic alterations in the experience of self and world (Frischholtz, 1985; Putnam, 1985; Kluft, 1985; Spiegel, Hunt, and Dondershine, 1988). Based on a wealth of clinical observations, these models define a causal continuity be-tween trauma in childhood and subsequent adult symptoms. Hyp-nosis is often effectively used in the treatment of dissociative disorder and posttraumatic stress disorder, but the idea that there is a direct causal relationship between early trauma and dissocia-tive pathology remains problematic (for a comprehensive review see Tillman, Nash, and Lerner [1994]). One of the most pressing issues in this regard is how narratives generated in psychotherapy (and hypnotherapy) square with historical events.

Though psychoanalytic theorists like Roy Schafer (1983) have been beating the hermeneutic drum for many years now, and researchers have issued many an empirical caution about the reconstructive nature of memory, there is a deeply entrenched conviction among practitioners that when our patients report a "memory" of a childhood trauma it must in some essential way be true. But there is now a growing sensitivity to the possibility that at least some reports of early trauma may not in fact be true (Tavris, 1993). That is not to say that all adults who suddenly report a memory of early trauma are somehow indulging in a believed-in fantasy. It is to say that in some cases the trauma will have happened and in some cases not. In the latter case it may indeed be derivative of oedipal fantasy.

From a purely logical point of view, two types of mnemonic errors are possible when an adult psychotherapy patient reflects on whether she was traumatized or not as a child. The patient may believe he or she was not traumatized when such an event did in fact occur (a false negative), or the patient may believe he or she was traumatized when the event did not in fact occur (a false positive). We contend that it is exceedingly important to realize that the problem of false positives and the problem of false negatives are distinct. The existence of one type of error does not necessarily eliminate the possibility of the other type of error. If patients sometimes report a traumatic event when it did not happen (a false positive), this does not require us to reject the possibility that patients may fail to remember such an event when it *did* occur (a false negative). If cultural and psychological factors can create a need to believe that certain events occurred when they did not (false positives), then these same factors can operate in such a way as to engender *not* remembering certain events when they did in actuality occur.

A great deal of public attention has focused on the advisability of using hypnosis to "enhance recall" for recent and remote events. There are still many clinicians willing to uncritically testify to the effectiveness of hypnosis in this regard. Nevertheless, there is consensus within the scientific community on six points (reviews of this rich literature include: Nash, 1987; McConkey, 1992; Kihlstrom, 1994; Kihlstrom and Barnhardt, 1993). First, hypnotizing a person and giving suggestions for improved memory has not been shown to be more effective than are other nonhypnotic interrogation techniques. Second, any increase in accurate memories during hypnosis is accompanied by an increase in inaccurate memories. Third, use of hypnotic age regression techniques does not enable adults to literally respond like children. Nor does it insure that what they "remember" actually happened. Fourth, because hypnosis involves explicit suggestion, subjects are more vulnerable to leading questions on the part of the interrogator. Fifth, hypnosis may compromise the subject's ability to distinguish memory from imagination or fantasy. Sixth, when hypnotic techniques are used, subjects later report being more certain of the content, even when it is inaccurate. Thus, confidence levels of the witness are artificially inflated, which can then prejudice a jury. For these reasons the American Medical Association (AMA Council on Scientific Affairs, 1958) and the Society for Clinical and Experimental Hypnosis (1986) advised extreme caution in its use. Many courts have followed suit (Laurence and Perry, 1988).

There is evidence that hypnosis contributes to the problem of false positive memories (that is, remembering things that did not in fact happen). The evidence from the lab and the field is very clear. No responsible clinician or researcher can simply ignore the possibility of this form of memory error. For the purpose of *therapeutic progress*, hypnosis and other psychotherapy techniques may be indicated. But, for the quite distinct purpose of investigation (for finding out the historical truth) these techniques can obscure rather than clarify what actually happened in the past, and hypnosis can be part of that problem. It seems incumbent on therapists to remain abreast of scientific developments in this area, and to inform patients that introduction of hypnosis into the therapeutic mix may be problematic, legally and emotionally.

In a sense, however, hypnosis has been unfairly singled out by the media and the courts on this issue. Of the hundreds of expressive therapeutic techniques now extant, hypnosis is the only one for which there are substantial data on memory and its accuracy. For various historical reasons, no other therapy technique has been so scrupulously examined as to its effect on memory. Because of this, hypnosis has become a kind of whipping boy for the sins of psychotherapy in general. The media and the courts focus on the memory-distorting effects of hypnosis precisely because hypnosis researchers are the ones who have most rigorously documented how plastic memory is in treatment. They have painfully and tediously documented the role of expectation, suggestion, imagination, and fantasy as codeterminants of what people report remembering, in treatment and outside of it. It is not that these factors are absent in other expressive therapies, it is just that if one wants to find out what science has to say about how memories can be distorted in therapy, one is going to encounter hypnosis, and not much of anything else. Hypnosis research has delivered an important and disturbing message to society at large: Passionately believed-in recollections about the past are not always what they appear to be. This message is so profoundly upsetting to cherished conventional notions of memory that courts, and some elements of the mental health community, yearn to "kill the messenger." The issue is much more complex than this. The problem is not just the nature of hypnosis per se, but the nature of memory as it emerges in the context of any psychotherapy.

On this question of recovered memories then, when we are faced with patients who experience themselves as suddenly and agonizingly remembering a previously forgotten trauma, either in the course of hypnosis or in spontaneous flashback states, we should above all else recognize the enormous clinical importance of this material. We should indeed consider that these reports might represent memory traces of an historical event (in this sense an undoing of a false negative error). But we owe it to ourselves, the patients, the patients' family, and society at large, to be mindful that a literal reliving of an historical event is not humanly possible. Memories do not literally "return" in pristine form, unsullied by contemporary factors like suggestion, transference, values, social context, and fantasies. In short, false memories can and do occur. Further, it is the special responsibility of clinicians to be mindful that getting better in therapy does not bestow upon the patient a mantle of infallibility. Indeed what we call insight may be partly a process of creation, and only partly one of discovery.

Below, the junior author (M.N.) shares two cases with the reader which had reasonably successful outcomes: The first case is of a patient who came to believe that he was exposed to a specific and traumatic event that almost certainly did not occur (example of a false positive); the second is of a patient who had initially not remembered a traumatic event, which almost certainly did occur (a false negative). Hypnosis was used (though sparingly) in both therapies. These cases were presented in a journal article (Nash, 1994), and are here reprinted with permission.

A UFO ABDUCTION: AN EXAMPLE OF A PROBABLE FALSE POSITIVE MEMORY ERROR

A 31-year-old single, white male patient consulted me reporting recent multiple flashbacks of a previously unremembered traumatic incident that occurred when he was 17 years old. He was acutely anxious, preoccupied with the incident, experiencing nightmares, interpersonally withdrawn, physiologically hyperreactive, and in short quite indistinguishable from PTSD patients. Upon interview and testing he was revealed to have a somewhat ruminative cognitive style and clearly not psychotic. This was a quite successful young professional man whose sexual, family, interpersonal, and work adjustment had been reasonably satisfactory.

He related to me that he had always known that something odd had happened to him when he was 17. What he had *always* remembered was that on a hot summer day he and a male friend had taken a trip to a particularly scenic and isolated part of the Rocky mountains, only a few miles from home. He and his friend both remember walking along a path together about twilight, near a stand of Red Woods. Then they came upon something very odd. It was a kind of brightly glowing grub on the path. They both moved up to the grub for a closer look. Suddenly there was a bright flash of light which startled them both. Then there was another flash of light. They had no idea what these lights were. In some distress, they briskly walked back to the car. The odd thing was that when they returned home they discovered that it was 11:30 at night. They had lost approximately two hours of time. The patient reported that this occurrence was the sort of scary story he and his friend would relate at appropriate times to friends around a campfire. It had always puzzled him, but in a fanciful and not distressing way. Three months before he consulted me he had picked up one of the popular books about UFO abductions, and this caused quite a bit of distress. He read sixty pages and was so terrified that he had to put the book down. He contacted the author of the book who happened to be conducting a workshop in a neighboring state. In short, the patient and his friend visited the author; they were both hypnotized by him twice during the weekend. While my patient's friend reported no memories of being abducted, my patient had two extraordinary hypnotic experiences filled with vivid details of the aliens, their spacecraft, and a peculiar machine that they attached to his penis to obtain samples of sperm (this instrument is commonly reported among abductees). Further, other memories of previous abductions occurred during the hypnosis. The author's conclusion was that while the patient's friend had not really been abducted, the patient had. As is seen so often in these cases the patient began to wonder whether there had been many more incidents of abduction throughout his life. As I mentioned earlier he was acutely anxious, sleep disordered, prone to nightmares, and physiologically hyperreactive. Thus, he came to me in a great deal of turmoil, acutely anxious, hoping that I might help him clarify what did and did not happen.

I believe I successfully treated this highly hypnotizable man over a period of three months using standard uncovering techniques and employing hypnosis on two occasions. My stance with him was that the abduction material as elaborated by the original hypnosis must be immensely important, but I told him that my operating hypothesis was that it was not literally true. Hypnosis and free association did enable him to elaborate more details of the abduction with some attending dramatic abreaction. My persistent attention to symbolic manifestations of conflictual material contained in the abduction material, while decidedly unappreciated by him initially, did yield some insight around tolerating his own passive–dependent longings. About two months into this therapy his symptoms abated: he was sleeping normally again, his ruminations and flashbacks had resolved, he returned to his usual level of interpersonal engagement, and his productivity at work improved. What we did, worked. Nevertheless let me underscore this—he walked out of my office as utterly convinced that he had been abducted as when he walked in. As a matter of fact he thanked me for helping him "fill in the gaps of my memory."

Here we have a stark example of a tenaciously held conviction about the past, which is almost certainly not true in all its detail, but which, nonetheless, has all the signs of a previously repressed traumatic event. I could discern no difference between this patient's clinical presentation around the trauma and that of my sexually abused patients. Nevertheless the patient seemed to get better as he was able to elaborate on the report of trauma and integrate it into his own view of the world. Appendix A (see p. 242) is a brief note by this patient 12 years post-treatment. We asked him to respond to the above clinical vignette and candidly share with the reader *his* understanding of if, how, and why the therapy worked.

AN EARLY SEXUAL SEDUCTION: AN EXAMPLE OF A PROBABLE FALSE NEGATIVE MEMORY ERROR

A 46-year-old man presented with complaints of depression, social withdrawal, excessive sleeping, violent outbursts, sexual problems over the previous two months, and some mild suicidal ideation. The patient was a well-educated individual from the Southwestern region of the United States with a sputtering career in electronic engineering. He was married, and currently taking courses at the community college which would redirect his career. He reported inconstant parenting in a rural community, with a father who died when he was quite young, and a mother who seemed prone to overly dramatic hysterical outbursts. From early adolescence through his midtwenties the patient reported experimenting with drugs. But it was alcohol which became a serious problem. Throughout this period he seems to have been a vocational underachiever. Though he completed his B.A. he was exceedingly dissatisfied with himself, prone to emotional outbursts. Through AA he had abstained from alcohol use entirely for the ten years prior to treatment with me. But he remained an underachiever vocationally.

My initial formulation was of an introjective depression such that the patient experienced himself as unworthy of pleasure: sexually, at work, and in relationships with authority figures. There was a figural component of self-punitiveness that moved the patient to undo and spoil anything phallic, from an erection to a work product, to school. I anticipated a therapy that would address issues of inhibited aggression, and would be saturated with themes of competition, power, and guilt.

What brought the patient into treatment was the two-month exacerbation of symptoms above noted. Interestingly this was co-incident with the emergence of two very troubling and intrusive unbidden images. One was of himself at the age of 9, being surrounded by a group of older threatening children in an unfamiliar house. This image was vague, but nonetheless highly charged with fear. He wondered if something sexual had happened at that time. The second was an image of himself curled up on his bed at home, sucking his thumb. By the time therapy began the patient was becoming increasingly preoccupied with what these images could mean. As is my custom, I acknowledged his curiosity about the intrusive images, and assured him that they must be important and that we should try to understand them. But I also shared with him the fundamentals of my clinical formulation and recommended that we focus our work on addressing his dramatically self-destructive flight from his own feelings and needs. He was amenable to this approach.

A period of five sessions followed in which I introduced the patient to hypnosis, finding him to be highly hypnotizable. Initial work on the intrusive images was quite productive of intense emotion (mostly fear) but bereft of specific new content. Eventually, however, the patient began to elaborate on the first image as being of a familiar (not unfamiliar) house. It seemed to be a house in his rural Texas home, the house of an older child whom he knew only tangentially. Though details were still wanting, he could identify a distant cousin who remained in the background during whatever attack there was, if any. He remembered lying face down with his buttocks exposed. He also remembered boys with erections, apparently masturbating. At this point (about twelve sessions into the therapy) the focus of our work returned to the initial formulation and symptom cluster involving introjective depression. Outside of hypnosis we explored and worked through his conflicts over "standing out" in any way, almost always utilizing the images of the trauma as an anchor. It was during this work that some of his more florid symptoms began to resolve: Sex with his wife became reasonably satisfying, his perfectionism at work was eased, his procrastination and self-sabotage at school ceased, his insomnia resolved. At this point, I was satisfied, but he was not. He wanted to know more precisely what did and did not happen to him at age 9. In this case there was a fairly definitive means of finding out, one which he hesitated to pursue: He could contact his cousin to ask him.

After much equivocation on this issue he finally decided to ask his cousin about the incident and to invite him to one of our last therapy sessions. His cousin was a 45-year-old oil contractor who lived out of town. Though reluctant initially, with acute embarrassment the patient's cousin declared that he remembered the incident quite clearly. Apparently there were four or five boys (variously related to one another) who during that time would become involved in mutual masturbation and sex play among themselves. During the incident in question the patient had stumbled upon their activities and was unwillingly incorporated into them. There was no sodomy, but the patient was masturbated upon by "several" of the boys. The cousin claimed to have been appalled by the incident, but unwilling to stop it. He was surprised to find that after the incident the patient acted like it never happened.

It seems reasonable to infer from the third party verification in this case that an emotionally charged sexual event did indeed occur to the patient when he was 9 years old. We cannot know the definitive details of the incident with certainty, but we do know that the patient reported a period of not remembering the incident; that affect-laden imagery emerged relative to the incident later in his life; and that fuller (though not complete) elaboration of the incident was associated with hypnosis and psychotherapy.

OVERVIEW OF BOTH CASES

For the purpose of clinical efficacy all we need to know is that the patients were helped to resolve a cluster of debilitating symptoms in part by enabling them to elaborate more fully their mnemonic experience, and by helping them to integrate these experiences into their own self-narrative. The issue of historical truth is another matter. In the UFO abduction case at least, getting better had nothing to do with real insight, recovery of real memories, or uncovering of the truth in any historical sense. Whether the mnemonic experience derives from highly symbolic imaginal material, screen memory, or actual memory traces, it is possible that constructing a compelling self-narrative provides some symptom relief. This is where the purposes of clinical utility and explication of developmental psychopathology may diverge. Clinically, the therapy was reasonably successful; but we cannot use this success alone to validate my patient's stories of how his symptoms arose and what they mean historically.

Summarizing then, when we are faced with patients who experience themselves as suddenly and agonizingly remembering a previously forgotten trauma, either in the course of therapy or in spontaneous flashback states, we should above all else recognize the enormous clinical importance of this material. We should indeed consider that these reports might represent memory traces of an historical event (in this sense an undoing of a false negative error). But we owe it to ourselves, the patients, the patients' family, and society at large, to be mindful that a literal reliving of an historical event is not humanly possible. Memories do not literally *"return"* in pristine form, unsullied by contemporary factors like suggestion, transference, values, social context, and fantasies elaborated at the time of (and subsequent to) the event. In short, false positives can and do occur. We believe that the field must acknowledge the reality of both types of inferential errors concerning self-report of early trauma: false positives and false negatives.

PART II: THE HYPNOANALYTIC TREATMENT OF TRAUMATIC MEMORIES AND DEVELOPMENTAL DEFICIT CAUSED BY EARLY INCEST[1]

Incest so deeply violates the moral standards of our society that, by and large, for centuries we have denied its existence;

---

[1]An earlier version of this section of chapter 8 was published in Dutch by Erika Fromm and Daniel P. Brown in Onno van der Hart, Ed. (1992), *Trauma, dissociatie en hypnose* (*Trauma, dissociation and hypnosis*). Amsterdam/Lisse: Swets & Zeitlinger, pp. 221–248.

particularly its existence in the middle and upper classes. Freud came close to recognizing it as the core cause of all hysteria, but then construed such reports as oedipal fantasy in most cases. However, since about 1980 there has been an increase in the number of reported incest cases, by psychotherapists, social scientists, and law enforcement agencies. Incest is a potentially severe traumatic experience. Not only girls, but also boys can be the victims. Incest can leave deep emotional scars on the victim which do not heal by themselves, nor can they easily be removed.

DEFINING INCEST

Clinicians and sociologists have come to see that incest is a widespread social problem (Sgroi, 1982; Russell, 1986; Draijer, 1988). According to recent surveys, the most common type of incest occurs across generations; that is, between a child and a parent, stepparent, grandparent, or aunt or uncle (Russell, 1986; Courtois, 1988). Peer incest that occurs between a child and an (older) sibling, has not been studied as extensively and may be more common than so far known.

Incestuous activity is likely to involve a progression of activities over time beginning with nonsexual activities—such as affectionate holding or bathing the child and progressing to an increasing sexualization of the relationship, to fondling, and eventually to penetration with finger and genital (Meiselman, 1978; Sgroi, 1982; Draijer, 1988).

Beginning with Burgess's pioneering work (1975), many clinicians have speculated that incest is not primarily sexual in nature but rather is an act of aggression and dominance. When incest occurs, the adult imposes his (or her) own needs upon the child.

THE PREVALENCE OF INCEST

Until the late 1970s the existence of incest in the Western world was largely denied. In the 1980s and early 1990s our society began to recognize it as a common trauma in the lives of many.

But since 1992 there has also been a backlash, created by the False Memory Syndrome Foundation that again attempts to deny it.

Various extensive surveys have been conducted on childhood sexual experience with adults by Draijer, 1988 (for the Dutch Government); Russell, 1986, on a large and carefully selected sample on the West Coast Bay Area of the United States; Sedney and Brooks, 1984; Boon and Draijer, 1993, and others.

Draijer (1988) planned and conducted an excellent national survey in Holland which showed that 32.2 percent of all Dutch women have had unwanted sexual contact before the age of 16. Nearly half of them, 15.6 percent, were most often abused inter-generationally by family members (fathers, stepfathers, grandfathers, or uncles). In *at least* 3 percent to 18 percent of the incest cases, the perpetrators were brothers, stepbrothers, or cousins. The only other genuinely random sample survey (Russell, 1986) similarly reported that by age 18, 38 percent of all women in the Bay area of California have been victimized by some form of unwanted sexual contact with one or more adults, or a person who is at least five years older. Authorities in the field believe that the current estimates are still conservative (Herman, 1981), since not all victims are willing to report their sexual victimization and many have repressed or dissociated the traumatic experiences. The typical "conspiracy of silence" (Butler, 1978) is the main reason why so many incest cases remain unreported or untreated. Mothers often collude with the incestuous involvement between father and daughter or brother and sister by denying that it is occurring (Meiselman, 1978).

THE PERPETRATORS

The perpetrators of incest are fathers, brothers, uncles, and occasionally grandfathers. They always demand that the child not tell anyone about the incest, and threaten the child with the loss of both parents' love if the child should break the silence. The mother usually has some vague knowledge of what goes on between the father and the child, but looks the other way, and does not help the child or give her the chance to unburden herself.

RISK FACTORS FOR INCEST

A parental history of incest greatly increases the risk for a child (Goodwin, McCarthy, and DiVasto, 1981). Such parents either repeat the abuse that was inflicted on them (sometimes in a dissociated state) or they fail to protect their children, like their parents did.

THE SHORT- AND LONG-TERM EFFECTS OF INCEST

Bad after-effects vary across victims from few symptoms to severe psychopathology (Herman, Russell, and Trocki, 1986; Conte and Schuerman, 1987; Koch, 1980; Draijer, 1990). Recent clinical studies have tended to categorize (1) the emotional sequelae, such as anxiety, phobias, depression, anger, guilt and shame; (2) somatic effects, such as nausea and vomiting, pain, and sleep or eating disturbances; (3) behavioral symptoms, such as school problems, running away, delinquency, substance abuse and alcoholism, self-mutilation, early marriage and pregnancy, and the repetition of traumatic abusive relationships; and (4) sexual problems, such as confusion of sexual orientation, problems of desire such as inhibited sexual desire or promiscuity, and problems of arousal and climax, such as vaginitis, frigidity or impotence, anorgasmia, premature or delayed ejaculation (Gomez-Schwartz, Horowitz, and Sauzier, 1985; Finkelhor and Browne, 1986; MacFarlane and Waterman, 1986; Draijer, 1988, 1990; Courtois, 1988).

Many experts believe that incest may result in a developmental arrest along one or several lines of normal development (Rosenfeld, 1979; Gaddini, 1983; Brown and Fromm, 1986; Draijer, 1988, 1990).

The areas of normal development most likely to be affected are: sexual development; relationship to others; the self; the development of self-esteem; affect tolerance; cognitive and character development. Sexual functioning is the area in which long-term effects are most likely to manifest themselves (Molnar and Cameron, 1975; Finkelhor, 1979; Gelinas, 1983; Draijer, 1990).

The frequency of sexual problems in the population of incest survivors is significantly higher than in the general population (Lukianowiez, 1971; Weeks, 1976; Meiselman, 1978).

Another very common area in which long-term effects of incest occur is that of relationships with others. Incest is a betrayal of trust in a significant family relationship during childhood (Freyd, 1994). The long-term effects of such betrayal on the capacity for attachment relationships are only just beginning to be understood. Common difficulties include difficulty in forming object relationships, and maintaining some detachment from relationships or keeping some distance from intimate involvement (Herman, 1981; Lindberg and Distad, 1985; Draijer, 1990).

Incest can also interfere with the development of the self and of self-esteem. Some types of childhood incestuous involvement, especially when complicated by sadistic aggression or an excessive need to deny the reality of incest (Rieker and Carmen, 1986), can interfere with the normal development of a cohesive sense of self either by having caused dissociation or by leaving the victim vulnerable to fragmentation (Soll, 1984). The individual either reports that her or his self consists of separate parts, or he or she experiences bounded separate selves, as is the case in the multiple personality (Coons, 1980; Watkins and Johnson, 1982; Putnam, 1985; Braun, 1990; Kluft, 1990). While self fragmentation represents the more extreme case of self pathology following incest, impairment of self-esteem is frequently present in incest survivors (Finkelhor, 1979; Herman, 1981; Gelinas, 1983). Many incest survivors see themselves as somehow different from others (Krener, 1985). They experience themselves as "damaged goods" (Sgroi, 1982).

An additional common area of self pathology is the inhibition of self development, a kind of pseudomaturity (Lustig, Dresser, Spellman, and Murray, 1966; Meiselman, 1978). This interferes with normal play and active exploration of interests common to childhood. Since play and discovery are vehicles of self-exploration in childhood (as well as of exploring the outside world) self development is inhibited. The range of potential interest and ambitions becomes restricted.

Incest can also interfere with the normal development of affect. The intense stimulation of sexual and aggressive impulses may lead to their long-term dysregulation. Sexual and aggressive impulses may find too much or too little expression. Incest survivors at times are highly promiscuous and at other times manifest inhibited sexual desire. Mature sexual adaptation is relatively rare among victims. They may be passive and nonassertive or highly irritable and full of rage. Seldom are they *appropriately* angry. The normal capacity for affect tolerance may be impaired, so that some incest survivors have little ability to tolerate intense, or even minor, affects (Brown and Fromm, 1986). Many experts have noted that the necessity to deny the reality of the trauma may contribute more than other factors to the overall psychological harm (Rieker and Carmen, 1986).

Perhaps the single most consistent predictor of the long-term effects of incest is age at onset of incest. Incest victims, at pre-school age, typically are less symptomatic than school age victims (Adams-Tucker, 1982; Gomez-Schwartz et al., 1985). The real psychological harm done to preschoolers may not appear until much later in life, in the form of the development of the self and self-esteem, damage to the capacity to form object relations, and to effect affect regulation (Brown and Fromm, 1986) or to the overall mental organization (Cohen, 1981). School-age incest victims are more likely to manifest a variety of obvious symptoms, either internally based symptoms such as anxieties, phobias, fears of situations, or externally based symptoms such as learning difficulties and conduct problems. Adolescents manifest more acting out than other age groups (Sloan and Karpinski, 1942).

TREATMENT

Uncovering and Abreaction
Until recently treatment approaches for adult incest survivors have generally adhered to an uncovering model of treatment with abreaction of affect. According to this model it is assumed that the goal of treatment is to remember completely and to encourage the full expression of feelings associated with the incest trauma (Breuer and Freud, 1883–1885). Many contemporary models for the treatment of incest are still based on assumptions about the value of uncovering, although emphasis has shifted

from remembering and expression per se to the integration of the traumatic memories.

While there may be no dispute about integration of the memories and affects associated with the incest trauma as being therapeutically useful, some caution is indicated for those who adhere to a strict abreactive approach to therapy. Abreaction per se may be harmful to the incest survivor. Many incest survivors come to therapy in the denial phase of posttraumatic recovery. They are likely to present with so-called disguised PTSD (Gelinas, 1983) wherein the only manifest symptoms are anxiety-related symptoms or depression. The therapist's too rapid encouragement to uncover the memories and affects associated with the presumed trauma may overwhelm the patient's defense. The patient's symptom picture may then shift rapidly from the denial phase to the intrusive phase of posttraumatic adjustment. Such rapid shifts may render her so distressed and fearful that she drops out of treatment. Moreover, since the therapist in such a case has inadvertently contributed to the patient's undue distress by emphasizing uncovering too early in treatment, the therapeutic relationship has become a retraumatizing relationship, not an emotionally corrective experience.

Recovery from the complicated trauma of early incest is possible only in the context of a long-term therapeutic *relationship* with a caring, warm, and empathic therapist who times things well (Brown and Fromm, 1986; Olio and Cornell, 1993; Nash, 1994).

More than in any other emotional illness, with cases of early incest it is necessary to respect the defenses for quite a while, particularly the tenacity of the dissociation or the repression. The therapist must not pierce these defenses too early, no matter how clearly the patient's material seems to show that here one is dealing with a case of early incest. Mental and emotional fragmentation, a psychotic break, might occur if the patient is robbed of these necessary protective mechanisms too early.

In some cases the repressed material wells up as symbolic imagery or through symbolic behavior. A male patient asked for hypnoanalysis after he had a work-related accident in which a sharp-edged metal object injured him near the anus. In the hospital he went into a *severe* panic and quite unnecessarily feared for his life. A few days later, this clearly heterosexual man went into another panic in which he was convinced that he was a homosexual. In therapy he later disclosed that he had always had a great fear about driving across the white lines that separate car lanes on wide streets. Only in a place where there were no lines, or where the lines were interrupted, could he cross from one lane to another. His fantasy, even long before his work accident, had been that one of the white lines would tilt up like a stick and penetrate him anally. Severely trembling and practically overwhelmed by fear, he eventually remembered in trance that his grandfather had sexually assaulted him from behind when he was 4 years old.

Symbolic and behavioral manifestations are disguised confessions of the trauma that has occurred; so are screen memories. A screen memory is an unconsciously produced false memory that disguises the real event and is felt by the patient to be somewhat less horrible than what actually happened to him or her.

If a PTSD patient is first seen in the denial phase, the clinician may fail to detect evidence of the trauma when taking the history. Early incest victims are much more easily diagnosed during the intrusive phase of the illness, via the communications given through symbolism and screen memories.

Hypnosis per se can be a useful *diagnostic* tool for cases of repressed incest. Incest patients often have an unusual reaction to the initial hypnotic experience. To the surprise of the patient as well as to that of the therapist who does not know yet that the patient is suffering from PTSD, traumatic memories may dramatically intrude into consciousness during early hypnotic sessions. Or the patient may experience severe generalized, panicky anxiety while being hypnotized, but does not remember the traumatic event. In such cases the ideational content of the trauma has been defensively isolated from the affect connected with it. Very poor hypnotic responsiveness coupled with great agitation in the initial hypnotic experience should also make the diagnostician suspect a posttraumatic stress disease.

Hypnoanalysis and the Long-term Effects of Incest

Because hypnosis is a means of gaining access to memories and affects not consciously available, it is the treatment of choice for various types of trauma (Brown and Fromm, 1986).

Hypnosis is introduced first as a means of relaxation. Induction and deepening are induced by suggesting waves of relaxation and relaxing imagery. The patient is encouraged to use self-hypnosis for the purpose of generating a relaxed state whenever he or she is tense or uncomfortable, but not for uncovering when he is without the hypnotherapist who can support him. A good deal of guided imagery is used in the therapy hours, but in the beginning the therapist avoids suggesting scenes that in any way could be associated with the trauma. The patient is also encouraged to allow his own imagery to emerge spontaneously while he is with the therapist. Usually the sequence of images that unfolds over time is a series of representations of the trauma in progressively less and less disguised symbolic forms, as well as screen memories. Gradually the patient achieves partial recovery of the traumatic memories and some conscious memory, or reexperiences the affects associated with the trauma. Both in the hypnotic state and in the waking state, patient and therapist together go over the material that the patient has produced in hypnosis, in order to help the patient integrate into waking memory the forgotten traumatic events. Indirect hypnoprojective techniques, such as cloud gazing, drawing in hypnosis, and anagrams, also are used to help the patient become consciously aware of the childhood trauma. Because trust in the parents, trust in adults, trust in the world has been shattered in the child who has been incestuously raped by the person who should have protected him or her (Freyd, 1995), it is particularly important for the therapist to put himself into the role of a reliable, nurturing, good and durably giving parental figure. Only thus can the patient develop new trust in people, eventually face the trauma in all its starkness, and overcome it.

The hypnoanalyst must provide a safe and facilitating environment in which the borderline patient can recapitulate or experience for the first time with a better parent figure the early phases of normal self-development. These are the periods from age 4 months to 3 years when the child normally struggles on the one hand with the desire to merge with the mother, and on the other hand with the fear of being engulfed by her; and then with dependency needs and the opposing needs for autonomy (Mahler, Pine, and Bergman, 1975; Masterson, 1976, 1981; Adler, 1985). The hypnoanalyst must provide soothing when the patient is anxious; help to develop object constancy and overcome "splitting"; and above all freely and unstintingly give a great deal for a long time. For incest victims who have suffered developmental deficit, the hypnoanalyst needs to provide an emotional environment that is nurturing, stable, protective, and constant. She or he must provide a "holding environment" (Winnicott, 1960), in which the patient is in a safe climate and can explore his or her own self in the relationship with the hypnoanalyst. Only through such a relationship with a deeply caring therapist can the patient fully internalize a sense of demarcation between the "me" and the "not me," the self and the other. When the patient has progressed along the developmental line of the self to the next phase, the level of narcissism (age 1–3), he or she needs to experience what Kohut (1971) has called "the gleam in the mother's eye." The therapist must take on the role of the proud mother who thinks her child is a genius and praises him for every minute success he has in his or her outside life or in therapy. The purpose here is to develop self-confidence in the patient, and thus to repair the developmental deficit. The therapeutic process with patients who have suffered from severe developmental deficit due to early training should parallel the phases of normal preoedipal development as indicated in Table 8.1.

With early incest cases (as well as with other cases of PTSD) intermittent resistance to trance characteristically occurs. Often material will come up for a while, and then, when the patient is not yet ready to face it, hypnotizability and the willingness to work with hypnosis decrease markedly. When the patient again becomes willing to close in on the trauma, she or he will ask to use hypnosis again, and hypnotizability will increase, often returning to its original level or exceeding it.

Treatment of early childhood incest, particularly where it involves developmental deficit (fixation or regression to the preoedipal states of the development of the self) is technically one of the most difficult types of hypnotherapy or hypnoanalysis that one can undertake. It necessitates more symbolic handling of the material that comes up than do most other kinds of cases. The use of imagery and age regression involving screen memories rather than the original traumatic ones, the use of drawings and

TABLE 8.1

Hypnoanalytic Methods for Treatment of Early Incest

1. Relaxation therapy.
2. Therapist takes on role of good, giving mother.
3. Working toward internalization of the good love object.
4. Gaining control over "splitting" as a defense.
5. Integrating love and hate objects and achieving solid object- and self-constancy.
6. Ego building and enhancing the patient's control over affect.
7. Praising the patient for any, even the most minute, successes in the therapy and in real life.
8. Developing solid personality structure and realistic evaluation of self and others.
9. Careful, slow uncovering of the repressed trauma by means of:

> patient's spontaneous hypnotic imagery
> guided imagery
> suggested hypermnesia
> automatic drawing
> dissociation of observing and experiencing ego
> interpretation of screen memories and symbolic acts
> projective fantasies
> age regression
> dreams and free association

10. Working through rage against incestuous attacker by means of vengeful hypnotic imagery.
11. Playful exploration of new interests and activities, first to be done in hypnotic fantasies, later in reality.
12. Working through the fear of sex.

anagrams, and the employment of delays, are all techniques that can allow repressed material to unfold at the patient's own speed. Even when the hypnoanalyst, through the patient's unconscious symbolic communications, has become aware of the trauma that the patient has suffered, she or he must not overwhelm the patient by confronting her with "the truth" or pushing her to become aware of the full truth. When handled correctly, the patient will eventually come to it, but it may take three years of hypnoanalysis. Uncovering should be done only when the patient in hypnotherapy has developed enough ego strength to face the trauma. First the uncovering occurs in the form of screen memories or acting out; only later when the patient has gained solid object constancy and self-constancy, when there is no more splitting the world into the good and the bad people, and when the structures of the self have become solid, can one go to the uncovering in terms of the original trauma. If there is a danger of the patient fragmenting under the impact of having to face the original trauma in all its starkness, that is, if the patient's ego is not strong enough to withstand such disclosure, feelings of rage and vengeance first must be worked out in imagery in hypnosis on the person who in the screen memory represents the real rapist, or in doll play. After the material has been uncovered and worked through, and after feelings of shame also have been worked through, there follows a phase of liberation, of increased self-development, and of autonomy. And after that, one helps the patient work through the remaining sex phobia, in the same way in which one would work with a neurotic. However, even with the best of hypnoanalysis, some patients will never be able to achieve normal relaxed enjoyment of sexuality.

The hypnoanalyst must provide a safe and facilitating environment in which the borderline patient can recapitulate, or experience for the first time, the early phases of normal self development with a good parent figure.

Table 8.1 sums up the hypnoanalytic methods one uses in the treatment of developmental deficit caused by early incest.

In order to treat early incest cases successfully the therapist must be a person who has real empathy and treats the patient with tender loving care, as a good mother would do, for a long time. But then there comes a time when, also like a good mother, the therapist must encourage the patient to get out of the regressive, dependent position and go forward, become autonomous, develop her own mature and fulfilling life, and leave the horrible trauma that has happened to her behind instead of forever wallowing in it. The past cannot be changed; but the future, if one works on it, can be bright.

APPENDIX A

In response to the clinical vignette, I'll begin by establishing that my confusion, frustration, and struggle regarding my unexplainable experiences continues. The difference today, compared to when I first approached Mike Nash, is that I have learned how to accept these confusing memories without allowing them to interfere with my day to day life.

The guidance I received from Mike was centered on accepting that a situation which is part of my "Life Story" may not ever be understood or explained, nor does it necessarily need to be, rather accepting these events as a reality and moving on without distraction was the base of our work. My experience is one where "the truth" is unobtainable, and given that, the role Mike played was one of "damage control," damage in the sense of emotional trauma, coming to terms with an experience which is totally unacceptable in the reality of the professional world I reside in, and once again, that cannot be explained.

9

Hypnosis in Short-Term

Psychoanalytic

Psychotherapy

Almost from the beginning there was pressure from within the burgeoning psychoanalytic movement to shorten the duration of treatment. For the most part Freud resisted such attempts, though in an address to the International Congress in 1918 he tacitly recognized the role of hypnosis in the rapid amelioration of shell shock during the Great War and acknowledged that the benefits of psychoanalysis could be extended if: "The pure gold of analysis [might be] freely alloyed with the copper of direct suggestion" (Freud, 1918, p. 168). Ferenczi in particular championed the cause of providing briefer intervention to more patients (Ferenczi and Rank, 1925). Later, Alexander and French (1946) proposed substantial and controversial modifications in the management of transference-countertransference to promote therapeutic experiences which were at once more focused and time-limited. In the past thirty years there has been a mushrooming of comprehensive models of short-term psychoanalytic intervention, some with the unapologetic goal of modifying long-standing pathology (Malan, 1963, 1976, 1979; Mann, 1973; Davanloo, 1978; Sifneos, 1972, 1979; Mann and Goldman, 1982; Strupp and Binder, 1984). Relying heavily upon the seminal work of the senior author and recent innovations in short-term psychoanalytic psychotherapy, this chapter examines when and how hypnosis can augment dynamically oriented brief therapies.

SOME PRELIMINARY CONSIDERATIONS ABOUT TIME-LIMITED UNCOVERING THERAPIES AND HYPNOSIS

Generally speaking, proponents of short-term psychoanalytic psychotherapies attempt to achieve their goals across three distinct intervention phases (Malan, 1963, 1976, 1979; Mann, 1973; Sifneos, 1972, 1979; Davanloo, 1978; Mann and Goldman, 1982; Strupp and Binder, 1984):

1. *The initial assessment phase.* Patient history, interpersonal characteristics, and ego functioning determine the initial appropriateness of short-term treatment approaches. Usually patient selection is limited to fairly circumscribed problems arising in psychologically intact, neurotic-level patients.
2. *Identification of the core dynamic conflict.* The goals of the therapy are specific and focused, not involving broad changes in characterological maturity (Davanloo is an exception here);
3. *Resolution of core dynamic conflicts via altered psychoanalytic technique.* Though narrowly focused, the pace of the interpretive work is accelerated through technical alterations which guide the management of transference, resistance, and regression.

There is a solid base of clinical and research evidence to support the claim that hypnosis is well suited to the aims and process of brief uncovering therapies, across all three of these phases. Brown and Fromm (1986) and Brown (1992), in an exhaustive review of the clinical literature, conclude that hypnosis can speed the course of symptom improvement in traditional psychoanalytic psychotherapies and psychoanalytic psychotherapies. Recent laboratory findings suggest that hypnosis involves a topographic regression which may promote emotional articulation of conflictual material, enhance access to symbolic processes, and encourage deautomatization of ingrained, maladaptive defensive operations (Nash, 1987). Frankel (1976) and Orne (1977) found evidence that the cognitive and perceptual shifts experienced by hypnotic subjects may prepare the way for conflict resolution and insight. But the flesh and blood of any therapeutic effect of hypnosis is undoubtedly associated with its facilitation of dramatic, immediate, and accessible transference reactions (Fromm, 1968b; Nash, 1988). These intense transference reactions underlie the enormous clinical potential of hypnosis, but at the same time present special challenges in pacing and dosage of interpretative work.

Before considering how hypnosis can be employed across the above phases of short-term intervention, it is necessary to elaborate upon three relevant aspects of hypnosis. First, hypnosis involves a topographic regression (Nash, 1987, 1988). If ill-managed this regression can eventuate in untoward dependence on the therapist, an outcome to be avoided at all costs according to most short-term therapists. Use of a permissive approach, and an emphasis on modulation of disruptive affect, support of mastery, and conflict-resolution can serve to deflect the patient away from the more iatrogenic aspects of ego passivity and infantile dependence.

Second, the issue of hypnotic susceptibility becomes especially relevant in the selection–assessment phases of short-term psychotherapy. Though perhaps not normally distributed in a classic sense (Woody, Bowers, and Oakman, 1992), hypnotic susceptibility, like intelligence, is a stable trait which does not vary much across time and situations. Interestingly, success in purely supportive hypnotic interventions (e.g., smoking cessation, weight loss) does not appear to hinge on the patient's susceptibility level. On the other hand, hypnotic susceptibility does seem pivotal in determining the outcome of interventions focusing on pain alleviation and insight: Moderate to high hypnotizability is modestly related to success under these circumstances. One should note, however, that approximately two-thirds of individuals fall within the moderate to high hypnotizability range, and almost all subjects can experience hypnosis to some extent (J. R. Hilgard, 1965). Nevertheless, trial hypnosis with a patient is suggested by many clinicians as a way to assess their responsiveness to hypnosis, and as a way of disabusing the patient of the usual misconceptions about the phenomena themselves. There are a number of brief standarized protocols which can serve this purpose (E. R. Hilgard, Crawford, and Wert, 1979; Morgan and J. R. Hilgard, 1975, 1978–1979a,b). In addition there is now a well-normed and standardized automated procedure to measure hypnotizability utilizing interactive computer technology (Grant and Nash, 1995).

Finally the relative expressiveness of the therapeutic intervention must be considered. Brown and Fromm (1986) outline four hypnotherapeutic paradigms: symptomatic relief, supportive ego strengthening hypnotherapy, dynamic hypnotherapy, and hypnotherapy of developmental deficit. Proponents of short-term psychoanalytic psychotherapies generally aim for change that is more substantial than symptom alleviation, but they defer to long-term therapies the task of pervasive and dramatic character change. Clearly then, the relevant strategies for hypnotic intervention in short-term therapies are supportive ego strengthening, and dynamic hypnotherapy. Supportive hypnotherapy is designed to modulate disruptive affect, reinforce ego syntonic adaptive defensive and coping strategies, and support mastery and conflict resolution. Dynamic hypnotherapy is primarily expressive in intent and designed to provide insight and working through of significant arenas of conflict for patients with encapsulated symptoms.

HYPNOSIS AND THE INITIAL ASSESSMENT PHASE
OF SHORT-TERM PSYCHOTHERAPY

It is exceedingly dangerous to gloss over the differences across models of short-term psychotherapy in regard to patient selection. While there is some consensus concerning exclusion and inclusion criteria, there are still areas of contention. At the risk of oversimplifying the often quite elegant selection paradigms, we will concentrate here on two areas of general agreement, exclusion criteria and inclusion criteria, both of which address the same underlying critical patient characteristic: intact ego functioning.

Exclusion/Inclusion Criteria
Malan (1976) outlined nine criteria which should exclude patients from short-term treatments: psychotic involvement, serious

suicide attempts, drug addiction, gender confusion, long-term hospitalization, more than one course of electroconvulsive therapy (ECT), chronic incapacitating obsessive–compulsive symptoms, chronic incapacitating phobic symptoms, and gross destructive or self-destructive acting out. Operating from a more empirical basis, Strupp and Binder (1984) found a cluster of patient characteristics to predict outcome in their form of short-term psychodynamic psychotherapy. These were: emotional discomfort with symptoms, a capacity for basic trust, a willingness to consider conflicts in interpersonal terms, a willingness to examine feelings, a capacity for mature relationships, and motivation for the treatment offered.

Ego Functioning as Overarching Criterion
As Davanloo (1978) pointed out the exclusion and inclusion criteria index a unitary aspect of psychological status: ego functioning. More than other clinical theorists, Davanloo intentionally fashioned the initial interview to be a comprehensive assessment of ego functions, including quality of human relationships, affect containment, psychological mindedness, motivation for treatment, cognitive intactness, capacity for an observing ego, and level of psychosexual adjustment. Strupp and Binder acknowledge that a traditional history/mental status examination may not provide the necessary information concerning the patient's level of ego functioning. While they direct clinicians to relevant psychological assessment techniques, hypnosis can also be used in the initial assessment phase to probe for ego resiliency and interpersonal efficacy.

Because hypnosis involves a shift to a more receptive ego state (Fromm, 1979), and concomitant emergence of usable primary process material, the clinician using hypnosis may be especially well-positioned to assess, not only the ego's capacity to tolerate regression, but its characteristic ways of doing so. When employed in this way hypnosis operates much like a projective technique. The clinician provides enough hypnotic imagery to supply structure, but gives the patient free rein to elaborate on this structure in whatever way seems natural. The question becomes: Can the patient tolerate and manage this kind of challenge in ways that might facilitate affect expression, conflict resolution, and insight?

Does processing through imagery enable the patient to temporarily relax resistance, suspend censorship, and adaptively problem solve, or is resistance mobilized in a brittle and desperate attempt to contain overwhelming threat (Kubie, 1943; Horowitz, 1970; Shorr, 1972; Reyher, 1963)? Thus use of hypnosis represents a new variation on an old theme. For years short-term theorists have championed use of trial interpretations during the assessment period. In a sense what we are suggesting is that hypnosis might be used as a trial regression. We now demonstrate how hypnosis can be used to assess two aspects of ego functioning which are core components of any patient selection system.

Assessment of Affect Tolerance
As Davanloo (1978) points out, assessing affect tolerance in one or two initial sessions is quite difficult, because patients usually wish to avoid experiencing and expressing troubling emotions. Nevertheless, the patient's ability to mobilize and tolerate a range of dystonic affect (e.g., guilt, shame, fear) is cited as a core precondition for most short-term treatments.

Case Example. A 33-year-old married white male presented at intake with complaints about swallowing. There were intrusive thoughts about swallowing too much/not enough, aspirating saliva or mucus, and the unacceptability of spitting. There was a long and fruitless search for traditional medical solutions to the problem, involving many types of specialists. Medical evaluations repeatedly revealed no physical basis for the functional difficulties around mucus, coughing, and swallowing. The patient maintained a relatively fulfilling relationship with his wife and two children. Though his work efficiency was somewhat compromised by his symptoms, the patient's career as a business administrator was flourishing. Thus, indications for short-term intervention were the circumscribed nature of his complaint, good motivation, and neurotic-level functioning. The major question mark was whether this overideational man could experience and tolerate the affect which would inevitably accompany any form of expressive therapy. If the patient proved to be unable to utilize affect, a supportive/cognitive therapy aimed at symptom relief might prove more effective. If, on the other hand, affect-laden material could be properly expressed and contained, something beyond symptom relief might have a reasonable chance of success. Accordingly, on the third evaluation intake session hypnosis was induced with some preliminary ideomotor suggestions to establish the patient's hypnotic responsiveness. As he was moderately hypnotizable the patient was given the following suggestion during hypnosis:

> In a little while I am going to stop talking, and when I do, you are going to have a dream; a real dream; just the kind you might have when you are asleep at night. But there will be two differences. First, this dream will be about your swallowing. This dream will be about what your swallowing means. Second, this dream will be dramatic; it will have some feelings involved. So, you are going to have a dream. A real dream. A dramatic dream about what this swallowing business really means.

The dream thus evoked was indeed very rich: He dreamt that he was a little boy again, driving in his father's car, as he did many times as a youngster. The car was filled with cigarette smoke and his father would only open the windows briefly to spit out phlegm after coughing. As the patient described how sick he felt, and how irritating the smoke was, his eyes actually began to tear in the session. The car became so smoke-filled that he could see nothing. He could only hear his father's cough; and feel his own wet, irritated eyes and throat. He was angry, and he knew he was crying. After some postdream questioning during hypnosis, it became quite clear that this patient's fairly circumscribed obsessional symptoms about swallowing reflected unresolved conflicts about being suffocated and even poisoned by authority figures, especially his father. Thus, it appeared that intense feelings (anger, grief, and an abiding attachment to his father) could be accessed by this young man, and could become available for use in a short-term intervention.

Assessment of Motivation

The theorist most identified with the importance of assessing the patient's motivation for change is Sifneos (1979). Two distinctions concerning motivation should be noted here. First, some determination should be made as to the patient's conscious and unconscious attitudes about treatment. Second, what is the balance between the patient's wish for change versus symptom relief? Is there a robust desire for change, or (for instance) is there a pervasive unconscious desire to satisfy infantile needs for supply? Hypnotic techniques may provide some interesting avenues to explore unconscious motivation for change.

Case Example. A 26-year-old married female patient presented with a thunderstorm phobia. During the spring she would become almost immobilized with fear during even the most innocuous showers. Television weather forecasts of violent storms would render the patient anxious for days prior to the anticipated "stormy day." While she reported that her symptoms had "come and gone" over the years, an upsurge in the frequency and intensity of symptoms coincided with her recent marriage, one that was proving to be problematic. Her initial request was for medication for her "nervous problem," though she was curious as to whether hypnosis might be of some use. Although this patient presented with some positive indicators for a short-term psychoanalytic treatment (conscious motivation was high, affect tolerance seemed acceptable, she was bright with neurotic-level pathology) there was ample reason to doubt her motivation for change.

Upon her second intake visit the patient was hypnotized, and with some difficulty, was able to experience a relaxed state in which she responded to some but not all suggestions. To examine the patient's motivation for change the clinician administered suggestions for age progression:

> In a little while I am going to count to 5 and as I count ahead, you will move ahead in time, and as I count, time will move ahead, at each count one month will go by, . . . so that by the time I reach *five*, it will be August. During all those months you will have been in treatment with me, and you will have overcome this fear of storms. You will be at peace because you will know what this fear of storms really means. When I reach the count of 5 it will be a stormy night in August. It will be a very stormy night in August when you are at home with your husband. It will be very stormy

and you will have gone through five months of treatment with me quite successfully. You will have found out what all this fear of storms means. When I reach the count of 5 it will be a stormy night in August, but you will have gone through therapy here, and you will tell me all about what happens. . . .

The patient described a moderately vivid experience of being with her husband at home on a stormy night. Imagining the lightening and thunder visibly shook her. But she soon described herself as arising from her living room chair and going to the bathroom medicine cabinet. She described taking a pill, settling in her chair, and the storm went away, as if by magic. She described looking at her husband and thinking how petty and unfair she had been with him about her troubles.

The patient's age progression was judged to reveal little genuine motivation for the rigors of insight oriented therapy. A brief systematic desensitization supported by pharmacotherapy was moderately successful in reducing levels of fear during storms. There were no reported changes in the problematic marriage.

IDENTIFICATION OF THE DYNAMIC FOCUS

All psychoanalytically oriented models of short-term intervention emphasize the importance of establishing a dynamic focus for the work with each patient. Luborsky (1984) refers to this focus as the "core conflictual relationship theme"; Strupp and Binder (1984) as the "cardinal symptom," "specific intrapsychic conflict," or "maladaptive conviction about the self." But however labeled, if a short-term intervention is to be maximally efficient, the therapist and patient, together, must come to some conclusion regarding the dynamic focus of the therapy (Sifneos, 1972; Malan, 1976; Armstrong, 1980; Davanloo, 1980; Strupp and Binder, 1984; Luborsky, 1984).

Of course what stands in the way of this collaborative effort by therapist and patient is the resistance. Even among patients who are motivated, responsive, and who present with specific complaints, establishing a dynamic focus can be complicated by complex and unconscious defensive machinations by the patient.

While Davanloo (1980) champions an aggressive model of trial interpretations during the initial assessment phase as a means of confronting resistances and determining the patient's core neurotic difficulties, this relentlessly systematic confrontation of patient resistances is viewed by others as problematic. Strupp and Binder (1984) acknowledge that such early and direct confrontation of resistances may be immensely productive with some patients, many less resilient patients may experience these confrontations as harsh disaffirmations, engendering a disruption in the collaborative therapeutic relationship. In addition to the less intrusive analytic strategies of support, containment, and interpretation of defense (rather than impulse) in the early phases of therapy, hypnosis can sometimes be employed to unblock such treatment stalemates.

Use of hypnosis during this phase in therapy comprises a viable alternative to the more confrontational aspects of purely interpretive work. By capitalizing on the enhanced positive transference engendered by hypnosis, and the concomitant topographic regression, the therapist establishes an atmosphere of gentle collaboration, in which the patient is invited to attend to resistances as they are occurring. The focus here is not so immediately on resolution of such resistances, but on their identification. There are two types of resistance which can be addressed with hypnosis in this phase of the evaluation. First, hypnosis can sometimes be quite helpful in illuminating the resistance to the awareness of the dynamic conflict itself. Second, to the extent that the patient's neurotic pattern becomes enacted with the therapist, hypnosis can provide a "window" on the nature of that interaction for both the patient and the therapist—in short, giving both parties an opportunity to observe the resistance to the awareness of the transference as it is happening. As any viable clinical formulation of the neurotic core must account for impulse and defense, clarification of resistance becomes an essential feature of any evaluation interview in short-term therapy models.

Addressing Resistance to the Awareness of Dynamic Conflict
Patients will employ a host of defenses to avoid encountering the affect and meaning associated with the core dynamic conflict. If the patient begins to secure some recognition that he or she is

participating in these obfuscations (e.g., intellectualization, passive dependent posturing, isolation of affect, denial, along with various projective and narcissistic mechanisms) the dynamic formulation emerges with less attendant turmoil and experienced disaffirmation. Hypnosis, by facilitating a modulated topographic regression, affords the therapeutic dyad an opportunity to examine the process of resistance in a more imagistic and affect-laden environment. Often patients then find that they embody their defensive operations in robust and tangible images, sometimes surprisingly dramatic. This can then be the somatoaffect substrate which supports verbal articulation and insight.

Case Example. Presenting with complaints of depression and difficulty in maintaining intimate relationships a 28-year-old single white male arrived fifteen to twenty minutes late for each of his first three sessions. Even the most innocuous intepretations of this behavior were met with courteous, somewhat amused denials until a metaphor for the resistance appeared during a hypnotic procedure. During hypnotic age regression to age 10 designed to explore dynamic material related to his family of origin, the patient looked down at his body and began to laugh. When asked about this he stated that his body "looks like it is 10 years old, but I am still thinking like an adult." The therapist responded: "Yes, you really want to know what 10 feels like, and in a way perhaps you do not want to know. So here you are 10 years old and not 10 years old all at the same time . . . a kind of compromise that feels safe. We can be curious about compromises that make things safer. We can be curious about being 10 and not being 10, being in therapy and not being in therapy all at the same time . . ." When asked to close his eyes and report where he is at age 10, he stated that all he sees is "fog." He can see his father and his mother in the kitchen but all is foggy. The therapist invited the patient to pay attention to this fogginess and this feeling that he is, and at the same time is not, age 10, to embrace the fog as something that is his.

> This fog, this feeling of being 10, and not being 10 in some way represents your mixed feelings about what this being 10 means. What would it mean to really know? Now watch this fog, feel it,

and as you do it will lift somewhat, it will clear to some extent.
There will undoubtedly be some obscurity because it may not be
time for all the fog to lift. But soon the fog will become clearer
and as it does you will see and know more about what it means to
be 10 and to see mom and dad.

The reader should note that this work addresses the resistance, without attempting to immediately resolve it. This otherwise hypnotically responsive patient resisted the therapist's
suggestions to experience age 10, for precisely the same reason
he was late for therapy sessions: He feared losing himself in the
encounter with the therapist. Upon termination of hypnosis the
patient was able to connect the fog with his ambivalence about the
past and about the therapy. While the more primitive aggressive
manifestations of resistance as willful defiance of the therapist,
he was able to acknowledge his resistance as a security operation
against anticipated threat. As therapy progressed fog became a
tangible metaphor for resistance, one that enabled the patient to
observe himself in the act of deploying defenses, even in regards
to feeling about the therapist. Variations on this theme echoed
throughout the therapy (e.g., "Gees, I guess the fog is rolling in
again isn't it?")

As in any form of psychoanalytic psychotherapy the therapist
using hypnosis encounters and respects the defensive function of
resistances while at the same time inviting the patient to gain a
clearer understanding of when, how and what he or she is
avoiding. Hypnosis is merely another technique which can be
joined with silence, clarification, confrontation, interpretation,
and other analytic activities addressing the means and motive
of defense.

Hypnosis in the demonstration of transference
In his seminal work on analysis of the transference Gill (1982a, b)
outlined two types of resistance encountered in regard to the
transference: resistance to the awareness of the transference and
resistance to the resolution of the transference. The former types
are of particular importance in short-term models of psychoanalytic psychotherapies precisely because attention to these resistances can clarify the dynamic focus and simultaneously test the

patient's capacity to observe these defensive operations in the heat of the clinical moment. Both Sifneos (1979) and Davanloo (1986) repeatedly and aggressively challenge the patient's construction of the ongoing therapeutic interaction, sometimes evoking very strong emotional reactions. The rationale for this relentlessness is to so exhaust the patient's defenses as to render the experience of the transference more immediately available to both patient and therapist. Of course one of the problems with this approach is that some patients will not be able to tolerate the rigors of such high-pressure maneuvers, and will regress to more primitive (and tractable) defenses.

In such instances hypnosis may be used to bring into focus important transference reactions in a timely fashion, but with less attendant threat to the working alliance. Among patients who are responsive, hypnosis can facilitate productive attention on the ongoing transferential material in a way that accesses unconscious conflicts and affect, but does not so acutely challenge the defenses. The relative suspension of secondary process in favor of more imagistic modes of experiencing during hypnosis enables the ego to bind intolerable manifestations of the transference to images which are sufficiently vague or disguised that their implications are sufficiently unrecognizable for the time being. Nevertheless important uncovering work can proceed. Perhaps even more critically in the beginning phases of the therapy, the patient is extended a gentle invitation to reflect on his or her own experience of the therapist in a context which communicates, not a pressured confrontation, but a hardy (and even relentless) curiosity.

Case Example. A 31-year-old single woman presented with depression, perfectionism, and unsatisfactory relationships with men. During the second intake session she told three stories about situations where men expect more from her than she can deliver: a teacher, her father, and coworker. The persistent and strained quality of these stories seemed to suggest that they might be references to the transference; that is, she had experienced me as demanding and critical in our previous session. But invitations to consider this idea were met with pained denial.

In a later session hypnosis was attempted, in part, to challenge and highlight her resistance to the awareness that she was having important feelings about me. Accordingly, after an initial induction and series of ideomotor suggestions, the patient was instructed to have a dream about "hypnosis and me." "You will have a dream about me doing hypnosis with you and what it means. This might be directly evident from what you dream, or you may dream about this quite indirectly, but you will have a dream about me doing hypnosis with you, and what it means."

The patient reported that she is in the classroom where she has seen me teach. I am lecturing to her and the other students, but I never ask anyone else questions, only her. Soon she is unable to hear my questions or make sense of what I am saying. But I look angry with her because she does not know the answers. She feels humiliated.

This work with hypnosis proved pivotal. As we explored the meaning of this dream outside of hypnosis it became evident that her perfectionism is a desperate defense against intrusive fears of being shamed and humiliated by those she loves. She could now explore this dynamic material as it unfolded in the therapeutic relationship.

By assisting patients to explore the nature of their resistance and transference feelings, and by finding new ways to address these neurotic repetitions through ego-supportive and anxiety modulating suggestions, patients come to experience a "softening" of defenses. Because patients are encouraged to explore these defensive reactions outside hypnosis, a clearer picture of the neurotic core emerges.

RESOLUTION OF THE DYNAMIC CONFLICT

While interpretation of resistance is an essential feature of any short-term psychoanalytic intervention, the goal is, of course, the eventual interpretation and resolution of dynamic conflict. Fantasies and impulses underlying maladaptive, defensive repetitions must eventually be encountered, interpreted, and worked through if enduring change is to be obtained.

Hypnosis can be of immense value in this phase of the therapy. The model we advocate here encourages the therapist to employ hypnosis as a means of expanding and enriching the patient's ego capacities while the rigorous uncovering work proceeds. The therapist must take care that unconscious conflicts are not uncovered too quickly and defenses pierced too sharply. This is, of course, in stark contrast to the way Freud and his contemporaries employed hypnosis at the turn of the century. For example, a young Freud, operating from a purely cathartic model of psychopathology, would hypnotize patients and in a most stern, authoritarian tone demand that the patient "Remember! Remember!" Contemporary use of hypnosis in a psychoanalytic context respects the patient's unconscious conflicts and his or her need for protective mechanisms. As noted above, when resistances are encountered they are interpreted with attention to timing, tact, and dosage, there is no attempt to demolish them. Even when unconscious affect-laden material is uncovered in the course of an hypnotic session, it is not assumed that the patient will have access to it following termination of hypnosis. Indeed we concur with Brown and Fromm that the therapist suggest: "When you return to the waking state, you will be able to bring up with you as much as you will be able to face" (Brown and Fromm, 1986, p. 143).

Two uncovering processes typically addressed in psychoanalysis and psychoanalytic psychotherapies can be facilitated by use of hypnosis: abreactive discharge of warded-off emotion and tracing the antecedents of conflictual relationship schemata. Below we offer case examples of how each process can proceed using hypnosis.

Discharge of Warded-Off Emotion

Although sometimes offering a sense of relief from "pent-up" emotions, abreaction is itself not an analytic technique per se. However, in certain cases involving trauma it can prepare the ground for interpretive work by giving the patient a sense of conviction about the reality of a remote event which might otherwise remain vague and unavailable. An hypnotic technique that can assist with this process is the "silent abreaction" as first articulated by Helen Watkins (1980). What follows is a case example of how this technique can be adapted in time-limited psychoanalytic therapies.

Case example. A 28-year-old female patient with three children was referred for depression. Following nonhypnotic work on resistance it became plain that she expected men, including the male therapist, to dominate and abuse her. Unfortunately her usual response to this unconscious expectation was nurturance of and submission to the man in question. With the resistance thus illuminated the patient began to remember incidents of early sexual abuse (age 6) by her maternal grandfather. Though there was considerable detail, these brutal episodes were remembered with only limited emotional involvement. Feelings were still quite vague, though the memories were clear. Concomitantly, indirect signs of increasingly pressing rage emerged: irritability at family members, uncharacteristic sleep disturbances, conversion reactions, and motor agitation. But these signs of barely contained emotion remained quite unavailable for her use in the therapy hour. Accordingly the therapist employed an hypnotic technique designed to bring emotion into the foreground of her awareness.

During hypnosis the therapist suggested that she imagine going back to the bedroom where the brutal attacks took place. No one would be there but her. The door is closed and she would not make a sound, "not a peep." It was suggested that she "examine the bed very, very carefully, telling me every detail." She carried this out with her usual precision. The therapist mentioned that soon she would find a very sturdy new oak baseball bat, and as she and the therapist explored her feelings she began quietly, silently, but thoroughly to demolish the bed with the baseball bat. And as she did the tears streamed down her face as she whispered through her clenched teeth how she hated him, his "ugly body," and his "sick mind." With every word she struck the bed. For over fifteen minutes she raged quietly.

There is nothing about insight here. Instead the work of this hour was restricted to elaboration and expression of affect. The patient reported some initial confusion followed by a quiet sense of exhausted relief which seemed to persist for several days. What was mutative occurred during sessions subsequent to the hypnosis as the patient discovered words that could meaningfully articulate the enormity of her rage, not just at her grandfather, but at all figures whom she construed as being maliciously dominating (for quite some time this included the therapist). Tracing and retracing contemporary manifestations of this recurrent interpersonal scenario of brutal domination/anxious submissiveness enabled this patient to realize a significant reduction in her depression and in her tendency to provoke in others the very domination which she so detested.

The Case of the Weeping Knee. The senior author (E.F.) reports the following case: Emily, a 72-year-old woman, had had arthritis of the knee and had needed a knee replacement. The knee eventually had healed well, but after a while a small wound just below the knee had opened up from which a watery liquid would ooze in drops; in the first year slowly and then at such a rate that the dressing had to be changed every hour. It was not pus, it was serum. Gradually Emily developed more and more pain in her leg again, which eventually became so severe that she could not walk at all, and had to be in a wheelchair.

She consulted many orthopedists and surgeons in three major medical centers to no avail. One after the other told her that there was no hope, her leg had to be amputated. She was desperate. At this point she contacted me (E.F.), asking hesitantly whether perhaps she could be helped with hypnosis. I saw her on three consecutive days, each time for a period of between 1 and $2^1/2$ hours. The first day was spent in taking a careful history and giving her a pleasant hypnotic experience. I did not test her hypnotizability but got the impression that she was in a medium trance. She was a health professional, had had a beautiful daughter, and was widowed when the child was 2 years old. With hard work, on a small salary, she brought up the beautiful and very talented daughter by herself and put her through college and graduate school. The daughter married and had two children five years apart. At the age of 28, when the younger child was just 2 months old, she suddenly died of a cerebral aneurism. After some twenty years of widowhood, the patient found another man who had lost his wife recently, and whom she remarried.

The two great tragedies in the patient's life struck me and I felt for her deeply. I resolved to do as a hypnoanalyst whatever I could to save her from another tragedy, the threatened amputation of the leg. I could not help but think about the case all day long.

On the next day, while the patient was in the waking state, I asked her whether she had ever been able to mourn her first husband and her daughter after their deaths, and whether she had been able to cry after her daughter's death. The patient said, "No, I couldn't. I immediately had to take care of my two little grandchildren, the 2-month-old and the 5-year-old." And then after a little silence she said: "Come to think of it, I couldn't cry after the death of my first husband either."

It seemed to me as if this might be the key. Perhaps her body during the last years, through that small wound on her knee, was weeping out the tears for the loss of her daughter and her first husband that she never had been able to shed when the tragedies occurred. So I hypnotized her and made exactly this interpretation to her. Before giving the interpretation I told her that because she was a psychodynamically trained mental health worker, and because I was going to stay in her city for only one more day (which she had known before), I was going to do a daring interpretation. Perhaps it would work, perhaps it would not.

After that, I interpreted to her that perhaps the droplike watery liquid that exuded from her knee wound were the tears she had never been able to weep for her daughter and first husband. She pulled in her breath sharply, was quiet for a few minutes as if in deep thought, and then said, "That's right. That's absolutely right. That strikes me as if it is *it.*" We talked for a good while, both in and out of hypnosis in order for her to gain real insight, consciously as well as unconsciously.

When I saw her the next day she told me jubilantly and incredulously that an hour or two after our session the leg had stopped exuding fluid and she had no longer needed to change the dressing at all. She had also been able to cry for a long time, particularly about her daughter. She said she felt shaky.

In order to settle the interpretation more solidly, I repeated content wise, while she was in hypnosis and out of hypnosis, what we had done the day before, and also gave her the posthypnotic suggestion that during the weeks to come she could cry and shed tears through her eyes as much as she needed in order to mourn her dead. I also gave her the name of a hypnotherapist in her home town to whom she could turn in case she would need more help.

The symptom never returned; and half a year later her amazed orthopedic surgeon agreed that the leg did not need to be amputated. However he found that part of the prosthesis which went from the artificial knee cap into the lower leg no longer fitted, and he replaced that. (The reason for the prosthesis not fitting any longer was that after she had shed enough tears, the edema in her leg disappeared). She could walk easily with a cane and no longer needed a wheelchair.

At a follow-up two years later the situation was the same; no recurrence of the symptom.

Tracing the Antecedents of Conflictual Relationship Schemata

Following the affect, pursuing its displacements and condensations, and retracing its course across objects remains the most rewarding avenue for elucidation and resolution of core conflictual material. What follows is a case that illustrates how hypnosis can be employed in support of this process.

Case Example. A 37-year-old married female patient presented with a long-standing untreated depression with recent acute suicidal features. This woman also suffered from serious pain for which she had undergone several courses of surgery over the past five years, with little success. The patient was a bright, but emotionally constricted woman who had little capacity to be directly angry or assertive with her husband. She overidealized her husband and strove to be his "perfect little girl." During the initial intake session she reported that the previous evening she had placed a loaded pistol in her mouth: She had played with the idea of pulling the trigger. She was hospitalized for what turned out to be less than ten days. While in the hospital the patient was seen daily for psychotherapy. The initial focus of therapy was the relief of her pain, since this was her only conscious reason for wanting to commit suicide. The therapy proceeded quickly in two phases: the unraveling of her conversion of anger to somatic pain; and the emergence of the original interpersonal matrix in which this anger was embedded.

During the third session in the hospital the patient was hypnotized and found to be highly responsive. Accordingly she was asked to have a dream about what her pain means. She vividly described a beautiful day on a beach in the Caribbean. She was alone, sunning herself on a white sand beach. The noises of the surf and the gulls were soothing and peaceful. As she visually scanned the scene she chanced to glance at her own body. There she noticed that coming out of the right side of her abdomen was "a white cloth, half in and half out." When asked to describe this white cloth, she said that it was white cotton; it emerged about seven or eight inches from her side; and it was gently waving in the breeze. She was bewildered by this, but certain that the cloth had something to do with her pain. Mindful of the patient's unconscious resentment of her submissive posture in important relationships, and mindful that premature interpretation of the expressive/phallic aspects of this imagery might be counterproductive so early in the work, the therapist queried whether this white cloth might be "a flag of surrender." Stunned for a moment, she wondered aloud whether she could ever stop wearing "this thing." For several subsequent sessions which did not employ hypnosis the patient productively considered whether surrender and pain might be connected for her. Interestingly her pain began to recede as she articulated her husband's oppressive insistence on her having a recent abortion. During a later hypnosis session the "white cloth" gradually emerged entirely from her abdomen. She could now examine it much more closely. Interestingly her examination of the "white flag" was attended by angry fantasies of wanting to strangle her husband with it (now ironically it had become a weapon). While she was entirely pain-free for the first time in months, she was left with a raw anger at her husband which was quite frightening to her. When she returned home from the hospital she reported "blowing up" at her husband for seemingly trivial oversights.

The second phase of this therapy began as the patient was invited to examine this anger more closely, to follow its course to the very source. Hypnosis was used on only one occasion in which the therapist employed the "affect bridge" (J. G. Watkins, 1971). Here hypnosis was used to magnify and intensify an important emotion (in this case anger). When the patient was experiencing the emotion with vivid intensity an age regression was quickly suggested: an age regression to an important time when this same intense feeling was in play. The response of the patient was a bit unusual for two reasons. First the age regression settled on a relatively recent, but no less important incident at the age of 19. Second, there was practically no conscious experience of anger as she described the incident. As the patient regressed to age 19 she coolly reported walking down the steps of her parents' home (where she lived at the time she was age 19). She was thinking about a very attractive young man she had met during the summer. A brief romance had developed that summer but he had to leave town for three months. He left, but promised he would write. As the patient imagined walking from the stairs of her parents' home to the living room she was wondering why he had never written. It had been over two months and she had not received a single letter. As she somewhat glumly and silently entered the living room she noticed her mother standing by the fireplace with a sealed letter in her hand, about to pitch it into the flames. The patient realized that she had caught her mother in the act of destroying what turned out to be the seventh or eighth letter from the young man. Again one particularly noteworthy aspect of the patient's story was that she was not in the least bit consciously aware of being angry at her mother. She numbly submitted to her mother's explanation that the boy was "not really suited for you." She returned to her room feeling that what her mother did was probably wrong, "but she really was just trying to look out for me."

As the therapy shifted to a once-a-week, outpatient format the therapy could now trace the demoralizing and humiliating surrenders she had made to the pathogenically intrusive mother: a mother who interpreted even the most innocent manifestation of separation-individuation as literally "sin." Of course the patient was remarkably persistent in her attempts to enact this same scenario with the therapist (e.g., "Is it sinful to feel this way about her?"; "Isn't it horrible/sick that I have these feelings?"). This patient's will had been crushed by her beloved mother. As she began to consciously experience anger at a previously overidealized mother, her depression lifted markedly. Just as importantly, a neurotic burden was lifted from her marital relationship. Couples therapy could now begin in earnest.

CONCLUSIONS

As a young Freud struggled to formulate a distinctive meta-psychology to guide clinical technique it was important, even necessary, for him to define what psychoanalysis was *not*. Because in those latter years of the nineteenth century treatment of hysteria was dominated by hypnosis, it was natural enough that hypnotic suggestion came to be the all-purpose foil for psychoanalysis. If psychoanalysis was to have its own identity, hypnosis had to be jettisoned. After all, to the extent that suggestion is unexamined transference it is anathema to the uncovering ethos of analysis. Deviations from the traditional technical canon were often quite justifiably labeled as "merely suggestion," because they enabled the patient to avoid the rigors of self-examination. But by categorically rejecting hypnosis on the basis of its demonstrated potential to obscure the unconscious when misused, the psychoanalytic community lost a tool which, when employed judiciously, can reveal defensive operations and prepare the patient for expressive work. For, when employed in a psychoanalytically informed manner, hypnosis is not used to "suggest the symptoms away" as was so often the case at the turn of the century. It is employed in service of expression. It can facilitate a "softening" of defenses that enables patients to productively explore emotions, memories, and transferential reactions. These are precisely the properties of hypnosis that render it so well suited to use in brief dynamic psychotherapies where there is a premium on early attention to resistance and transference reactions.

Hypnosis can be smoothly integrated into the assessment, focusing, and interpretive phases of short-term psychoanalytic therapies. In this sense its utility has much in common with other more traditional psychoanalytic technical maneuvers like interpretation of dreams, invitations to free associate, silence, and fantasy. With some patients the timely use of hypnosis, even when employed on only one or two occasions, can yield new and helpful material that might otherwise be unavailable. Far from obscuring or compounding resistance, hypnosis can in fact reveal it. In sum, hypnosis can be a valuable adjunctive technique in time-limited psychoanalytic interventions when it is used with the right person at the right time and with a balanced respect for impulse and defense.

10

Psychological Processes
That Are Altered in
Hypnosis and How These
Changes Potentiate
Psychotherapy and
Psychoanalysis

Hypnosis is an altered state of consciousness, in some ways different from the waking state. Jean Holroyd (1987), in a thoughtful article, has discussed nine of the characteristics of hypnosis that help to increase the effectiveness of psychotherapy when hypnosis is used as an adjunct therapy. They are:

1. Attention changes (more focused or more free flowing);
2. Imagery;
3. Dissociation;
4. Decrease in reality orientation;
5. Heightened suggestibility;

6. Mind–body interface (motor paralyses, automatic movements, altered sensation or perception, somewhat changed physiology);
7. Feeling of compulsion to do what the hypnotist suggests;
8. Affect becoming more available;
9. Fusional or archaic involvement with the hypnotist (i.e., transference).

As so often happens in the scientific field, two researchers at the same time, and independently of each other, prepared papers on the psychological processes that are altered in hypnosis and through their alteration increase the effectiveness of psychotherapy. One of the authors of the current book (E.F.) was the other researcher who came up with such a list and started to write a paper on it when Holroyd sent E.F. her paper on this topic. The lists overlapped to a great extent; eight points were the same. Fromm's projected paper contained three points in addition to Holroyd's nine points, namely, regression in the service of the ego, heightened awareness, and the avoidance of some transference resistances. Fromm then decided not to finish or publish her own paper, but has used her eleven points in lectures and many workshops all over the world as teaching material. Here is Fromm's list, followed in parentheses by the equivalent points in Holroyd's list:

1. Transferences develop faster (9);
2. Transference resistances can more easily be avoided or circumvented (no corresponding point by Holroyd);
3. Attention changes (1);
4. Ego receptivity (= suggestibility) increases (5);
5. Awareness: heightened permeability between conscious and unconscious, as shown, for example, in hypermnesia (no homologous point by Holroyd);
6. Increased imagery or primary process (2);
7. Dissociation (3);
8. Fading of the general reality orientation (4);
9. Involuntarism (Holroyd's points 6 and 7 roughly cover involuntarism);
10. More affect becomes available (8);

11. Regression in the service of the ego (no equivalent point by Holroyd).

TRANSFERENCES DEVELOP FASTER

The interpretation of transferences is the most important tool of psychoanalysis. Therefore psychoanalysts spend a good deal of time in the beginning of every analysis on fostering the transference neurosis. Fostering of the transference is unnecessary when one uses hypnosis as an adjunct therapy, because a strong regression tendency coupled with positive transference is practically always present as soon as the patient comes for therapy. The myths that have surrounded hypnosis for centuries have created the impression in the general public that the hypnotist is omniscient and omnipotent, can "look through you," knows your innermost thoughts and conflicts, and can solve them. Thus, a situation already exists in which the patient when he or she comes for hypnotherapy—or probably even before that—has put the hypnotherapist into the position in which the preoedipal child sees the parent, that of an all-wise, all-powerful figure. In Kohut's terms (1984), right from the outset the patient makes the hypnotherapist into an idealized selfobject.[1] Of course, in hypnoanalysis there are also times in which the patient experiences strong negative transference feelings.

In psychoanalysis the patient feels his way cautiously in the relationship with the analyst, not only in the beginning, but throughout. By contrast, in hypnosis the patient early on experiences strong positive transference feelings and deep affects which provide a great deal of material for analysis. Wolberg in 1945 already recognized that this is so and these facts provide a distinct advantage for hypnoanalysis over psychoanalysis (1945).

AVOIDANCE OR CIRCUMVENTION OF RESISTANCES, PARTICULARLY TRANSFERENCE RESISTANCES

When the patient is in the hypnotic state, transference resistances can more easily be avoided or circumvented by the hypnotist's carefully and respectfully worded suggestions. Or the

[1]Many of us are very uncomfortable with being put into this position of being considered all-wise, and also feel that the patient's problems can only be solved if the patient works on them *with* us. The latter we tell the patient right from the start on.

hypnoanalyst can temporarily withdraw attention from the topic that aroused resistance, and shift it somewhere else, until the time is ripe for the patient to come back to that topic. Hypnotherapists are carefully trained in such maneuvers, which shorten the total time needed for analysis. Because patients are suggestible in trance, and their attention shifts easily, they allow themselves to be led to work on various of their problems at the right time(s), which makes it unnecessary to get bogged down for many months in transference resistances.

Blocking can easily be counteracted by suggesting to the patient (in an open-ended way) that an image will appear to him that will in some way be related to the conflict he is currently working on. Or, the hypnoanalyst can make suggestions such as that the patient now is floating to his (earlier established) safe and relaxing place where it will be easier to talk.

ATTENTION CHANGES

Another of the characteristics of hypnosis is that in trance there are vast vacillations of attention. At times, in the hypnotic state, attention is highly concentrated, at other times it is free floating and wide ranging. The hypnotized patient lets the stream of consciousness flow by (James, 1902) and effortlessly picks out of it, here and there, important memories and feelings. Thus it is a state in which free association need not be learned. It occurs naturally and easily.

EGO RECEPTIVITY

Earlier theoreticians conceived of hypnosis as a state characterized by heightened suggestibility (Hull, 1933; Weitzenhoffer, 1957; and many others). This theory was particularly popular at a time when authoritarian hypnosis was being used and the patient was simply told what to do. But even in permissive hypnosis, suggestions still play a role, though they are given in an open-ended way ("perhaps you would like to. . . "; or "perhaps you might want to consider. . . ;" leaving the choice or decision up to the patient).

On the basis of our psychoanalytic background, we, the authors of this book, have proposed thinking of suggestibility as being heightened ego receptivity; that is, the ability to open oneself up to suggestions coming from the hypnotherapist as well as to promptings from within. The hypnotic state with its heightened ego receptivity potentiates psychoanalysis and other psychotherapies because the ego receptivity decreases resistance in the interpersonal situation with the hypnotherapist and also makes it more possible for the patient to become aware of hitherto unconscious thoughts and affects.

AWARENESS IN TRANCE DIFFERS FROM THAT IN THE WAKING STATE

In the state of trance, the human being makes closer contact with the unconscious, and has an awareness of things that in the waking state he or she is not aware of, or is not quite aware of. Fundamental experiences of the self and the world such as memory, perception, cognition, and sensation can be profoundly altered during hypnosis.

Fromm (1965b) differentiated between awareness and consciousness and pointed out that they are not the same. In the waking state, one can preconsciously be aware of a stimulus, and even unconsciously be aware of an affect or a memory without the stimulus, affect, or memory reaching conscious awareness. In hypnosis, the deeper the patient is in trance, the more likely it is that the light of awareness—like a flashlight—is illuminating deeper and deeper levels of the unconscious. Prime examples of this difference between awareness in the hypnotic and in the waking state are Breuer and Freud's (1893–1895) early hysteria patients. Under hypnosis they remembered and reported the incestuous experiences they were subjected to in childhood, but when brought back to the waking state, they had no memory of them. In hypnosis, more light shines on that which is repressed or otherwise defended against, and it comes into awareness.[2]

---

[2]We are convinced that some of these hypermnestic memories were true memories, while others were oedipal fantasies. Regardless of whether they were true memories or wishful thoughts, patients were not aware of them in the waking state, and were really shocked when Freud told them what they had told him in hypnosis.

In modern, permissive hypnosis we gently encourage patients to bring these hypermnestic memories back up with them into the waking state by telling them before waking that they can bring up with them anything they have experienced in hypnosis if they "know deep inside of themselves" (i.e., unconsciously) that they will be able to face it in the waking state. Clearly, if the patient does remember in the waking state emotions and memories that before were below the repression barrier, it will benefit the therapy.

INCREASED IMAGERY AND PRIMARY PROCESS

Imagery, thinking in pictorial, sensory ways rather than in language and sequential logic, is another hallmark of hypnosis. It is the language of fantasy and of dreams; and, in a way, hypnosis is a dreamlike state. Primary process is the langugage of the unconscious. As it increases markedly in the hypnotic state, it shows again that in hypnosis there is a much closer contact with the unconscious than there is when a person is awake. This, of course, is a great aid in hypnoanalysis and several other types of hypnotherapy. It increases awareness of emotional conflict, it is highly useful in psychodynamic explorations, and it facilitates creative problem solving.

DISSOCIATION

As psychoanalysts, we tend to accept only those patients who have at least some ability to separate (or dissociate) the observing ego from the experiencing ego (i.e., to observe their own emotions and actions in order to understand them). In hypnosis, dissociation is a naturally occurring process, both in this sense as well as in the sense of its being easy to encourage the patient to separate parts of the self (e.g., the observer from the experiencer; or various ego states in ego state therapy [Watkins, 1978, 1992]).

The dissociation method can be used in the relief of any time-limited increase of pain. We would not advise using it in cases of permanent pain. In undiagnosed pain, any kind of hypnotic treatment of the pain is definitely counterindicated; for obvious reasons. Pain is a signal that should not be overlooked. For other methods to treat pain hypnotically, see Brown and Fromm (1987, pp. 59–88).

THE FADING OF THE GENERAL REALITY ORIENTATION (GRO)

In hypnosis, the general reality orientation seems to fade into the background (Shor, 1959).[3] When a person goes into trance, he or she withdraws the greater part of his or her awareness from the outside surroundings and concentrates on their own inner processes, and on the voice and the interrelationship with the hypnotist. As peripheral attention is withdrawn from most of the outside world, more attention is available to be invested in becoming aware of one's own conscious and preconscious processes as well as of the relationship with the hypnotherapist. The increase in primary process thinking also is partly due to the suspension of reality orientation. It, and the increase in fantasy and imagery, make available for psychoanalytic exploration rich treasures of unconscious fantasies. In addition, the patient gains access to prelogical types of thinking which, when used temporarily, can increase creativity and recentering of the ways in which the person thinks about his or her conflicts. Thus the fading of the general reality orientation can lead to the finding of better solutions, both in psychoanalytic psychotherapy as well as in other therapies, such as behavior modification or cognitive psychotherapy.

INVOLUNTARISM

A curious phenomenon that appears in most hypnotic subjects is the fact that they want to have the therapist tell them what they should do, and that upon the suggestion of the hypnotist

---

[3]Shor (1959), the inventor of this concept, called it the Fading of the General*ized* Reality Orientation (GRO). We prefer Gener*al* Reality Orientation.

the patient automatically seems to perform certain actions involuntarily (e.g., arm levitation, effective posthypnotic suggestions, etc.). Involuntarism often is greeted by the patient with wonderment, sometimes with amusement. The desire to please the therapist, and to do what the therapist suggests, can be helpful to patients who want to get rid of problems due to habit formation and addictions, such as smoking and certain types of overeating. For instance, the hypnotherapist may give a posthypnotic suggestion to a smoker that every time he reaches for a cigarette a big octagonal stop sight will appear in front of his eyes that will help him to forego the cigarette and throw it away. For some problems we do not need to find a root and a dynamic meaning. They can be handled symptomatically without causing new symptoms. If symptomatic treatment does not provide the hoped-for results, then one employs hypnoanalytic uncovering of the underlying dynamics.

With regard to research in hypnosis, the subject's desire to give the hypnotist what he or she wants is the bane of hypnosis researchers' existence. If the subject has some idea about the researcher's hypothesis, he or she tends to produce the results the researcher wants. Therefore it is very necessary not to let the subject know what one's hypotheses are. If the patient knows, he or she will "kindly" produce the results the researcher hopes for. The results then are all for naught, and must be discarded. The double-blind method therefore must be used in many hypnosis research projects.

INCREASE IN AVAILABLE AFFECT

In hypnosis, affect becomes more available. This can be seen in the spontaneous occurrence of strong emotions during trance as well as in the easy arousal of emotion by suggestion. In hypnosis, patients experience emotions more strongly than in the waking state. All kinds of emotions can be aroused or increased by simple suggestion ("And now you will find that all of a sudden you feel very sad . . . or very happy; and that you have it in your own hands[4] to increase this feeling of happiness by imagining that your fingers are curling around a dial or a knob which can be turned clockwise or counterclockwise. When your hand turns it clockwise your feelings will become much stronger. Should you become overwhelmed by your feelings—or fear you would be overwhelmed—your hand automatically will turn the knob counterclockwise and the feeling will decrease and become manageable.'').

Affect regulation (both increase and decrease of experienced affect) can be therapeutically important. One can let a patient who gets overwhelmed by affect, decrease the affect for a while and work on strengthening his or her ego to the point where strong affects can be faced; while in patients who too rarely experience affect, an increase of affect can easily be effected in trance.

Childhood memories cathected with strong affect are more readily recalled in hypnosis than bland childhood memories. Therefore, hypnotic induction of strong affect also is a therapeutic help in the recovery of important memories.

REGRESSION IN THE SERVICE OF THE EGO

Regression in the service of the ego is one of the major characteristics of hypnosis and hypnoanalysis. Basically, it is a combination of three points discussed above: increase in primary process thinking, a natural loosening of defenses, and the fact that the general reality orientation, with its customary logical thinking, fades into the background of awareness.

We have on our list three factors that do not appear on Holroyd's list, namely point 2, the avoidance or deft circumvention of transference resistances, point 5, heightened permeability between the unconscious and the conscious, and point 11, regression in the service of the ego.

Because of our ego psychological orientation, and our constant attempts to help patients gain autonomy and coping skills,

---

[4]The hypnoanalyst's wording a suggestion in the language of imagery as well so that it contains a double entendre (such as in this case, "you have the control knob in your own hands . . .") greatly increases the potential in therapy.

we do not feel that Holroyd's point 7 (feeling of compulsion or necessity to do what the hypnotist suggests) really contributes as much to the success of therapy as Holroyd feels it does. Nor do we have on our list a "mind–body interface" factor (her point 6), under which Holroyd orders such phenomena as motor paralyses, automatic movement, altered sensations or perceptions, changed physiology, or shifted cerebral lateralization. However, the hypnotic technique of automatic writing which she mentions there, we agree, potentiates psychoanalysis because it reveals unconscious motivations, thoughts, and affects. It is an aid in uncovering.

On the whole, however, we are in agreement with Holroyd, and feel, as she does, that hypnosis used as an adjunct therapy greatly potentiates psychotherapy and psychoanalysis.

Another hypnoanalyst who has written about hypnotically augmented psychotherapy is Michael Jay Diamond (1986). His article deals with the contributions hypnotically well-trained clinicians make to increase the effects or shorten the time needed in psychoanalysis and psychotherapy. They are:

1. Hypnotherapists are trained to very carefully and subtly word everything they say so that the therapeutic message can be fully heard by the patient, consciously as well as unconsciously, and *via* a multitude of channels. In the training of hypnoanalysts a great deal of effort is spent on developing this ability (see chapter 4 of this volume, and Brown and Fromm, 1986, chapter 4).
2. Maximizing expectation and hope in the patient.
3. Accessing bodily experiences through mental ideas (ideomotor suggestions); and, *vice versa*, symbolizing difficult to describe conflicts *via* bodily images.
4. Handling resistances respectfully and thus maintaining the therapeutic alliance until the patient's need to protect himself defensively is decreased.
5. Employing hypnotic phenomena in an ego supportive, adaptive way that leads to encourage the patient to strive for gaining coping skills and mastery.
6. Using archaic levels of relationship, i.e., promoting in hypnoanalysis a more secure, firmer "holding environment" (Winnicott, 1965) in which work can proceed.

7. Stressing healthy, adaptive portions of the patient's ego functioning in order to promote ego strengthening and psychological health.

8. While we fully endorse the hypnotherapist using his or her capacity for empathic encounter with patient material in the context of evenly hovering attention, we do not agree with Diamond's (1986) advice that the hypotherapist should enter trance concurrently with the patient.

   Some endorse the hypnotist going into trance with the patient; others strongly disagree and never use it. We feel that it is the therapist's duty to be very alert and awake in order to observe the facial and bodily expressions of the patient and, while he or she is in this altered state of weakened defenses, to protect the patient from affect that may be stronger than he or she can handle.

9. Permitting responsible creativity. What Diamond discusses here applies to the therapist. When the therapist uses hypnosis, he or she can be much more flexible, creative, and innovative than more orthodox psychoanalysts are. Diamond writes:

> Clinicians skilled in hypnosis have introduced a veritable plethora of responsibly creative psychotherapeutic innovations, ranging from Breuer and Freud's (1893–1895) "talking cure" of hypnotic catharsis to [Milton] Erickson's (1980) strategic use of metaphor and indirect hypnotic communication promoting mastery and cognitive restructuring. These and many other hypnotherapists have provided abundant evidence for the perceptive, thoughtful, surprising, and often humorous ways of doing effective psychotherapy [Diamond, 1986, p. 244].

Irving Kirsch (Kirsch, Montgomery, and Sapirstein, 1995), a cognitive–behavioral psychotherapist, and his coworkers, Guy Montgomery and Guy Sapirstein, have reanalyzed statistically the literature on hypnosis as an adjunct to cognitive–behavioral psychotherapy. In what they call their meta-analysis, they found that hypnosis also is a useful adjunct to cognitive–behavioral psychotherapy. Their results indicate a very substantial effect. The average patient receiving cognitive–behavioral *hypno*therapy benefited a good 70 percent more than matched patients who received the same kind of treatment without hypnosis.[5]

In summary, it can be said that every psychotherapist should have the knowledge of hypnotic techniques as a tool in his or her tool chest, so it can be used to enhance the effects or to shorten the time needed for psychotherapy.

Excellent three-day continuing education workshops for psychoanalysts and other mental health workers are taught by the Society for Clinical and Experimental Hypnosis in various parts of the country once a year; six times a year by the Institute for Clinical Hypnosis and Research in Chicago (Stephen Kahn and Erika Fromm); six times a year by Daniel Brown and Associates in Boston; and several times per year by Marianne Anderson in New York. These continuing education workshops are taught on various levels, to M.D.'s to psychologists with a Ph.D. or a Psy.D., and to clinical social workers, as well as with regard to a wide variety of patient populations.

---

[5]When Kirsch (1994) reanalyzed his data, for a paper written later but published a bit earlier than the Kirsch, Montgomery, and Sapirstein article, he realized that actually the typical patient treated with adjunct hypnosis was up to 90 percent better off than those who were treated without it.

References

Adams-Tucker, Christine (1982), Proximate effects of sexual abuse in childhood: A report on 28 children. *Amer. J. Psychiat.*, 139:1252–1256.

Adler, Gerald (1985), *Borderline Psychopathology and Its Treatment.* New York: Aronson.

Alexander, Franz, & French, Thomas M. (1946), *Psychoanalytic Therapy: Principles and Applications.* New York: Ronald Press.

———— ———— (1948), *Studies in Psychosomatic Medicine.* New York: Ronald Press.

American Medical Association (1958), Medical use of hypnosis. *J. Amer. Med. Assn.*, 168:186–189.

Armstrong, Stephen (1980), Dual focus in brief psychodynamicpsychotherapy. *Psychother. & Psychosomat.*, 33:147–154.

Atwood, Gilbert (1971), An experimental study of visual imagination and memory. *Cognit. Psychol.*, 2:290–299.

Baker, Elgan L. (1981), An hypnotherapeutic approach to enhance object relatedness in psychotic patients. *Internat. J. Clin. & Exper. Hypnosis*, 29:136–147.

———— Nash, Michael R. (1987), Hypnotherapeutic approaches to the treatment of anorexia nervosa and bulimia. *Amer. J. Clin. Hypnosis*, 29:185–193.

Bányai, Eva I., & Hilgard, Ernest R. (1976), A comparison of active-alert hypnotic induction with traditional induction. *J. Abnorm. Psychol.*, 85:218–224.

Barabasz, Arreed F., & Barabasz, Marianne (1989), Effects of restricted environmental stimulation: Enhancement of hypnotizability for experimental and chronic pain control. *Internat. J. Clin. & Exper. Hypnosis*, 37:217–231.

Barabasz, Marianne, & Spiegel, David (1989), Hypnotizability and weight loss in obese subjects. *Internat. J. Eating Disorders*, 8:335–341.

Barsky, Arthur J., & Klerman, Gerald L. (1983), Overview: Hypochondriasis, bodily complaints, and somatic styles. *Amer. J. Psychiat.*, 140:273–283.

Bates, Brad L. (1994), Individual difference in response to hypnosis. In: *Handbook of Clinical Hypnosis*, ed. J. W. Rhue, S. L. Lynn, & I. Kirsch. Washington, DC: American Psychological Association Press, pp. 23–54.

Bellak, Leopold (1955), An ego psychological theory of hypnosis. *Internat. J. Psycho-Anal.*, 36:375–379.

277

Bernheim, Hippolyte (1886a), *De la suggestion et de ses applications a la therapeu- tique.* Paris: Octave Doin.

———— (1886b), *Suggestive Therapeutics: A Treatise on the Nature and Uses of Hypno- tism,* trans. C. A. Herter. New York: G. P. Putman's Sons.

Beutler, Larry E., Crago, M., & Machado, P. P. P. (1991), The status of program- matic research. In: *Psychotherapy Research,* ed. L. E. Beutler & M. Crago. Washington, DC: American Psychological Association, pp. 325–328.

Bogen, J. E. (1973), The other side of the brain: An appositional mind. In: *The Nature of Human Consciousness,* ed. R. Ornstein. San Francisco: Freeman, pp. 101–125.

Bolocofsky, David N., Spinler, Dwayne, & Coulthard-Morris, Linda (1985), Effec- tiveness of hypnosis as an adjunct to behavioral weight management. *J. Clin. Psychol.,* 41:35–41.

Boon, Suzette, & Draijer, Nel (1993), *Multiple Personality Disorder in the Nether- lands.* Amsterdam/Lisse: Swets & Zeitlinger.

Bowers, Kenneth S. (1979), Stress, disease, and hypnosis. *J. Abnorm. Psychol.,* 88:490–505.

———— (1992), Preconscious processes: How do we distinguish mental represen- tations that correspond to perceived events from those that reflect imagi- nal processes? Paper presented at a NIMH workshop entitled: *Basic Behavioral and Psychological Research: Building a Bridge.* Rockville, Mary- land, November.

———— (1993), The Waterloo-Stanford Group C Scale of Hypnotic Susceptibility: Normative and comparative data. *Internat. J. Clin. & Exper. Hypnosis,* 41:35–46.

Bowers, Patricia G. (1978), Hypnotizability, creativity and the rọle of effortless experiencing. *Internat. J. Clin. & Exper. Hypnosis,* 26:184–202.

———— (1982–1983), On not trying so hard: Effortless experiencing and its correlates. *Imagin. Cognit. & Person.,* 2:3–13.

———— (1986), Understanding reports of nonvolition. *Behav. & Brain Sci.,* 9:469–471.

Braid, James (1843), *Neurypnology, or the Rationale of Nervous Sleep Considered in Relation with Animal Magnetism, Illustrated by Numerous Cases of Its Successful Application in the Relief and Cure of Disease.* London: John Churchill.

Braun, Bennett G. (1990), Dissociative disorders as sequelae of incest. In: *Incest- related Syndromes of Adult Psychopathology,* ed. R. P. Kluft. Washington, DC: American Psychiatric Press, pp. 227–245.

Breuer, Josef, & Freud, Sigmund (1893–1895), Studies on hysteria. *Standard Edition,* 2. London: Hogarth Press, 1955.

Brom, Daniel, Kleber, Rolf J., & Defares, P. B. (1989), Brief psychotherapy for posttraumatic stress disorders. *J. Consult. & Clin. Psychol.,* 57(5):607–612.

Brown, Daniel P. (1992), Clinical hypnosis research since 1986. In: *Contemporary Hypnosis Research,* ed. E. Fromm & M. Nash. New York: Guilford Press, pp. 427–458.

———— (1995), Pseudomemories, the standard of science and the standard of care in trauma treatment. *J. Amer. Soc. Clin. Hypnosis,* 37:1–24.

———— Fromm, Erika (1986), *Hypnotherapy and Hypnoanalysis.* Hillsdale, NJ: Lawrence Erlbaum Associates.

———— ———— (1987), *Hypnosis and Behavioral Medicine.* Hillsdale, NJ: Lawrence Erlbaum Associates.

Buie, Dan H., & Adler, Gerald (1982), Definitive treatment of the borderline personality. *Internat. J. Psychoanal. Psychother.,* 9:51–87.

Burgess, Ann W. (1975), Family reaction to homicide. *Amer. J. Orthopsychiat.,* 45:391–398.

Burns, A., & Hammer, Gordon (1970), Hypnotizability and amenability to social influence. Paper presented at the meeting of the Society for Clinical and Experimental Hypnosis, Philadelphia, October, 1970.

Butler, S. (1978), *Conspiracy of Silence: The Trauma of Incest.* San Francisco: New Guide Publications.

Cartwright, Rosalind D. (1972), Sleep fantasy in normal and schizophrenic persons. *J. Abnorm. Psychol.,* 80:275–279.

Chaves, John F. (1993), Hypnosis in pain management. In: *Handbook of Clinical Hypnosis,* ed. J. Rhue, S. Lynn, & I. Kirsch. Washington, DC: American Psychological Association, pp. 511–532.

Chertok, Leon (1977), Freud and hypnosis: An epistemological appraisal. *J. Nervous & Ment. Dis.,* 165:99–109.

Cochrane, Gordon, & Friesen, John (1986), Hypnotherapy in weight loss treatment. *J. Consult. & Clin. Psychol.,* 54:489–492.

Coe, William C., & Sarbin, Theodore R. (1991), Role theory: Hypnosis from a dramaturgical and narrational perspective. In: *Theories of Hypnosis: Current Models and Perspectives,* ed. S. J. Lynn & J. W. Rhue. New York: Guilford Press, pp. 303–323.

Cohen, Jonathan A. (1981), Theories of narcissism and trauma. *Amer. J. Psychother.,* 35:93–100.

Colgan, Stephen M., Faragher, E. B., & Whorwell, P. J. (1988), Controlled trial of hypnotherapy in relapse prevention of duodenal ulceration. *Lancet,* i:1299–1300.

Collison, David A. (1978), Hypnotherapy in asthmatic patients and the importance of trance depth. In: *Hypnosis at Its Bicentennial: Selected Papers,* ed. F. H. Frankel & H. S. Zamansky. New York: Plenum, pp. 261–274.

Conte, Jon R., & Schuerman, John R. (1987), Factors associated with an increased impact of child sexual abuse. *Child Abuse & Neglect,* 2:210–211.

Coons, Philip M. (1980), Multiple personality: Diagnostic considerations. *J. Clin. Psychiat.,* 41:330–336.

Cornwell, Julie, Burrows, Graham D., & McMurray, Nancy (1981), Comparison of single and multiple sessions of hypnosis in the treatment of smoking behavior. *Austral. J. Clin. & Exper. Hypnosis,* 9:61–76.

Council on Scientific Affairs, American Medical Association (1985), Scientific status of refreshing recollection by the use of hypnosis. *J. Amer. Med. Assn.,* 253:1918–1923.

Courtois, Christine A. (1988), *Healing the Incest Wound: Adult Survivors in Therapy.* New York: W. W. Norton.

Crasilneck, Harold B., & Hall, James A. (1975), *Clinical Hypnosis: Principles and Applications*. New York: Grune & Stratton.

——— ——— (1990), Hypnotic technique for treating warts. In: *Handbook of Hypnotic Suggestions and Metaphors*, ed. D. Corydon Hammond. New York: Norton, pp. 223–224.

Crawford, Helen J., & Barabasz, Arreed F. (1993), Phobias and intense fears: Facilitating their treatment with hypnosis. In: *Handbook of Clinical Hypnosis*, ed. J. W. Rhue, S. J. Lynn, & I. Kirsch. Washington, DC: American Psychological Association Press, pp. 311–338.

Davanloo, Habib (1978), *Basic Principles and Techniques in Short-Term Dynamic Psychotherapy*. New York: Spectrum.

——— (1980), *Short-Term Dynamic Psychotherapy*. New York: Jason Aronson.

——— (1986), Intensive short-term dynamic psychotherapy with highly resistant patients. I. Handling resistance. *Internat. J. Short-term Psychother.*, 1:107–133.

Deikman, Arthur J. (1971), Bimodal consciousness. *Arch. Gen. Psychol.*, 25:481–489.

Dement, William, & Kleitman, Nathaniel (1957), Cyclic variations in EEG during sleep and their relation to eye movements, body motility and dreaming. *J. Electroencephalogr. & Clin. Neurophysiol.*, 9:673–690.

Diamond, Michael J. (1984), It takes two to tango: Some thoughts on the neglected importance of the hypnotist in an interactive therapeutic relationship. *Amer. J. Clin. Hypnosis*, 27:3–13.

——— (1986), Hypnotically augmented psychotherapy: The unique contributions of the hypnotically trained clinician. *Amer. J. Clin. Hypnosis*, 28:238–247.

——— (1987), The interactional basis of hypnotic experience: On the relational dimensions of hypnosis. *Internat. J. Clin. & Exper. Hypnosis*, 35:95–115.

——— Friedman, A. P. (1983), *Headache*. Hyde Park, NY: Medical Examination Publishing.

Dixon, N. F. (1981), *Preconscious Processing*. New York: Wiley.

Draijer, Nel (1988), *Seksuele misbruik van meisjes door verwanten: Een landelijk onderzoek naar de omvang, de aard, de gezinsachtegronden, de emotionele betekenis, en de psychische en psychosomatische gevolgen.* (Sexual abuse of girls by members of the family: Nation-wide research with regard to the extent, its nature, family backgrounds, emotional meaning and psychological psychosomatic effects.) Den Haag: Ministerie van Sociale Zaken en Werkgelegenheid.

——— (1990), *Seksuele traumatisering in de jeugd. Gevolgen op lange termijn van seksueel misbruik van meisjes door verwanten.* (Sexual traumatization in childhood: Long-term consequences of sexual abuse of girls by relatives.) Amsterdam: SUA.

DuBreuil, Susan C., & Spanos, Nicholas P. (1993), Psychological treatment of warts. In: *Handbook of Clinical Hypnosis*, ed. J. W. Rhue, S. J. Lynn, & I. Kirsch. Washington, DC: American Psychological Association Press, pp. 623–643.

Dunbar, F. (1943), *Psychosomatic Diagnosis.* New York: Harper.

Epstein, Seymour (1994), Integration of the cognitive and the psychodynamic unconscious. *Amer. Psychol.,* 49:709–724.

Erdelyi, Matthew H. (1985), *Psychoanalysis: Freud's Cognitive Psychology.* New York: Freeman.

Erickson, Milton H. (1980), *The Collected Papers of Milton H. Erickson on Hypnosis.* 4 vols., ed. E. L. Rossi. New York: Irvington.

Evans, Fred J. (1966), The case of the disappearing hypnotist. Paper presented at the American Psychological Association convention, New York, September.

Ewer, T. C., & Stewart, D. E. (1986), Improvement in bronchial hyperresponsiveness in patients with moderate asthma for treatment with a hypnotic technique. *Brit. Med. J.,* 1:1129–1132.

Federn, Paul (1952), *Ego Psychology and the Psychoses,* trans. & ed. E. Weiss. New York: Basic Books.

Feinstein, David, & Morgan, Michael (1986), Hypnosis in regulating bipolar affective disorders. *Amer. J. Clin. Hypnosis,* 29:29–38.

Ferenczi, Sandor (1909), Introjection and transference. In: *Sex in Psychoanalysis.* New York: Brunner, 1950, pp. 35–93.

———— Rank, Otto (1925), *Development of Psychoanalysis,* trans. C. Newton. New York: Nervous and Mental Disease Publishing Co.

Finkelhor, David (1979), *Sexually Victimized Children.* New York: Free Press.

———— Browne, A. (1986), Initial and long-term effects: A conceptual framework. In: *A Sourcebook on Child Sexual Abuse,* ed. D. Finkelhor. Beverly Hills, CA: Sage, pp. 180–198.

Frankel, Fred H. (1976), *Hypnosis: Trance as a Coping Mechanism.* New York: Plenum Medical.

———— (1990), Hypnotizability and dissociation. *Amer. J. Psychiat.,* 147:823–829.

———— Misch, Robert C. (1973), Hypnosis in a case of long-standing psoriasis in a person with character problems. *Internat. J. Clin. Exper. Hypnosis,* 2:121–130.

Frauman, David C., Lynn, Steven J., & Brentar, John (1994), Prevention and therapeutic management of "negative effects" in hypnotherapy. In: *Handbook of Clinical Hypnosis,* ed. J. W. Rhue, S. J. Lynn, & I. Kirsch. Washington, DC: American Psychological Association, pp. 95–120.

French, Thomas M., & Fromm, Erika (1964), Dream Interpretation: A New Approach. *Classics in Psychoanalysis,* Monogr. 5. Madison, CT: International Universities Press, 1986.

Freud, Sigmund (1890), Psychical (or mental) treatment. *Standard Edition,* 7:282–302. London: Hogarth Press, 1953.

———— (1891), *On Aphasia: A Critical Study,* trans. E. Stengel. New York: International Universities Press, 1953.

———— (1895), Project for a scientific psychology. *Standard Edition,* 1:283–397. London: Hogarth Press, 1966.

———— (1900), The interpretation of dreams. *Standard Edition,* 4 & 5. London: Hogarth Press, 1953.

—— (1905a), Fragment of an analysis of a case of hysteria. *Standard Edition*, 7:1–122. London: Hogarth Press, 1953.

—— (1905b), Jokes and their relation to the unconscious. *Standard Edition*, 8:9–236. London: Hogarth Press, 1960.

—— (1905c), Three essays on the theory of sexuality. *Standard Edition*, 7:130–243. London: Hogarth Press, 1953.

—— (1909), Jokes and their relation to the unconscious. *Standard Edition*, 14:275–300. London: Hogarth Press, 1957.

—— (1910), An autobiographical account. *Standard Edition*, 20:7–70. London: Hogarth Press, 1959.

—— (1912), The dynamics of transference, *Standard Edition*, 12:97–108. London: Hogarth Press, 1958.

—— (1914), On the history of the psycho-analytic movement. *Standard Edition*, 14:7–66. London: Hogarth Press, 1957.

—— (1915), Thoughts for the times on war and death. *Standard Edition*, 14:275–300. London: Hogarth Press, 1957.

—— (1916–1917), Introductory Lectures on Psychoanalysis (Part III). *Standard Edition*, 16. London: Hogarth Press, 1962.

—— (1917), A metapsychological supplement to the theory of dreams. *Standard Edition*, 14:222–235. London: Hogarth Press, 1957.

—— (1918), Lines of advance in psycho-analytic therapy. *Standard Edition*, 17:157–168. London: Hogarth Press, 1955.

—— (1920), *A General Introduction to Psychoanalysis*. New York: Boni and Liveright.

—— (1921), Group psychology and the analysis of the ego. *Standard Edition*, 18:65–143. London: Hogarth Press, 1955.

—— (1923), The ego and the id. *Standard Edition*, 19:12–59. London: Hogarth Press, 1961.

—— (1924), A short account of psychoanalysis. *Standard Edition*, 19:189–209. London: Hogarth Press, 1961.

—— (1925), An autobiographical study. *Standard Edition*, 20:1–70. London: Hogarth Press, 1959.

—— (1933), New introductory lectures on psycho-analysis. *Standard Edition*, 22:7–182. London: Hogarth Press, 1964.

Freyd, Jennifer Joy (1995), Betrayal trauma: Traumatic amnesia as an adaptive response to childhood abuse. *Ethics and Behavior*, 4:307–329.

Freytag, Fredericka F. (1959), *The Hypnoanalysis of an Anxiety Hysteria*. New York: Julian Press.

Frischholz, Edward J. (1985), The relationship among dissociation, hypnosis, and child abuse in the development of multiple personality. In: *Childhood Antecedents of Multiple Personality*, ed. R. P. Kluft. Washington, DC: American Psychiatric Press, pp. 99–120.

Fromm, Erika (1965a), Awareness versus consciousness. *Psychological Reports*, 16:711–712.

—— (1965b), Hypnoanalysis: Theory and two case excerpts. *Psychotherapy: Theory, Research, & Practice*, 2:127–133.

———— (1968a), Dissociative and integrative processes in hypnoanalysis. *Amer. J. Clin. Hypnosis,* 10:174–177.

———— (1968b), Transference and countertransference in hypnoanalysis. *Internat. J. Clin. Exper. Hypnosis,* 16:77–84.

———— (1970), Age regression with unexpected reappearance of a repressed childhood language. *Internat. J. Clin. Exper. Hypnosis,* 2:79–88.

———— (1972), Ego activity and ego passivity in hypnosis. *Internat. J. Clin. Exper. Hypnosis,* 20:238–251.

———— (1977), An ego psychological theory of altered states of consciousness. *Internat. J. Clin. Exper. Hypnosis,* 25:372–387.

———— (1978–1979), Primary and secondary process in waking and in altered states of consciousness. *J. Altered States of Consciousness,* 4:115–128.

———— (1979), The nature of hypnosis and other altered states of consciousness: A psychoanalytic theory. In: *Hypnosis: Research Developments and New Perspectives,* ed. E. Fromm & R. E. Shor. New York: Aldine Publishing, pp. 81–103.

———— (1984), Hypnoanalysis—with particular emphasis on the borderline patient. *Psychoanal. Psychol.,* 1:61–76.

———— (1987), Significant developments in clinical hypnosis during the past 25 years. *Internat. J. Clin. Exper. Hypnosis,* 35:215–230.

———— (1988), Self-hypnosis and the creative imagination. In: *The Incarnate Imagination: Essays in Theology, the Arts & Social Sciences in Honor of Andrew Greeley. A Festschrift,* ed. I. H. Shafer. Bowling Green, OH: Bowling Green State University Popular Press, pp. 15–24.

———— (1992), Dissociation, repression, cognition, and voluntarism. *Consciousness and Cognition,* 1:40–46.

———— Brown, Daniel P. (1992), Hypnoanalyse voor traumatische herinneringen en ontwikkelingstekorten ten gevolge van incest. In: *Trauma, Dissociatie en Hypnose (Trauma, Dissociation and Hypnosis),* ed. Onno van der Hart. Amsterdam/Lisse: Swets & Zeitlinger, 1992, pp. 221–248.

———— ———— Hurt, Stephen W., Oberlander, Joab Z., Boxer, A. M., & Pfeifer, G. (1981), The phenomena and characteristics of self-hypnosis. *Internat. J. Clin. Exper. Hypnosis,* 29:189–246.

———— Eisen, Marlene (1982), Selfhypnosis as a therapeutic aid in the mourning process. *Amer. Clin. Hypnosis,* 25:3–14.

———— Gardner, G. Gail (1979), Ego psychology and hypnoanalysis: An integration of theory and technique. *Bull. Menn. Clin.,* 43:413–423.

———— Hurt, Stephen W. (1980), Ego-psychological parameters of hypnosis and altered states of consciousness. In: *Handbook of Hypnosis and Psychosomatic Medicine,* ed. G. D. Burrows & L. Dennerstein. New York: Elsevier/North-Holland, pp. 13–27.

———— Kahn, Stephen (1990), *Self-Hypnosis: The Chicago Paradigm.* New York: Guilford Press.

———— Lombard, Lisa, Skinner, S. H., & Kahn, Stephen (1987–1988), The modes of the ego in self-hypnosis. *Imag., Cog. & Personality,* 7:335–349.

————— Nash, Michael R. (1992), *Contemporary Hypnosis Research*. New York: Guilford Press.

————— Oberlander, Mark I., & Gruenewald, Doris (1970), Perceptual and cognitive processes in different states of consciousness: The waking state and hypnosis. *J. Project. Tech. Personal. Assess.*, 34:375–387.

Fromm-Reichmann, Frieda (1948), Notes on the development of the treatment of schizophrenics by psychoanalytic psychotherapy. *Psychiat.*, 11:263–273.

————— (1954), Psychotherapy of schizophrenia. *Amer. J. Psychiat.*, 11:410–419.

Gaddini, Renata (1983), Incest as a developmental failure. *Child Abuse & Neglect*, 7:357–358.

Galin, D. (1974), Implications for psychiatry of left and right cerebral specialization: A neurophysiological context for unconscious processes. *Arch. Gen. Psychiatry*, 31:572–583.

Gelinas, Denise J. (1983), The persisting negative effects of incest. *Psychiat.*, 46:312–332.

Gill, Merton M., Ed. (1967), *The Collected Papers of David Rapaport*. New York: Basic Books.

————— (1982a), *Analysis of Transference Volume 1: Theory and Technique*. Madison, CT: International Universities Press.

————— (1982b), The analysis of the transference. In: *Curative Factors in Dynamic Psychotherapy*, ed. S. Slipp. New York: McGraw-Hill, pp. 104–126.

————— Brenman, Margaret M. (1959), *Hypnosis and Related States: Psychoanalytic Studies in Regression*. New York: International Universities Press.

Godowin, Jean, McCarthy, T., & Divasto, Peter (1981), Prior incest in mothers of abused children. *Child Abuse & Neglect*, 3:953–957.

Gomez-Schwartz, Beverly, Horowitz, Jonathan M., & Sauzier, Maria (1985), Severity of emotional distress among sexually abused preschool, school-age and adolescent children. *Hospital Community Psychiat.*, 35:503–508.

Grant, Carol D., & Nash, Michael R. (1995), The Computer-Assisted Hypnosis Scale: Standardization and norming of a computer-administered measure of hypnotic ability. *Psychol. Assess.*, 7:49–58.

Gruenewald, Doris, Fromm, Erika, & Oberlander, Mark I. (1972), Hypnosis and adaptive regression: An ego-psychological inquiry. In: *Hypnosis: Research Developments and Perspectives*, ed. E. Fromm & R. Shor. Chicago: Aldine Atherton, pp. 495–509.

————— ————— ————— (1979), Hypnosis and adaptive regression: An ego-psychological inquiry. In: *Hypnosis: Research Developments and Perspectives*, 2nd ed., ed. E. Fromm & R. Shor. Chicago: Aldine Atherton, pp. 619–635.

Hartland, John (1965), The value of "ego-strengthening" procedures prior to direct symptom removal under hypnosis. *Amer. J. Clin. Hypnosis*, 8:89–93.

————— (1971), Further observations on the use of "ego strengthening" techniques. *Amer. J. Clin. Hypnosis*, 14:1–8.

Hartmann, Heinz (1939), *Ego Psychology and the Problem of Adaptation*, trans. David Rapaport. New York: International Universities Press, 1958.

Heitler, James B. (1976), Preparatory techniques in initiating expressive psycho-therapy with lower-class unsophisticated patients. *Psycholog. Bull.*, 83:339–352.

Henry, William P., & Strupp, Hans H. (1992), Vanderbilt University: The Vanderbilt center for psychotherapy research. In: *Psychotherapy Research*, ed. L. E. Beutler & M. Crago. Washington, DC: American Psychological Association, pp. 166–174.

Herman, Judith (1981), *Father-Daughter Incest.* Cambridge, MA: Harvard University Press.

—— Russell, Diane, & Trocki, K. (1986), Long-term effects of incestuous abuse in childhood. *Amer. J. Psychiatry*, 143:1293–1296.

Hilgard, Ernest R. (1974), Toward a neo-dissociation theory: Multiple cognitive controls in human functioning. *Perspect. Biol. Med.*, 17:301–316.

—— (1977), *Divided Consciousness: Multiple Controls in Human Thought and Action.* New York: Wiley.

—— (1986), *Divided Consciousness: Multiple Controls in Human Thought and Action,* rev. ed. New York: Wiley.

—— (1992), Dissociation and theories of personality. In: *Contemporary Hypnosis Research*, ed. E. Frómm & M. Nash. New York: Guilford Press, pp. 69–101.

—— Crawford, Helen J., & Wert, A. (1979), The Stanford Hypnotic Arm Levitation Induction and Test (SHALIT): A six-minute induction and measurement scale. *Internat. J. Clin. Exper. Hypnosis*, 27:111–124.

—— Hilgard, Josephine R. (1975), *Hypnosis in the Relief of Pain.* Los Altos, CA: William Kaufmann.

Hilgard, Josephine R. (1965), Personality and hypnotizability: Inferences from case studies. In: *Hypnotic Susceptibility*, ed. E. R. Hilgard. New York: Harcourt, Brace & World, pp. 343–374.

—— (1970), *Personality and Hypnosis: A Study of Imaginative Involvement,* 2nd ed. Chicago: University of Chicago Press, 1979.

—— (1979), Imaginative and sensory-affective involvements in everyday life and in hypnosis. In: *Hypnosis: Developments in Research and New Perspectives*, 2nd ed., ed. E. Fromm & R. Shor. New York: Aldine, pp. 483–517.

—— LeBaron, Samuel (1984), *Hypnotherapy of Pain in Children with Cancer.* Los Altos, CA: William Kaufmann.

Holroyd, Jean (1980), Hypnosis treatment for smoking: An evaluative review. *Internat. J. Clin. Exper. Hypnosis*, 28:341–357.

—— (1987), How hypnosis may potentiate psychotherapy. *Amer. J. Clin. Hypnosis*, 29:194–200.

Horowitz, Mardi J. (1970), *Image Formation and Cognition.* New York: Appleton-Century-Crofts.

—— (1992), The effects of psychic trauma on mind: Structure and process of meaning. In: *Interface of Psychoanalysis and Psychology*, ed. J. Barron, M. Eagle, & D. Wolitzky. Washington, DC: American Psychological Association, pp. 489–500.

Hull, Clark L. (1933), *Hypnosis and Suggestibility: An Experimental Approach*. New York: Appleton-Century-Crofts.

Hyman, G. J., Stanley, R. O., Burrows, G. D., & Horne, D. J. (1986), Treatment effectiveness of hypnosis and behavior therapy in smoking cessation: A methodological refinement. *Addict. Behav.*, 11:335–365.

Jackson, Stanley W. (1969), The history of Freud's concepts of regression. *J. Amer. Psychoanal. Assn.*, 17:743–784.

Jacobson, Rebecca, & Edinger, Jack D. (1982), Side effects of relaxation training. *Amer. J. Psychiat.*, 139:952–953.

James, William (1902), *The Varieties of Religious Experience*. New York: Longmans, Green, 1935.

Janet, Pierre (1893), L'Amnésie continue. *Revue Générale des Sciences*, 4:167–179. Reprinted In: Janet, P. (1898), *Néuroses et idées fixes*, I:109–155. Paris: Félix Alcan.

Jencks, Stephen F. (1985), Recognition of mental distress and diagnosis of mental disorder in primary care. *J. Amer. Med. Assn.*, 253:1903–1906.

Johnson, M. K., Hashtroudi, S., & Lindsay, D. (in press), Source monitoring. *Psycholog. Bull.*

Jones, Ernest (1955), *The Life and Work of Sigmund Freud, Vol. 1*. New York: Basic Books.

Karon, Bertram (1963), The resolution of acute schizophrenic reactions. *Psychother.: Theory, Research, Practice*, 1:27–43.

Kernberg, Otto (1968), The treatment of patients with borderline personality organization. *Internat. J. Psycho-Anal.*, 49:600–619.

―――― (1975), *Borderline Conditions and Pathological Narcissism*. New York: Jason Aronson.

―――― (1976), *Object Relations Theory and Clinical Psychoanalysis*. New York: Aronson.

Kihlstrom, John F. (1987), The cognitive unconscious. *Science*, 237:1445–1452.

―――― (1990), The psychological unconscious. In: *Handbook of Personality: Theory and Research*, ed. L. Pervin. New York: Guilford Press, pp. 445–464.

―――― (1994), Exhumed memory. In: *Truth in Memory*, ed. S. J. Lynn & N. P. Spanos. New York: Guilford.

―――― Barnhardt, T. M. (1993), The self-regulation of memory for better and for worse, with and without hypnosis. In: *Handbook of Mental Control*, ed. D. M. Wegner & J. W. Pennebaker. Englewood Cliffs, NJ: Prentice-Hall.

―――― Diaz, W. A., McClellan, G. E., Ruskin, P. M., Pistole, Donna D., & Shor, Ronald E. (1980), Personality correlates of hypnotic susceptibility: Needs for achievement and autonomy, self-monitoring and masculinity-femininity. *Amer. J. Clin. Hypnosis*, 22:225–229.

Kirsch, Irving (1994), Clinical hypnosis as a non-deceptive placebo. *Amer. J. Clin. Hypnosis*, 37:95–106.

―――― Lynn, S. J. (1995), The altered state of hypnosis: Changes in the theoretical landscape. *Amer. Psychol.*, 50:846–858.

―――― Montgomery, Guy, & Sapirstein, Guy (1995), Hypnosis as an adjunct to cognitive behavioral psychotherapy: A meta-analysis. *J. Consult. Clin. Psychol.*, 63:214–220.

Klein, K. B., & Spiegel, David (1989), Modulation of gastric acid secretion by hypnosis. *Gastroenterol.*, 96:1383–1387.

Kleinhauz, Morris, Dreyfuss, David A., Beran, Barbara, & Azikri, D. (1979), Some after-affects of stage hypnosis: A case study of psychopathological manifestations. *Internat. J. Clin. Exper. Hypnosis*, 27:155–159.

Klemperer, Edith (1965), Past ego states emerging in hypnoanalysis. *Internat. J. Clin. Exper. Hypnosis*, 13:132–143.

Kline, Milton V. (1958), *Freud and Hypnosis*. New York: Julian Press.

Kluft, Richard P. (1985), *Childhood Antecedents of Multiple Personality*. Washington, DC: American Psychiatric Press.

——— Ed. (1990), *Incest-Related Syndromes of Adult Psychopathology*. Washington, DC: American Psychiatric Press.

Koch, Michael (1980), Sexual abuse in children. *Adoles.*, 15:643–648.

Kohut, Heinz (1971), *The Analysis of the Self.* New York: International Universities Press.

——— (1977), *The Restoration of the Self.* New York: International Universities Press.

——— (1984), *How Does Analysis Cure?* ed. A. Goldberg with P. E. Stepansky. Chicago, IL: University of Chicago Press.

Krener, Penelope (1985), After incest: Secondary prevention? *J. Amer. Acad. Child Psychiat.*, 24:231–234.

Kris, Ernest (1936), *Psychoanalytic Explorations in Art.* New York: International Universities Press, 1972.

Kroger, William S. (1970), Comprehensive management of obesity. *Amer. J. Clin. Hypnosis*, 12:165–176.

Kubie, Lawrence S. (1943), The use of induced hypnotic reveries in recovery of repressed amnesic data. *Bull. Menn. Clin.*, 7:172–182.

——— (1961), Hypnotism: A focus for psychophysiological and psychoanalytic investigation. *Arch. Gen. Psychiat.*, 4:40–54.

——— Margolin, Sidney (1944), The process of hypnotism and the nature of the hypnotic state. *Amer. J. Psychiat.*, 100:611–622.

LaClave, Linda J., & Blix, Susanne (1989), Hypnosis in the management of symptoms in a young girl with malignant astrocytoma: A challenge to the therapist. *Internat. J. Clin. Exper. Hypnosis*, 37:6–14.

Laidlaw, Tannis M. (1993), Hypnosis and attention deficits after closed head injury. *Internat. J. Clin. Exper. Hypnosis*, 41:97–111.

Laurence, J. R., & Perry, C. (1988), *Hypnosis, Will, and Memory: A Psycho-Legal History.* New York: Guilford Press.

Lavoie, Germain, Sabourin, Michel, Ally, Gilles, & Langlois, Jacques (1976), Hypnotizability as a function of adaptive regression among chronic psychotic patients. *Internat. J. Clin. Exper. Hypnosis*, 24:238–257.

——— ——— Langlois, Jacques (1973), Hypnotic susceptibility, amnesia, and IQ in chronic schizophrenia. *Internat. J. Clin. Exper. Hypnosis*, 21:157–168.

Lerner, Paul M. (1992), Some preliminary thoughts on dissociation. Unpublished manuscript.

Levitt, Eugene E. (1993), Hypnosis in the treatment of obesity. In: *Handbook of Clinical Hypnosis*, ed. J. W. Rhue, S. J. Lynn, & I. Kirsch. Washington, DC: American Psychological Association Press, pp. 533–553.

Liébeault, A. A. (1866), *Du sommeil et des états analogues considérés surtout au point de vue de l'action moral sur le physique.* (Sleep and Related States, Conceived of from the Viewpoint of the Action of the Psyche upon the Soma.) Paris: V. Masson. Vienna: F. Deuticke, 1892.

Lindberg, Frederick H., & Distad, Lois J. (1985), Survival responses to incest: Adolescents in crisis. *Child Abuse & Neglect,* 9:521–526.

Lombard, Lisa, Kahn, Stephen, & Fromm, Erika (1990), The role of imagery in self-hypnosis: Its relationship to personality characteristics and gender. *Internat. J. Clin. Exper. Hypnosis,* 38:25–38.

London, Perry (1963), *The Children's Hypnotic Susceptibility Scale.* Palo Alto, CA: Consulting Psychologists Press.

Longo, David J., Clum, George A., & Yaeger, Nancy J. (1988), Psychosocial treatment for recurrent genital herpes. *J. Consult. Clin. Psychol.,* 56:61–66.

Luborsky, Lester (1984), *Principles of Psychoanalytic Psychotherapy: A Manual for Supportive-Expressive Treatment.* New York: Basic Books.

Lukianowicz, N. (1971), Incest. *Brit. J. Psychiat.,* 120:210–212.

Lustig, Myron, Dresser, J. W., Spellman, S. W., & Murray, T. B. (1966), Incest: A family group survival pattern. *Arch. Gen. Psychol.,* 14:31–40.

Lynn, Steven J., Neufeld, Victor, Rhue, Judith W., & Matorin, Abigal (1993), Hypnosis and smoking cessation: A cognitive-behavioral treatment. In: *Handbook of Clinical Hypnosis*, ed. J. W. Rhue, S. J. Lynn, & I. Kirsch. Washington, DC: American Psychological Association Press, pp. 555–585.

——— Rhue, J. W., & Weekes, J. R. (1990), Hypnotic involuntariness: A social cognitive analysis. *Psycholog. Rev.,* 97:169–184.

MacFarlane, Kee, & Waterman, Jill, with Conerly, S., Dramon, L., Durfee, M., & Long, S. (1986), *Sexual Abuse of Young Children.* New York: Guilford.

MacHovec, Frank J. (1986), *Hypnosis Complications. Prevention and Risk Management.* Springfield, IL: Charles C Thomas.

Mahler, Margaret S., Pine, Fred, & Bergman, Anni (1975), *The Psychological Birth of the Human Infant.* New York: Basic Books.

Malan, David H. (1963), *A Study of Brief Psychotherapy.* New York: Plenum Press.

——— (1976), *The Frontier of Brief Psychotherapy: An Example of the Convergence of Research and Clinical Practice.* New York: Plenum Press.

——— (1979), *Individual Psychotherapy and the Science of Psychodynamics.* London: Butterworth.

Mann, James (1973), *Time Limited Psychotherapy.* Cambridge: Harvard University Press.

——— Goldman, Rhonda (1982), *A Casebook in Time-Limited Psychotherapy.* New York: McGraw-Hill.

Marcel, Anthony J. (1983), Conscious and unconscious perception: Experiments on visual masking and word recognition. *Cognit. Psychol.,* 15:197–237.

Marlatt, G. Alan, & Gordon, Judith R. (1985), *Relapse Prevention: Maintenance Strategies in the Treatment of Addictive Behaviors.* New York: Guilford Press.

Marquardt, K., Sicheneder, L., & Seidenstucker, G. (1975), The influence of role induction on the success of systematic desensitization of socially anxious students. *Archiv-fur Psychiatrie-und Nervenkrankheiten,* 221:123–137.

Mason, A. A. A. (1955), A case of congenital ichthyosiform erythrodermia of Brocq treated by hypnosis. *Brit. Med. J.,* 2:422–423.

Masterson, James F. (1976), *Psychotherapy of the Borderline Adult: A Developmental Approach.* New York: Brunner/Mazel.

—— (1981), *The Narcissistic and Borderline Disorders: An Integrated Developmental Approach.* New York Brunner/Mazel.

McConkey, Kevin (1992), The effects of hypnotic procedures on remembering: The experimental findings and their implications for forensic hypnosis. In: *Contemporary Hypnosis Research,* ed. E. Fromm & M. Nash. New York: Guilford Press, pp. 405–426.

McGlashan, T. H., Evans, Fred J., & Orne, Martin T. (1969), The nature of hypnotic analgesia and placebo response to experimental pain. *Psychosom. Med.,* 31:227–246.

Meares, A. (1961), An evaluation of the dangers of medical hypnosis. *Amer. J. Clin. Hypnosis,* 4:90–97.

Meehan, Therese Connell (1990), A role for therapeutic touch: A review of the state of the art. In: *Touch: The Foundation of Experience,* ed. Kathryn E. Barnard & T. Berry Brazelton. Madison, CT: International Universities Press, pp. 365–382.

Meiselman, Karen C. (1978), *Incest: A Psychological Study of Cause and Effects with Treatment Recommendations.* San Francisco: Jossey-Bass.

—— (1990), *Resolving the Trauma of Incest: Reintegration Therapy with Survivors.* San Francisco: Jossey-Bass.

Melzack, Ronald, & Wall, Patrick (1988), *The Challenge of Pain,* 2nd ed. New York: Penguin Books.

Miller, Neal E. (1992), Some examples of psychophysiology and the unconscious. *Biofeedback and Self-Regulation,* 17:89–107.

Molnar, George, & Cameron, P. (1975), Incest syndromes: Observations in a general hospital psychiatric unit. *Can. Psychiat. Assn. J.,* 20:373–377.

Moore, R. K. (1964), Susceptibility to hypnosis and susceptibility to social influence. *J. Abnorm. Soc. Psychol.,* 68:282–294.

Morgan, A. H., & Hilgard, Josephine R. (1975), Stanford Hypnotic Clinical Scale (SHCS). In: *Hypnosis in the Relief of Pain,* ed. E. R. Hilgard & J. R. Hilgard. Los Altos, CA: William Kaufmann, pp. 209–221.

—— —— (1978–1979a), The Stanford Hypnotic Clinical Scale for adults. *Amer. J. Clin. Hypnosis,* 21:134–147.

—— —— (1978–1979b), The Stanford Hypnotic Clinical Scale for children. *Amer. J. Clin. Hypnosis,* 21:148–169.

Murphy, Lois B. (1962), *The Widening World of Childhood.* New York: Basic Books.

References

Nash, Michael R., Lynn, S. J., & Stanley, S. M. (1984), The direct hypnotic suggestion of altered mind/body perception. *Amer. J. Clin. Hypnosis*, 27:95–102.

—— (1987), What, if anything, is regressed about hypnotic age regression. *Psychol. Bull.*, 102:42–52.

—— (1988), Hypnosis: A window on regression. *Bull. Menn. Clin.*, 52:383–403.

—— (1994), Memory distortion and sexual trauma: The problem of false negatives and false positives. *Internat. J. Clin. Hypnosis*, 42:346–362.

—— Baker, Elgan L. (1993), Hypnosis in the treatment of anorexia nervosa. In: *Handbook of Clinical Hypnosis*, ed. J. W. Rhue, S. J. Lynn, & I. Kirsch. Washington, DC: American Psychological Press, pp. 383–394.

—— Spinler, Dwayne (1989), Hypnosis and transference: A measure of archaic involvement with the hypnotist. *J. Clin. Exper. Hypnosis*, 37:129–144.

Newsweek (May 23, 1960), "Hypnosis: Deep sleep—and danger," p. 107A.

Olio, Karen A., & Cornell, William F. (1993), The therapeutic relationship as the foundation for treatment with adult survivors of sexual abuse. *Psychother.*, 30:512–523.

Orne, Martin T. (1965), Undesirable effects of hypnosis: The determinants and management. *Internat. J. Clin. Exper. Hypnosis*, 13:226–237.

—— (1977), The construct of hypnosis: Implications of the definition of research and practice. *Annals of the New York Acad. Science*, 296:14–33.

—— Evans, Fred (1966), Inadvertant termination of hypnosis with hypnotized and simulating subjects. *Internat. J. Clin. Exper. Hypnosis*, 14:61–78.

—— Lynn, S. J., & Stanley, S. M. (1984), The direct hypnotic suggestion of altered mind/body perception. *Amer. J. Clin. Hypnosis*, 27:95–102.

Paivio, A. (1971), *Imagery and Verbal Processes*. New York: Holt.

Perry, Campbell, Gelfand, Robert, & Marcovitch, Phillip (1979), The relevance of hypnotic susceptibility in the clinical context. *J. Abnorm. Psychol.*, 88:592–603.

Peterfreund, Emanuel (1978), Some critical comments on psychoanalytic conceptualizations of infancy. *Internat. J. Psycho-Anal.*, 59:427–441.

Pettinati, Helen M., Ed. (1988), *Hypnosis and Memory*. New York: Guilford Press.

Piaget, Jean (1973), *The Child and Reality: Problems of Genetic Psychology*, trans. A. Rosin. New York: Grossman.

Piccione, Carlo, Hilgard, Ernest R., & Zimbardo, Phillip G. (1989), On the degree of stability of measured hypnotizability over a 25-year period. *J. Person. & Soc. Psychol.*, 56:289–295.

Putnam, Frank W. (1985), Dissociation as a response to extreme trauma. In: *Childhood Antecedents of Multiple Personality*, ed. R. P. Kluft. Washington, DC: American Psychiatric Press, pp. 65–97.

Rapaport, David (1950), *Emotions and Memory*, 2nd ed. New York: International Universities Press.

—— (1967), Some metapsychological considerations concerning activity and passivity. In: *The Collected Papers of David Rapaport*, ed. M. M. Gill. New York: Basic Books, pp. 530–568.

Ravndal, Edle, & Vaglum, P. (1992), Different intake procedures: The influence on treatment start and treatment response: A quasi-experimental study. *J. Sub. Abuse Treat.*, 9:53–58.

Reyher, Joseph (1963), Free imagery: An uncovering procedure. *J. Clin. Psychol.*, 19:454–459.

Rhue, Judy, Lynn, Steven, & Kirsch, Irving, Eds. (1993), *Handbook of Clinical Hypnosis*. Washington, DC: American Psychological Association.

Rieker, Patricia, & Carmen, Elaine (1986), The victim-to-patient process: The disconfirmation and transformation of abuse. *Amer. J. Orthopsychiat.*, 56:360–370.

Rodin, J. (1982), Obesity: Why the losing battle? In: *Psychological Aspects of Obesity*, ed. B. B. Wolman. New York: Van Nostrand Reinhold, pp. 30–87.

Rorschach, Hermann (1921), *Psychodiagnostik*. Bern: Huber.

———— (1932), *Psychodiagnostik: Methodik und Ergebnisse eins wahrnehmungsdiagnostischen Experiments*, 2nd ed., trans. P. Lemkau & B. Kronenberg. Bern and Berlin: Huber. New York: Grune & Stratton (distr.), 1942.

Rosen, Harold (1953), *Hypnotherapy in Clinical Psychiatry*. New York: Julian Press.

———— (1960), Hypnosis: Applications and misapplications. *J. Amer. Med. Assn.*, 172:683–687.

Rosenfeld, Alvin A. (1979), Incidence of a history of incest among 18 female psychiatric patients. *Amer. J. Psychiat.*, 57:161–172.

Rubinfine, D. L. (1981), Reconstruction revisited: The question of the reconstruction of mental functioning during the earliest months of life. In: *Object and Self: A Developmental Approach: Essays in Honor of Edith Jacobson*, ed. S. Tuttman, C. Kaye, & M. Zimmerman. New York: International Universities Press, pp. 383–395.

Russell, Diane E. H. (1986), *The Secret Trauma: Incest in the Lives of Girls and Women*. New York: Basic Books.

Scagnelli, Joan (1976), Hypnotherapy with schizophrenic and borderline patients: Summary of therapy with eight patients. *Amer. J. Clin. Hypnosis*, 19:32–38.

Schafer, R. (1983), *The Analytic Attitude*. New York: Basic Books.

Schilder, Paul (1923/1953), *Medical Psychology*. New York: International Universities Press. (This book was written in German in 1923, in the same year in which Freud published his book *The Ego and the Id*. It was translated into English in 1953 by David Rapaport.)

———— (1927), Foreword. In: *Lehrbuch der Hypnose* (A Textbook of Hypnosis). Vienna: Springer.

———— Kauders, Otto (1926), *Hypnosis*, trans. S. Rothenberg. *Nervous and Mental Disease Monograph Series*, Monogr. 46, 1956.

Schwartz, G. E., Davidson, R. J., & Maer, F. (1975), Right hemisphere lateralization for emotion in the human brain: Interactions with cognition. *Science*, 190:286–288.

Scott, Donald S., & Barber, Theodore X. (1977), Cognitive control of pain: Effects of multiple cognitive strategies. *Psychol. Rec.*, 2:373–383.

Searles, Harold (1965), *Collected Papers on Schizophrenia and Related Subjects*. New York: International Universities Press.

Sedney, Mary A., & Brooks, Barbara (1984), Factors associated with history of childhood experience in a nonclinical female population. *J. Amer. Assn. Child Psychiat.*, 23:215–218.

Sgroi, Suzanne M., Ed. (1982), *Handbook of Clinical Intervention in Child Sexual Abuse*. Lexington, MA: D. C. Heath.

Sheehan, Peter W., & Dolby, Robyn M. (1979), Motivated involvement of hypnosis: The illusion of clinical rapport through hypnotic dreams. *J. Abnorm. Psychol.*, 88:573–583.

—— McConkey, Kevin M. (1982), *Hypnosis and Experience: The Exploration of Phenomena and Process.* Hillsdale, NJ: Erlbaum.

Shor, Ronald E. (1959), Hypnosis and the concept of the generalized reality-orientation. *Amer. J. Psychother.*, 13:582–602.

—— (1972), *Psycho-Imaginative Therapy.* New York: Intercontinental Medical Book.

—— (1979), A phenomenological method for the measurement of variables important to an understanding of the nature of hypnosis. In: *Hypnosis: Developments in Research and New Perspectives*, 2nd ed., ed. E. Fromm & R. E. Shor. New York: Aldine, pp. 105–135.

—— Orne, Emily C. (1962), *Harvard Group Scale of Hypnotic Susceptibility, Form A.* Palo Alto, CA: Consulting Psychologists Press.

Sifneos, Peter (1972), *Short-term Psychotherapy and Emotional Crisis.* Cambridge, MA.: Harvard University Press.

—— (1979), *Short-term Dynamic Psychotherapy: Evaluation and Technique.* New York: Plenum Press.

Silverstein, Steven M., & Silverstein, Barry R. (1990), Freud and hypnosis: The development of an interactionist perspective. *The Annal of Psychoanalysis*, 18:175–194.

Sloane, P., & Karpinski, E. (1942), Effects of incest in the participants. *Amer. J. Orthopsychiat.*, 12:666–673.

Smith, Mark L., Glass, Gene V., & Miller, T. I. (1980), *The Benefits of Psychotherapy.* Baltimore, MD: Johns Hopkins University Press.

Smith, M. S., Womack, W. M., & Chen, A. C. N. (1989), Hypnotizability does not predict outcome of behavioral treatment of pediatric headache. *Amer. J. Clin. Hypnosis*, 31:237–241.

Society for Clinical and Experimental Hypnosis (1986), Scientific status of refreshing recollection by the use of hypnosis. *Internat. J. Clin. Exper. Hypnosis*, 34:1–12.

Soll, Maxwell J. (1984), Transferable penis and the self representation. *Internat. J. Psychoanal. Psychother.*, 10:473–493.

Spanos, Nicholas P. (1986), Hypnosis and the modification of hypnotic susceptibility: A social psychological perspective. In: *What Is Hypnosis? Current Theories and Research*, ed. P. L. N. Naish. Philadelphia: Open University Press, pp. 85–120.

—— (1989), Experimental research on hypnotic analgesia. In: *Hypnosis: The Cognitive-Behavioral Perspective*, ed. P. Spanos & J. F. Chaves. Buffalo, NY: Prometheus Books, pp. 206–240.

—— Chaves, John F. (1989), The cognitive-behavioral alternative in hypnosis research. In: *Hypnosis: The Cognitive-Behavioral Perspective*, ed. N. P. Spanos & J. F. Chaves. Buffalo, NY: Prometheus Books, pp. 9–16.

—— Perlini, Arthur H., & Robertson, Lynda A. (1989), Hypnosis, suggestion, and placebo in the reduction of experimental pain. *J. Abnorm. Psychol.*, 98:285–293.

———— Radtke, H. Lorraine, Hodgins, D. C., Stam, Henderikus J., & Bertrand, Lorne D. (1983), The Carleton University Responsiveness to suggestion scale: Normative data and psychometric properties. *Psychol. Rep.*, 53:523–535.

———— Stenstrom, Robert J., & Johnston, Joseph C. (1988), Hypnosis, placebo and suggestion in the treatment of warts. *Psychosom. Med.*, 50:245–260.

———— Williams, Victoria, & Gwynn, Maxwell I. (1990), Effects of hypnotic, placebo, and salicylic acid treatments on wart regression. *Psychosom. Med.*, 52:109–114.

Sperling, G. (1960), The information available in brief visual presentations. *Psychological Monographs*, 74 (11, whole number 498).

Spiegel, David, Bloom, Joan R., Kraemer, H. C., & Gottheil, E. (1989), Effect of psychosocial treatment on survival of patients with metastatic breast cancer. *Lancet*, 2:888–891.

———— Frischholz, Edward, Fleiss, J. L., & Spiegel, Herbert (1993), Predictors of smoking abstinence following a single-session restructuring intervention with self-hypnosis. *Amer. J. Psychiat.*, 150:1090–1093.

———— Hunt, Thurman, & Dondershine, Harvey F. (1988), Dissociation and hypnotizability in posttraumatic stress disorder. *Amer. J. Psychiat.*, 145:301–305.

Spiegel, Herbert, & Bridger, A. A. (1970), *Manual for the Hypnotic Induction Profile*. New York: Soni Medica.

———— Spiegel, David (1978), *Trance and Treatment: Clinical Uses of Hypnosis*. New York: Basic Books.

Spinhoven, Philip (1987), Hypnosis and behavior therapy: A review. *Internat. J. Clin. Exper. Hypnosis*, 35:8–31.

Spitz, René A. (1965), *The First Year of Life: A Psychoanalytic Study of Normal and Deviant Development of Object Relations*. New York: International Universities Press.

Sterba, Richard (1934), The fate of the ego in analytic therapy. *Internat. J. Psycho-Anal.*, 15:117–126.

Stern, Daniel N. (1985), *The Interpersonal World of the Infant: A View from Psychoanalysis and Developmental Psychology*. New York: Basic Books.

Stern, J. A., Brown, M., Ulett, A., & Sletten, I. (1977), A comparison of hypnosis, acupuncture, morphine, Valium, aspirin, and placebo in the management of experimentally induced pain. *Annals of the N.Y. Acad. Sci.*, 296:175–193.

Stolar, Donald W., & Fromm, Erika (1974), Activity and passivity of the ego in relation to the superego. *Internat. Rev. Psycho-Anal.*, 1:297–311.

Stoler, Diane (1990), Suggestions for vaginal warts. In: *Handbook of Hypnotic Suggestions and Metaphors*, ed. D. C. Hammond. New York: Norton, pp. 225–226.

Strupp, Hans H., & Binder, Jeffrey L. (1984), *Psychotherapy in a New Key: A Guide to Time-Limited Dynamic Psychotherapy*. New York: Basic Books.

———— Bloxom, Anne L. (1973), Preparing lower-class patients for group psychotherapy: Development and evaluation of a role-induction film. *J. Consult. Clin. Psychol.*, 41:373–384.

———— Hadley, S. W., & Henry, William P. (1977), *Psychotherapy for Better or Worse: An Analysis of the Problem of Negative Effects.* Montvale, NJ: Jason Aronson.

Stunkard, Albert J. (1972), Foreword. In: *Slim Chance in a Fat World: Behavioral Control of Obesity,* ed. R. B. Stuart & B. Davis. Champaign, IL: Research Press.

Tavris, Carol A. (1993), Beware the incest-survivor machine. *New York Times Book Review,* January 3, 1993.

Tellegen, Auke, & Atkinson, Gilbert (1974), Openness to absorbing and self-altering experiences ("absorption"), a trait related to hypnotic suscepti-bility. *J. Abnorm. Psychol.,* 83:268–277.

Tillman, Jane G., Nash, M. R., & Lerner, Paul M. (1994), Does trauma cause dissociative pathology? In: *Dissociation: Clinical, Theoretical, and Research Perspectives,* ed. S. Lynn & I. Kirsch. Washington, DC: American Psychological Association, pp. 395–414.

Tosi, D. J., Judah, S. M., & Murphy, M. A. (1989), The effects of a cognitive experiential therapy utilizing hyponosis, cognitive restructuring, and de-velopmental staging on psychological factors associated with duodenal ulcer disease: A multivariate experimental study. *J. Cog. Psychotherapy,* 3:273–290.

Turk, Dennis, Meichenbaum, Donald H., & Genest, Myles (1983), *Pain and Behavioral Medicine: A Cognitive-Behavioral Perspective.* New York: Guilford Press.

Tuttman, Saul (1982), Regression: Curative factor or impediment in dynamic psychotherapy? In: *Curative Factors in Dynamic Psychotherapy,* ed. S. Slipp. New York: McGraw Hill, pp. 177–198.

Van der Hart, Onno, Ed. (1992), *Trauma, dissociatie en hypnose (Trauma, Dissociation and Hypnosis).* Amsterdam/Lisse: Swets & Zeitlinger.

Wadden, Thomas A., & Anderton, Charles H. (1982), The clinical use of hypno-sis. *Psychol. Bull.,* 91:215–243.

Wagstaff, Graham F. (1989), Forensic aspects of hypnosis. In: *Hypnosis: The Cogni-tive-Behavioral Perspective,* ed. N. P. Spanos & J. F. Chaves. Buffalo, NY: Prometheus Books, pp. 340–357.

Walker, Barbara B. (1983), Treating stomach disorders: Can we reinstate regula-tory processes? In: *Psychophysiology of the Gastrointestinal Tract: Experimental and Clinical Applications.* New York: Plenum Press, pp. 209–233.

Wallas, Graham (1926), *The Art of Thought.* New York: Harcourt, Brace and Company.

Watkins, John G. (1949), *Hypnotherapy of War Neurosis.* New York: Ronald Press.

———— (1971), The affect bridge: A hypnoanalytic technique. *Internat. J. Clin. Exper. Hypnosis,* 19:21–27.

———— (1978), *The Therapeutic Self.* New York: Human Science Press.

———— (1987a), *Hypnotherapeutic Techniques.* New York: Irvington Publishers.

———— (1987b), *Practice of Clinical Hypnosis.* New York: Irvington Publishers.

———— (1992), *Hypnoanalytic Techniques: The Practice of Clinical Hypnosis.* Vol. 2, New York: Irvington, pp. 155–226.

———— Johnson, R. H. (1982), *We, the Divided Self.* New York: Irvington.

—— Watkins, Helen H. (1979–1980), Ego states and hidden observers. *J. Alt. St. of Cons.*, 5:3–18.

—— —— (1980), *I. Ego States and Hidden Observers. II. Ego-State Therapy: The Woman in Black and the Lady in White.* (Audio tape and transcript.) New York: Jeffrey Norton.

—— —— (1981), Ego state therapy. In: *Handbook of Innovative Therapies,* ed. R. J. Corsini. New York: Wiley, pp. 252–270.

—— —— (1990), Ego-state transference in the hypnoanalytic treatment of dissociative reactions. In: *Creative Mastery in Hypnosis and Hypnoanalysis: A Festschrift for Erika Fromm,* ed. M. L. Fass & D. Brown. Hillside, NJ: Lawrence Erlbaum.

Weeks, Randall B. (1976), The sexually exploited child. *So. Med. J.*, 69:848–850.

Weizenhoffer, André M. (1957), *General Techniques of Hypnotism.* New York: Grune & Stratton.

—— Hilgard, Ernest R. (1959), *Stanford Hypnotic Susceptibility Scale, Forms A and B.* Palo Alto, CA: Consulting Psychologists Press.

—— —— (1962), *Stanford Hypnotic Susceptibility Scale, Form C.* Palo Alto, CA: Consulting Psychologists Press.

—— —— (1967), *Revised Stanford Profile Scales of Hypnotic Susceptibility, Forms I and II.* Palo Alto, CA: Consulting Psychologists Press.

Welgan, Peter R. (1974), Learned control of gastric acid secretion in ulcer patients. *Psychosom. Med.*, 36:411–419.

Whorwell, P. J., Prior, A., & Colgan, S. M. (1987), Hypnotherapy in severe irritable bowel syndrome: Further experience. *Gut,* 28:423–425.

Winnicott, Donald W. (1951), Transitional objects and transitional phenomena. In: *Essential Papers on Object Relations,* ed. P. Buckley. New York: New York University Press, 1986, pp. 254–271.

—— (1960), The theory of the parent-infant relationship. In: *The Maturational Processes and the Facilitating Environment.* New York: International Universities Press, pp. 37–55.

—— (1965), *The Maturational Processes and the Facilitating Environment: Studies in the Theory of Emotional Development.* New York: International Universities Press.

Wolberg, Lewis R. (1945/1960), *Hypnoanalysis.* New York: Grune & Stratton.

—— (1948a), *Medical Hypnosis Vol. 1: The Principles of Hypnotherapy.* New York: Grune & Stratton.

—— (1948b), *Medical Hypnosis Vol. 2: The Practice of Hypnotherapy.* New York: Grune & Stratton.

Woody, Eric Z., Bowers, Kenneth S., & Oakman, Jonathan M. (1992), A conceptual analysis of hypnotic responsiveness: Experience, individual differences, and context. In: *Contemporary Hypnosis Research,* ed. E. Fromm & M. Nash. New York: Guilford Press, pp. 3–33.

Zeig, Jeffrey K. (1974), Hypnotherapy techniques for psychotic in-patients. *Amer. J. Clin. Hypnosis,* 17:56–59.

Zeigarnik, Bluma (1927), Über das Behalten von erledigten und unerledigten Handlungen. (On remembering finished and unfinished activities [German].) *Psychologische Forschung,* 9:1–5.

Name Index

Subject Index